T0305362

Measuring Organizational Performance

Measuring Organizational Performance

Metrics for Entrepreneurship and Strategic Management Research

Robert B. Carton

Assistant Professor of Entrepreneurship, Western Carolina University, USA

Charles W. Hofer

Regents Professor of Strategy and Entrepreneurship, University of Georgia Terry College of Business, USA

Edward Elgar
Cheltenham, UK • Northampton, MA, USA

Published by
Edward Elgar Publishing Limited
Glensanda House
Montpellier Parade
Cheltenham
Glos GL50 1UA
UK

Edward Elgar Publishing, Inc.
William Pratt House
9 Dewey Court
Northampton
Massachusetts 01060
USA

A catalogue record for this book
is available from the British Library

ISBN-13: 978 1 84542 620 0 (cased)
ISBN-10: 1 84542 620 7 (cased)

Printed and bound in Great Britain by MPG Books Ltd, Bodmin, Cornwall

Contents

The measurement series foreword

STRATEGIC MANAGEMENT AND ENTREPRENEURSHIP AS FIELDS OF STUDY

Strategic management and entrepreneurship are both relatively new fields of study. Both are, therefore, experiencing the myriad pains associated with 'growth', including issues related to the legitimacy and definitions of the fields themselves, as well as to the development of new knowledge regarding the various phenomena that they address.

Currently, both fields are healthy and vibrant – a fact substantiated by several indices, including: (i) an increasing number of articles and books being published in both fields; (ii) increasing professional meeting program time being devoted to papers, symposia and workshops addressing the issues of each field; (iii) an increasing number of scholars indicating both fields as the primary focus of their teaching and research; (iv) an increasing number of graduate students seeking PhDs in both fields; and (v) an increasing number of universities offering PhD programs in one or both of these fields.

In the 1970s, the field of strategic management was beginning to evolve as an academic discipline from the business policy and planning area, which had existed at most business schools as a 'capstone' course for their MBA and executive program curricula. Toward the end of that decade, I helped Dr Dan Schendel, currently the editor of the *Strategic Management Journal*, to organize a conference at the University of Pittsburgh around the theme 'Strategic Management: A New View of Business Policy and Planning'. Later, Dan and I published a Proceedings of that Conference under this title. In addition, we co-edited a series of 'advanced' strategic management texts, with the help of Richard Feldman of West Publishing Company, which addressed various important issues in this newly emerging field.

At that time, one of the major 'challenges' facing the fields of both strategic management and entrepreneurship, in the opinion of many of the scholars in them, was the lack of a substantial theoretical base for these fields. As a consequence, most of the research that was done in both fields at that time was of an exploratory nature. The major focus was on trying to describe the phenomenon of interest, and trying to abstract from 'best industry practices' some 'guidelines for success' that we might pass on to our students in the classroom.

Today, the creation of a theoretical base is no longer the key issue facing the fields of strategic management and entrepreneurship. In fact, if anything, there are almost too many theories and theoretical articles being developed with too little empirical research being done to support the various theoretical speculations that are being made by the scholars in both fields.

There is broad recognition of this problem, with frequent calls for more 'theory-based' research in both fields. However, what is lacking is not a theoretical base for doing such research, it is effective 'measures' of many, if not most, of the basic concepts that are key components of these theories.

I have had the honor and privilege of serving as the liaison between the Academy of Management's Entrepreneurship Division and the individuals and organizations that have sponsored the Heizer Award for Outstanding Research in New Enterprise Development for the past 30 years, and the Division and the National Federation of Independent Business (NFIB) Foundation Award for Outstanding Research in Entrepreneurship and Independent Business for the past 15 years. In addition, during the 1970s and early 1980s, I served as liaison between the Academy's Business Policy and Strategy Division and the General Electric Company when it sponsored the GE Award for Outstanding Research in Strategic Management and the A.T. Kearney Company when it sponsored the A.T. Kearney Award for Outstanding Research in General Management. In these roles, I had the opportunity to receive and read some of the leading dissertations done in the fields of entrepreneurship and strategic management over the past three decades.

The major trend that is immediately obvious when one examines these dissertations is increasing amounts of very high-quality doctoral research in both fields. Three other trends are also apparent, however: (i) increasing attention to the development of hypotheses and propositions based on various theories (that is, to theory-based research) in both fields; (ii) increasing sample sizes in most of the more recent dissertations; and (iii) less attention to and/or 'critical' discussion of the appropriate measures for the concepts that make up these hypotheses and propositions. Regrettably, this relative lack of attention to 'measurement issues' is one of the factors most responsible for the lack of greater progress in both fields.

THE IMPORTANCE OF MEASUREMENT

The importance of measurement is summed up by J.P. Peter in the *Journal of Marketing Research* (1979: 6), as follows:

Valid measurement is the *sine qua non* of science. In a general sense, validity refers to the degree to which instruments truly measure the constructs which they are intended to measure. If the measures used in a discipline have not been demonstrated to have a high degree of validity, that discipline is not a science.

There is little dispute among scholars that the purpose of most research in business is to provide a greater understanding of how the decisions made by managers impact organizational performance.

Unfortunately, even though scholars in most fields of business increasingly agree that shareholder wealth creation is the best measure of overall performance, none of the traditional measures of financial performance correlates with shareholder value creation strongly enough that it could be used as a surrogate for shareholder value creation. This is clearly problematic for the field.

A recent review of the *Academy of Management Journal*, the *Strategic Management Journal*, the *Journal of Management*, the *Journal of Business Venturing* and *Entrepreneurship Theory and Practice* revealed that the 138 research studies published between July 1996 and June 21 that assessed overall organizational performance used 133 different measures of that construct. In short, there are currently no 'generally accepted' measures of overall organizational performance that can be used across studies to help advance our knowledge base in either strategic management or entrepreneurship.

In addition, a similar review of research studies published between 1996 and 2001 in the *Academy of Management Journal*, the *Strategic Management Journal*, the *Journal of Management*, the *Journal of Business Venturing* and *Entrepreneurship Theory and Practice* that used the concept of organizational strategy as one of the study's independent variables revealed that none of these studies' authors measured that concept in precisely the same way. Furthermore, almost all of them used single-attribute indices to measure organizational strategy even though most major strategic management scholars 'define' strategy as a multi-attribute concept. The net result is that none of these studies' findings regarding organizational strategy has built on prior research findings regarding such strategy in a way that would allow one to develop a general set of conclusions regarding the influence of organizational strategy on the performance of the organizations studied.

In other words, there are major 'measurement' problems in both strategic management and entrepreneurship because there are currently no 'generally accepted' 'measures' for several of the major concepts of both fields, including 'overall organizational performance', 'organizational strategy', 'top management and/or entrepreneurial teams', 'organizational resources' and 'environmental opportunities'.

The major purpose of the Edward Elgar 'Measurement Series' is to address some of these measurement issues in the fields of strategic management and entrepreneurship.

THE ORIGIN OF THE MEASUREMENT SERIES

The origin of the Measurement Series lies in a series of 10 PhD dissertations done at the University of Georgia's Terry College of Business under the supervision of Dr Charles W. Hofer over a period of 20 years that won a total of 12 dissertation awards in the field of entrepreneurship during this period, that is, about 25 percent of all of the dissertation awards given in this field over this period of time.

The purpose of the initial dissertations done under Hofer's supervision was to try to identify the 'determinants of new venture performance' and these dissertations utilized a number of concepts from the field of strategic management to address this issue. Very early, however, it became clear that there were a number of 'measurement' issues that had to be addressed to do this research effectively. Consequently, each new dissertation in the series was designed to explicitly address one or more of these measurement issues. Figure 1 lists the dissertations in the series, and notes some of the key issues addressed by each dissertation.

The two most important factors from the perspective of potential users of the materials contained in the Measurement Series are

1. The fact that most of the measurement concepts and methods that will be covered in the series have been *used*, *tested* and *refined* in these 'award-winning' dissertations using relatively large-scale databases using data covering both robust and non-robust periods of economic activity.
2. The fact that the judges for these various dissertation awards included the most senior and respected scholars in the world in the field of entrepreneurship, that is: Raphael Amit, Candy Brush, Bill Bygrave, Arnold Cooper, Tom Dean, William Gartner, Robert Hishrich, Jerry Katz, Ian MacMillan, Patricia McDougall, Ron Mitchell, Paul Reynolds, Harry Sapienza, Kelly Shaver, Dean Sheppard, Howard Stevenson, Jeff Timmons, Nancy Upton, V. Venkatraman, Karl Vesper, Harold Welch and Shaker Zhara.

The bottom line is that the measurement concepts and methods that will be covered in the Measurement Series have been reviewed and deemed to be among the 'best' in the world by a set of judges consisting of the best scholars in the world in the field of entrepreneurship.

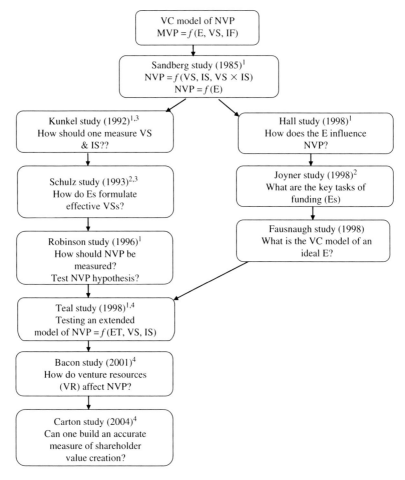

Notes:
1. Won a Heizer Award (5).
2. Won an NFIB Award (2).
3. Won a TIMS/ORSA Award (2).
4. Won a Carland Award (3).

Figure 1   Research on the determinants of new venture performance

THE MEASUREMENT SERIES

The Measurement Series will focus on 'measurement issues' associated with research in the fields of strategic management and entrepreneurship. Each book in the series will review the measurement issues associated with the topic(s) they cover, and then present one or more innovative model(s) for addressing these measurement issues. Each book will also provide questionnaires, data classification forms and discussions of how to use them.

The Measurement Series will begin with two books – one on the 'measurement of organizational performance' and one on the 'measurement of organizational strategy'.

Carton and Hofer's book, *Measuring Organizational Performance*, develops two new multi-attribute models for 'measuring' shareholder wealth creation – one covering one-year timeframes and the other covering three-year time periods. The accuracy and effectiveness of both measures was tested on largescale databases. Particular attention was paid to the ability of the measures to identify and differentiate between high- and low-performing firms, since the 'essence' of both strategic management and entrepreneurship is the development of new knowledge for improving overall organizational performance. Both measurement models correlated with shareholder value creation in high- and low-performing firms with an R^2 of over 0.60, a 500 percent improvement over the 'best' of the measures used in the myriad research studies conducted in both fields over the past decade. Moreover, both new organizational performance measures use only accounting data, so they can be used as proxies for measuring increases in shareholder value for both publicly and privately held firms, including small and family businesses.

Hofer's book, *Measuring Organizational Strategy*, reviews the various metrics that have been used to measure strategy over the past two decades, and then develops two multi-attribute strategy measurement models, one to measure business-level strategy and one to measure corporate-level strategy. Hofer's business-level strategy measurement model has been used in four PhD dissertations that have won six awards for outstanding research in the field of entrepreneurship, while his corporate-level strategy measurement model is the first major extension of Richard P. Rumelt's corporate strategy classification system put forward in the past 30 years.

Two further books covering the 'measurement of top management (or founding entrepreneurial) teams' and the 'measurement of organizational resources' are planned after the initial books are completed. In addition, books on the 'measurement of environmental opportunities' and 'content analysis in strategic management and entrepreneurship' are under consideration.

Charles W. Hofer
Editor of the Measurement Series

Preface

There is little dispute that one of the core purposes of both entrepreneurship and strategic management theory and research is the improvement of organizational financial performance (Venkatraman and Ramanujam 1986; Eisenhardt and Zbaracki 1992). However, there seems to be no consensus regarding the best, or even sufficient, measures of organizational performance. This is in no small part due to the many varied views on the most desirable outcomes of organizational effectiveness and because performance has often been characterized by the theory and purposes of the research being performed. Researchers further confound the problem by confusing determinants of performance with measures of performance (Cameron 1986).

In this book, we seek to develop an improved measure of overall organizational performance in order to provide entrepreneurship and strategic management researchers and managers with a better understanding of the implications of selecting variables for use in empirical studies and practice where overall organizational financial performance is the criterion of interest. The paradox of management research, as expressed by Cameron (ibid.), is that empirical studies tend to explain average performance, while the focus should be on understanding what makes firms either successful or unsuccessful. By developing better measures of overall organizational financial performance, researchers and managers should be able to better differentiate firms that are performing well, from those that are performing poorly.

Specifically for management practice, providing a greater understanding of which dimensions of performance covary with shareholder returns permits better strategic focus in for-profit companies. This information may allow management to track critical financial performance metrics that anticipate market reactions where actual market valuations are unavailable, such as for new ventures and privately held small and family-owned firms. Further, a better understanding of the relative and incremental information content of financial performance metrics can assist managers in selecting non-financial metrics to fill information gaps about overall organizational performance.

WHY ANOTHER BOOK ON FINANCIAL PERFORMANCE MEASUREMENT?

Measurement is the 'careful, deliberate, observations of the real world for the purpose of describing objects and events in terms of the attributes composing a variable' (Babbie 1998: 116). For a variable to be clearly and equally understood by many different individuals, it must be accurate, precise, quasi-invariant across observers, provide discrimination from other variables and be stable over time.

For entrepreneurship and strategic management scholars, the development of valid operationalizations of the key concepts and constructs used to form both independent and dependent variables in the models used in each field, is fundamental to the description and corroboration of theoretical relationships being tested in research, and is the essence of the measurement stream of research. In other words, the validity of research studies that use arbitrary dependent measures to represent overall organizational performance is highly questionable. Researchers need to know that the effects they are studying will reasonably be represented by the changes in the dependent variables. The use of different measures as proxies for 'performance' makes extension from one study to the next dubious.

WHAT IS COVERED IN THIS BOOK?

Four important questions are examined:

1. What is the 'essential' nature of overall organizational financial performance?
2. What are the primary constructs that represent the different dimensions underlying overall organizational financial performance?
3. What are the best measures of the primary constructs underlying overall organizational financial performance?
4. Can a model of overall organizational financial performance be developed that distinguishes between high- and low-performing companies?

These questions are important for several reasons. First, a multidimensional model of organizational performance has not been explicitly studied before. Second, a generalizable and more powerful measurement model of overall organizational performance could help resolve previously inconsistent research findings where different dependent variables were used to represent the same phenomenon. Third, understanding the relationship between the many different financial variables and the creation of shareholder value provides a better basis for understanding the quality of management decisions. Finally, a multidimensional model of overall organizational performance could significantly improve organizational stakeholders' understanding of the effectiveness of management. Such a model allows for the measurement of value creation and for reasonable comparison across companies that have chosen different paths to creating value.

The model developed in this research provides another tool for researchers to understand the simultaneous interaction of financial influences on the creation of shareholder value. Perhaps the most important contribution of the research is the development of a multidimensional composite measure that explains over five times the variance in market adjusted shareholder returns than the most frequently used variables in recent entrepreneurship and strategic management research.

1. Introduction and overview

The essence of the fields of entrepreneurship and strategic management can be summarized in three words – 'successful opportunity exploitation'. Most of the theory and research in the fields has focused on the areas of 'opportunity' and 'exploitation', for example, on what constitutes an opportunity, on how one identifies opportunities, on who does the exploitation, on the strategies necessary for effective exploitation, and so on. Some, although much less, attention has been focused on the issues of 'what constitutes success' or 'how one should measure success'. However, there seems to be no consensus regarding the best, or even sufficient, measures of organizational performance. This is in no small part due to the many varied views of what are desirable outcomes of organizational effectiveness and because performance has often been characterized by the theory and purposes of the research being performed. One indication of this lack of attention is the fact that almost none of the research studies done in the fields of entrepreneurship and small business have used the same measures of 'success', a fact that makes it difficult, if not impossible to generalize findings across studies.

In 1995, Robinson compared various measures of new venture performance, and concluded that 'shareholder wealth' was the 'best' measure for assessing the success of entrepreneurial ventures, a conclusion increasingly shared by both strategic management and finance scholars. Unfortunately, for the field of entrepreneurship, and to a lesser extent the field of strategic management, much, if not most, of what is really interesting in the area of 'opportunity exploitation' occurs before a venture has gone public, that is, before there is any easy way to measure 'shareholder wealth'. Moreover, both Robinson's study and others done in the fields of strategic management and finance have shown that most traditional financial performance measures, such as return on assets (ROA), return on equity (ROE), return on investment (ROI) and return on sales (ROS), do not strongly correlate with shareholder wealth creation. The objective of this research is to fill this void.

In general, this research addresses the measurement of organizational performance to provide researchers and managers with a better understanding of the implications of selecting variables for use in empirical studies and management practice where organizational financial performance is the criterion of interest. More specifically, the purpose of this research is to develop a measure of overall organizational performance that is based on traditional financial performance statistics that correlate strongly with overall shareholder wealth creation, so that both entrepreneurs and entrepreneurship scholars (as well as strategic management and finance scholars) will have a 'metric' that they can use from the date of organization creation onward to indicate whether the organizations they are leading or studying are on the road to success. Further, a better understanding of the relative and incremental information content of financial performance metrics can assist managers in selecting non-financial metrics to fill information gaps about overall organizational performance.

Since no prior research has empirically established the domain of organizational financial performance, this research is by necessity exploratory in nature. A three-part approach is adopted to address this problem. First, a model of overall organizational performance is inferred from empirical data that include the primary constructs of an organization's financial performance and empirical measures of these constructs. Next, the validity and reliability of the constructs and measures are tested. Finally, the overall model is statistically evaluated.

This research makes several unique contributions to the understanding of financial performance measurement for both research and management practice. Specifically,

1. it demonstrates that the changes in financial performance metrics provide unique and significant information about shareholder returns;
2. it identifies specific financial performance measures that discriminate, and those that do not discriminate, between high- and low-performing companies with respect to shareholder returns;
3. it tests the relative information content of individual financial performance measures with respect to shareholder returns;
4. it identifies distinct dimensions of financial performance and measures of them;
5. it develops and tests a multidimensional model of financial performance; and
6. it develops annual and three-year composite measures of financial performance, with previously unequaled explanatory power for shareholder value creation, for use when market data are not available.

WHAT IS PERFORMANCE?

Performance is a contextual concept associated with the phenomenon being studied (Hofer, 1983). In the context of organizational financial performance, performance is a measure of the change of the financial state of an organization, or the financial outcomes that result from management decisions and the execution of those decisions by members of the organization. Since the perception of these outcomes is contextual, the measures used to represent performance are selected based upon the circumstances of the organization(s) being observed. The measures selected represent the outcomes achieved, either good or bad.

Most management research focuses on the determinants of performance. For instance, Kunkel (1991) proposed that new venture performance was a function of new venture strategy and industry structure (expressed as a formula as $P = f(VS, IS)$). Kunkel tested the relationship between two independent variables and the dependent construct of new venture performance. The focus of Kunkel's research was on the hypothesized relationship between certain independent variables and certain dependent variables, while the focus of this research is just on the 'P'.

The independent variables are proposed as determinants of the changes in the dependent variables. The changes in the dependent measures are considered to represent 'performance' caused by the variations in the independent measures. The critical point here is that performance as a concept involves measurement of the effects of organizational actions.

The Concept of Organizational Performance

In general, the concept of organizational performance is based upon the idea that an organization is the voluntary association of productive assets, including human, physical and capital resources, for the purpose of achieving a shared purpose (Alchian and Demsetz, 1972; Jensen and Meckling, 1976; Simon, 1976; Barney, 2002). Those providing the assets will only commit them to the organization so long as they are satisfied with the value they receive in exchange, relative to alternative uses of the assets. As a consequence, the essence of performance is the creation of value. So long as the value created by the use of the contributed assets is equal to or greater than the value expected by those contributing the assets, the assets will continue to be made available to the organization and the organization will continue to exist. Therefore, value creation, as defined by the resource provider, is the essential overall performance criterion for any organization. How that value is created is the essence of most empirical research in management. Conversely, how that value is measured is the essence of this research.

Issues Associated with the Assessment of Value Creation

There are several issues associated with the assessment of value creation for organizations. First, value creation is situational since different types of organizations have different concepts of what outcomes are valuable. Second, organizations perform on multiple dimensions, such as growth, profitability and legitimacy, often trading positive outcomes in one dimension for worse outcomes in another. Third, performance is in part perceptually based upon what the observer finds 'valuable'. Finally, timing plays a role in value creation as opportunities created in the present, which will be realized in the future, are valued in the present based upon individual assumptions about future actions and conditions. These assumptions about future outcomes vary based upon the perceptions of the observer.

Value creation is situational
If performance is to be measured in terms of value created, it is incumbent upon researchers to select samples of organizations that have homogeneous concepts of value. Value may be tangible or intangible, operational or financial. Public companies (those traded on a recognized stock exchange) seek creation of shareholder value (increases in market value plus dividends paid) as their ultimate objective (Blyth et al., 1986; Rappaport, 1986; Porter, 1987; Stewart, 1991; Scott, 1998; Copeland et al., 2000; de Waal, 2001). For private companies, value creation may be a combination of both financial and non-financial objectives. When significant owners are also the managers of an organization, value creation for shareholders is more likely to include non-financial outcomes (Jensen and Meckling, 1976). These types of costs in public companies might be characterized as agency costs, but when the owners are also the managers, they are actually a component of the return to shareholders.

Non-financial returns to owner–managers would include lifestyle benefits, including work location, work duration, social interactions (such as when an owner continues to operate an underperforming business just so he/she will have a place to go and feel useful everyday) and ego. Other non-financial returns can be classified as constituency benefits, such as providing income for friends and family, helping people with special needs, such as goodwill industries, and providing employment for a depressed community. This discussion should not imply that public companies do not have non-financial objectives. They certainly do have agency costs, but they are not a specific objective of the organization. Rather, they are a cost of doing business. Therefore, they should not be considered as a positive part of organizational performance.

After six years of examining the concept of organizational effectiveness, Cameron (1986) concluded that there is no conceptualization of organizational effectiveness that is comprehensive. Therefore, similar to Hofer (1983), Cameron concluded that performance is a problem-, rather than a theory-driven construct.

Organizations perform on multiple dimensions

Even with a homogeneous sample with respect to the concept of value (such as publicly owned companies, family-owned businesses, or not-for-profit organizations), performance is a multidimensional construct, which permits value to be created on differing dimensions (Steers, 1975; Dess and Robinson, 1984; Cameron, 1986; Murphy et al., 1996). It is also possible to conceive of multiple measures of the value created. This fact is supported by the number of different dependent measures that have been used to measure organizational performance in research studies (Brush and Vanderwerf, 1992; Murphy et al., 1996).

There are many dimensions to performance and positive performance in one dimension may simultaneously result in negative performance in another dimension. For instance, if resource accumulation and profitability are hypothesized as separate dimensions of performance in the same model, adding resources in the form of equity may result in a lower risk-adjusted return on investment. This means that the company has performed well on one dimension, resource accumulation, while it has earned lower performance on the second construct, profitability. A new venture may be effective if it is accumulating resources and building market share, even at the expense of profitability. Conversely, a mature organization may be effective with stable resources and market share, and increasing productivity and profitability. Examining each dimension separately, without consideration of the other dimension will lead to decidedly different conclusions than examining the counterbalancing effects of the two dimensions simultaneously. To equate these levels of performance, a measure that covaries with each dimension is needed.

Interpretation of performance depends upon the observer's perspective

Value is in the eye of the beholder. Each organizational stakeholder will have a different perspective of what is 'valuable' based upon their purpose for associating with the organization. Passive investors have different perspectives of value creation than do active investors. Creditors may perceive value to be created by the organization's ability to generate positive cash flow and preserve the worth of collateral. Conversely, equity investors may perceive value in expending company resources to create future opportunities, even if it diminishes cash flow and tangible company assets in the short term.

Each group of organizational stakeholders will have a different view of organizational performance, making it incumbent upon a researcher to select a perspective of performance that conforms to the phenomenon of interest. In other words, a researcher should select a perspective of performance that coincides with the purpose of the research. The key is matching the appropriate model of organizational performance with the existing circumstances.

Assumptions about future performance influence perceptions of present value

The most difficult problem in developing a generalizable measurement model of performance is finding an indicator, or set of indicators, that reflect a weighted measure of all of the different dimensions of performance in the form of value created. An ideal measure must take into account information on both historical performance as well as expectations of future performance. It can be argued that performance should measure actions taken to date and not include the value of future expectations, since they may not materialize. However, the expectations of future performance depend upon the actions taken to date to create strategic alternatives and opportunities. Therefore, the value of the opportunities created relates to past actions and, accordingly, this value should be included in a performance measure as the risk-adjusted present value of the opportunities.

The realization of the anticipated value of opportunities is dependent upon future implementation. If the anticipated value of the opportunity is realized, the resulting increase in shareholder value in the implementation period will be equal to the discount rate applied to the expected return of the opportunity in the period when the opportunity was captured. The value created from opportunities in future periods will vary from the discount rate based upon the realized returns. In summary, performance measures should capture not only realized value creation, but also the value of opportunities created during the measurement period.

WHY STUDY PERFORMANCE MEASUREMENT?

There is little dispute that one of the core purposes of both entrepreneurship and strategic management theory and research is the improvement of organizational performance (Schendel and Hofer, 1979; Cameron and Whetten, 1983; Venkatraman and Ramanujam, 1986; Eisenhardt and Zbaracki, 1992). However, there seems to be no consensus regarding the best, or even sufficient, measures of organizational performance. This is in no small part due to the many varied views of what are desirable outcomes of organizational actions, and because performance has often been characterized by the theory and purposes of the research being performed. Researchers further confound the problem by confusing determinants of performance with measures of performance (Cameron, 1986).

It has long been reported that different measures of organizational effectiveness and performance have been used in management and entrepreneurship studies with little or no thoughtful discussion of why the measures used in the studies were chosen (Steers, 1975; Capon et al., 1990; Kaplan and Norton, 1992; Murphy et al., 1996). Little attention has been paid to the limitations that these measures may impose on the interpretation or generalizability of the results of the research (see Kunkel and Hofer, 1991; Brush and Vanderwerf, 1992; Cooper, 1993; Murphy et al., 1996; Robinson, 1995 as examples), and most have concluded that organizational performance is multidimensional in character (Cameron, 1980; Chakravarthy, 1986; Venkatraman and Ramanujam, 1986, 1987; Kaplan and Norton, 1992; Murphy et al., 1996). However, no study has successfully proposed and empirically tested a generalizable multidimensional model of organizational performance. This is a particularly challenging issue since changing environmental conditions may dictate that different performance dimension priorities exist at different times. For instance, during economic recessions, liquidity may be more crucial than profitability, while during economic booms, profitability and growth may take precedence.

Measurement is the 'careful, deliberate, observations of the real world for the purpose of describing objects and events in terms of the attributes composing a variable' (Babbie, 1998: 116). For a variable to be clearly and equally understood by many different individuals, it must be accurate, precise, quasi-invariant across observers, provide discrimination from other variables, and be stable over time. As a result, it is problematic that overall organization performance has been measured in research studies by dozens of variables that are generally not strongly correlated over time.

The validity of research studies that use arbitrary dependent measures to represent organizational performance is questionable. Researchers need to know that the effects they are studying will reasonably be represented by the changes in the dependent variables. The use of different measures as proxies for 'performance' makes extension from one study to the next dubious. Peter clearly summed up the importance of construct measurement as follows:

> Valid measurement is the *sine qua non* of science. In a general sense, validity refers to the degree to which instruments truly measure the constructs which they are intended to measure. If the measures used in a discipline have not been demonstrated to have a high degree of validity, that discipline is not a science. (1979: 6)

The topic of this research is particularly important for several reasons. First, a multidimensional model of organizational performance has not been explicitly studied before. Murphy et al. (1996) examined the dependent measures used in entrepreneurship research and through exploratory factor analysis found nine distinct performance constructs among the more then 50 different dependent variables reported upon. Venkatraman and Ramanujam (1987) empirically demonstrated that growth and profitability were distinctly different measures of performance, but did not attempt to propose a specific model for overall performance measurement. Robinson (1998) empirically tested the relationship between four separate independent variables (stage of the life cycle, industry concentration, entry barriers and product differentiation) with eight different measures of performance in new venture research and found significantly different results between each independent variable and the eight dependent variables. This further demonstrated the existence of multiple dimensions of performance.

Second, a generalizable and more powerful measurement model of performance has significant implications for future research and for reexamining the findings of prior research where less-powerful dependent variable measurement models were used. Such a model may help resolve multiple inconsistent theories where differing dependent variables were used.

Finally, a multidimensional model of organizational performance can significantly improve organizational stakeholders' understanding of the effectiveness of management. It allows for the measurement of value creation and for reasonable comparison across companies that have chosen different routes to creating value.

Therefore, the objective of this research is to develop a model of organizational performance. The model demonstrates that organizational performance is a multidimensional construct. In addition, it shows that the simultaneous consideration of these multiple dimensions is more appropriate for drawing conclusions about the effectiveness of managerial actions than considering each performance dimension separately.

WHAT QUESTIONS WILL BE ANSWERED BY THIS RESEARCH?

It is not the intention to propose cause and effect relationships between organizational actions and outcomes, but rather to develop a measurement model that captures greater information about the effects of organizational actions. Therefore, the first issue to be addressed is what is meant by organizational performance. This question is theoretical in nature and will be addressed through examination of prior theory and research.

Research Question 1:   What is the nature of organizational performance?

The outcome of the examination of the first research question leads to a second research question. As discussed above, performance is multi-dimensional. Accordingly, this research will seek to identify the primary dimensions of performance and demonstrate that they are distinct from one another. Murphy et al. (1996) found nine distinct performance constructs and Venkatraman and Ramanujam (1987) demonstrated that growth and profitability were distinct performance constructs. However, a comprehensive model of organizational performance has not been proposed and empirically tested.

Research Question 2:   What are the primary constructs underlying organizational performance?

If it is clearly shown that performance is multidimensional, the next area of investigation should be to identify appropriate measures for each construct. To accomplish this task, the relative and incremental information content of each measure will be examined. Those measures that provide better or more information about the construct of interest than other measures will be identified.

Research Question 3:   What are the best measures of the primary constructs underlying organizational performance?

Finally, the combination of dimensions of organizational performance and the indicators of these constructs constitute a model of organizational performance. This model will be tested to determine whether it can distinguish between high- and low-performing companies.

Research Question 4:   Can the model of organizational performance developed in this research distinguish between high- and low-performing organizations?

In summary, the focus of this research is the development and testing of a measurement model that accurately describes organizational financial performance. The purpose is not to examine determinants of performance, but rather to examine the nature of performance itself as a multidimensional construct.

THE ORGANIZATION OF THIS BOOK

Chapter 2 examines the prior literature with respect to empirical management research on organization performance measurement. In addition, the chapter includes a summary of the measures of organizational performance that were used in entrepreneurship and strategic management empirical studies published in five primary scholarly journals, over a five-year period.

Chapter 3 examines how the concept of overall organizational performance and effectiveness was characterized and investigated in prior theory and research. The chapter includes an argument for a single-constituency, multidimensional model of performance for for-profit organizations, from the perspective of the common stockholder.

Chapter 4 discusses the nature of the different categories of organizational performance measures. Since there is no authoritative list of performance categories in the prior literature, the categories of performance measures discussed in this chapter are based upon general classifications of such measures often found in finance and accounting texts. Five primary categories are proposed and the nature of the performance measures for each category is discussed.

Chapter 5 examines the strengths and weaknesses of individual performance measures that have been most frequently used in research and practice. Each of them is defined and samples of the arguments for these measures, as put forth by authors who have utilized the variables in empirical studies, are discussed. In addition, the validity of the arguments in favor of using these variables is examined and discussed. These variables include traditional accounting-based measures of performance, likelihood of financial survival measures, market-based measures and economic value measures.

Chapter 6 addresses the measurement attributes and specifications appropriate for the variables that scholars, especially those in the fields of entrepreneurship and strategic management, use for dependent variables when undertaking a research study. In this context, the chapter first reviews the role of measurement in theory building and testing. Next, it reviews the nature of empirical constructs and classification systems, and the criteria for them to be effective. The chapter concludes by applying the general concepts of measurement to the specific task of measuring organizational performance.

Chapter 7 details the research design. It includes a discussion of the philosophy underlying the research design and the critical assumptions for the operationalization of the study. Using Cameron and Whetten's (1981) seven questions for bounding and evaluating organizational effectiveness, the research design, the population of interest, and data-gathering and measurement issues for this research are detailed. Next, an exploratory approach to inferring a model of organizational financial performance from empirical data is presented. Finally, a discussion of the data analysis techniques used to test the model concludes the chapter.

Chapter 8 presents the exploratory work performed to examine individual measures of organizational financial performance as a first step in developing a measurement model of this construct. First, the relative information content of ratios calculated using ending balances for the denominator versus those calculated using average balances for the denominator, with respect to return to shareholders, is examined to determine whether they are statistically significantly different. Next, the results of statistical comparisons between high- and low-performing companies are presented to identify measures that discriminate between the two groups. The third section of the chapter examines the relative information content of various individual measures of financial performance. Finally, the incremental and relative information content of static measures versus change scores is examined.

Chapter 9 presents the exploratory work performed to develop and test different potentially useful models of organizational financial performance for annual and three-year timeframes. These models are inferred from empirical data, and include primary constructs representing separate dimensions of organizational financial performance as well as the measures of those constructs. The chapter concludes with the development and testing of financial performance composite measures for annual and three-year timeframes that may be useful when market-based measures are unavailable.

Chapter 10 presents the summary and conclusions of this research. The limitations of the study and application of the findings to entrepreneurship and strategic management research are discussed. Finally, the implications of the findings for management practice are discussed.

CHAPTER SUMMARY

Chapter 1 described the rationale for this research and specific research objectives to be accomplished. The focus of this research is to develop and test a measurement model that represents organizational performance. Four research questions were posed as the foundation for this research:

RQ1: What is the nature of organizational performance?

RQ2: What are the primary constructs underlying organizational financial performance?

RQ3:   What are the best measures of the primary constructs underlying organizational financial performance?

RQ4:   Can the model of organizational financial performance developed in this research distinguish between high- and low-performing companies?

The approach to answering these questions is to first determine what measures are actually used in empirical studies in entrepreneurship and strategic management and critically examine these measures' strengths and weaknesses. Next, the strengths and weaknesses of performance measures used in management practice are examined. Using this critique as background, key characteristics and attributes of effective performance measures are discussed. This analysis is then compared to theories of organizational performance measurement extracted from academic literature. Finally, based upon this review of academic research and theory, and real-world practice, a model of organizational performance is proposed and tested.

It is not the purpose of this research to examine determinants of performance, but rather to examine the nature of performance itself as a construct. The chapter concluded with a summary of the organization of the research and the material included in each succeeding chapter.

2. Performance measurement in management literature

This chapter will review prior research on the measurement of overall organizational performance. First, previous studies are identified, summarized and analysed. Next is an analysis of the measures of overall organizational performance used in empirical research in strategic management over the past five years. The chapter concludes with a synopsis of the 'current state of the art' *vis-à-vis* overall organizational performance measurement.

PRIOR STUDIES OF OVERALL ORGANIZATIONAL PERFORMANCE

Despite the importance of accurately measuring organizational performance in most areas of academic research, there have been very few studies that have directly addressed the question of how overall organizational performance is or should be measured. Perhaps more importantly, none of these studies seems to have significantly influenced how overall organizational performance is actually measured in most of the empirical research that uses this construct as a dependent measure.

In total, seven empirical studies on the measurement of organizational performance were identified: Dess and Robinson (1984), Rawley and Lipson (1985), Chakravarthy (1986), Venkatraman and Ramanujam (1987), Brush and Vanderwerf (1992), Robinson (1995) and Murphy et al. (1996). The following discussion summarizes and analyses these studies.

Dess and Robinson's Research

Dess and Robinson (1984) examined the usefulness of subjective performance measures as compared to objective measures. Specifically, they investigated the relationship between objective and subjective measures of return on assets (ROA), growth in sales and 'global' performance measures. The study involved three phases of data collection from 26 manufacturing organizations using onsite interviews of CEOs, mail surveys of the top management teams and a mail survey of CEOs. Conclusions were drawn from examining the zero-order correlations between the six variables of interest.

Dess and Robinson found that top management's subjective evaluation of performance was highly correlated with objective measures, suggesting that researchers may consider using subjective perceptual measures of ROA and sales growth under certain conditions. These conditions include when objective measures are not available and when the alternative is to remove the consideration of performance from the research design. Another finding reported in the study was that there is some evidence that the global measures of organizational performance overlap with subjective and objective measures of ROA and sales growth. However, the amount of unshared variance between the constructs implies that the global measures may capture some broader conceptualization of performance. In other words, there are more dimensions to overall organizational performance than ROA and sales growth.

Rawley and Lipson's Research

In 1985, Rawley and Lipson examined the relationships among several combinations of performance measures to demonstrate that different common measures of financial performance did not represent the same attributes. Of these comparisons, the only overall performance measures that they found to be related to each other at statistically significant levels were the Q ratio versus cash flow return on investment (CFROI) adjusted for the capital asset pricing model (CAPM) discount rate, and market-to-book value versus return on investment adjusted for inflation. The Q ratio was proposed by Callard and Kleinman (1985) as a substitute for Tobin's Q, and is calculated as the ratio of the value of individual business units divided by the inflation-adjusted purchase cost of assets. The other measures that they compared were clearly discriminant and do not measure the same construct. Table 2.1 summarizes their findings for the S&P 400 companies for the period 1982 through 1984.

Chakravarthy's Research

Chakravarthy (1986) empirically compared seven exemplar firms with seven 'maladapted' firms in the computer industry, as determined by corporate reputation. The criteria for selecting the samples were the criteria proposed by Peters and Waterman (1982) for 'excellent' firms. Chakravarthy hypothesized that the means of the two groups, excellent and non-excellent firms, would differ along common measures of performance. Accordingly, those measures of performance that demonstrated that the means of the two

Table 2.1   Summary of relationships among selected performance
measures from Rawley and Lipson (1985)

Variables compared	R^2
Price-to-earnings ratio vs. Earnings per share growth	0.12
Price-to-book ratio vs. Return on equity less CAPM cost of equity	0.19
Price-to-book ratio vs. Return on capital employed – CAPM cost of capital	0.34
Q ratio vs. CFROI less discount rate	0.65
Market-to-book ratio vs. ROI less inflation	0.71

groups were statistically significantly different would be the best measures of performance for use in strategic management research.

The two groups were first compared for return on sales, return on total capital and return on book equity. The results, using Tukey's standardized range test, did not demonstrate a statistically significant difference between the two groups. Chakravarthy concluded that profitability criteria are not capable of 'distinguishing differences in the strategic performances of the computer firms in the sample' (1986: 442).

Next, Chakravarthy compared the two groups of firms for differences in market-to-book value and industry-adjusted market-to-book value ratios. Again it was found that these performance measures were not capable of distinguishing between excellent and non-excellent firms in the sample from the computer industry.

In examining alternative measures of strategic performance, Chakravarthy compared the two groups of firms using Altman's Z-scores. His findings indicate that the Z-score was more successful at discriminating between the two groups. However, the linear discriminant function that produces the Z-score is empirically, rather than theoretically, based and focuses only upon a firm's ability to avoid bankruptcy. Chakravarthy concluded that while a good Z-score may be indicative of good short-term performance and a necessary condition for excellence, it does not sufficiently consider the long-term prosperity of a firm. Therefore, a good Z-score may be a necessary, but not a sufficient, condition for a firm to be excellent.

The most important finding of Chakravarthy's study was that the ability of a firm to produce slack resources was a discriminator of strategic performance. Chakravarthy demonstrated this by constructing a discriminant function using eight variables: (i) cash flow to total investment (CFBYIN); (ii) sales to total assets (SABYTA); (iii) research and development to sales (RDBYSA); (iv) market-to-book value (MBYB); (v) sales per employee

(SABYEM); (vi) debt to equity (DTBYEQ); (vii) working capital to sales (WCBYSA); and (viii) dividend payout to net income (DIVPAY). This function discriminated between excellent and non-excellent firms in 73 percent of their sample. The function created was:

$$0.12\ \text{CFBYIN} - 0.19\ \text{SABYEM} - 0.10\ \text{SABYTA} + 0.12\ \text{MBYB} -$$
$$0.28\ \text{DTBYEQ} + 0.34\ \text{RDBYSA} + 0.19\ \text{WCBYSA}$$
$$+ 0.29\ \text{DIVPAY} \geq 0.14\ \text{for excellence.}$$

The importance of this research was that no single profitability measure was capable of discriminating between the two groups of computer firms. This applied to both the accounting measures used and the market-based measure. As strategic performance deals with the future, Chakravarthy proposes that a firm needs slack resources to ensure its flexibility. Accordingly, in assessing strategic performance, the ability of a firm to produce slack resources is critical. The discriminant function developed includes multiple dimensions of performance, once again indicating the importance of multivariate measures of overall organizational performance.

Venkatraman and Ramanujam's Research

Venkatraman and Ramanujam (1987) empirically examined the degree of convergence across methods of measuring business economic performance, and in so doing demonstrated that sales growth, profit growth and profitability were discriminate measures of different dimensions of business economic performance. The purpose of this study was not to empirically derive the best measures of business economic performance in the context of the variables selected by researchers, but rather to test the convergence of methods used to obtain data on business economic performance.

Specifically, they compared two different modes of assessment, objective and perceptual, with two different sources of data, primary and secondary, using two different methods, multi-trait, multi-method (MTMM) and confirmatory factor analysis (CFA). The first finding of the study suggests that perceptual assessments of business economic performance by managers are strongly correlated with secondary data and consequently can be used as acceptable operationalizations of business economic performance. The second finding suggests that although both the MTMM and the CFA approaches provided support for the hypothesis of convergent validity between the measures, the CFA approach was more definitive and provided a better explanation. The implication is that CFA is a superior methodology for testing the convergent validity of measures of a construct.

Although it was not the primary aim of the study, Venkatraman and Ramanujam demonstrated that sales growth, profit growth and profitability were discriminate measures of different dimensions of business economic performance. They selected these measures based upon a review of the different performance dimensions typically used by different disciplines reported by Hofer (1983) and Woo and Willard's (1983) findings of key dimensions of performance based upon an analysis of PIMS data.

The results of this research suggest that CFA is a superior method to MTMM for testing the constructs for discriminant validity (that the performance constructs tested do not measure the same phenomenon). The sample for the study included primary and secondary data from 86 publicly traded companies. Sales growth was represented by the percentage change in sales for each company in the sample over a single year, adjusted for the industry average based upon the firm's primary SIC code. Profit growth was operationalized as the percentage change in net income over one year adjusted for the industry average. The profitability construct was represented by return on investment for one year adjusted for the industry average. The CFA indicated that the correlations between the three constructs were statistically significantly lower than unity. Accordingly, one finding of the research was that sales growth, profit growth and profitability were distinct constructs, implying that they did not measure the same performance phenomenon. The implication of this finding is that in isolation, none of the three variables individually measures the business economic performance construct. Consequently, the findings from a study that uses sales growth to represent business economic performance should not be equated to findings from a study that uses either profit growth or profitability to represent business economic performance.

Brush and Vanderwerf's Research

Brush and Vanderwerf (1992) examined 34 different studies in the entrepreneurship literature that explicitly used firm performance as the dependent variable. They found that 35 different measures of performance were used in those studies. This indicated that researchers perceived many different dimensions of performance, and that there was no agreement on what measures actually represent overall organizational performance. The most frequently used measures of performance were changes in sales, organizational survival, changes in number of employees, and profitability. Multiple objective measures were much more frequently employed than were subjective or perceptual measures of performance. Further, the primary means of data collection was mail surveys, and the primary sources of performance information were managers, executives, founders or owners.

Based upon the findings of their literature review, Brush and Vanderwerf examined methods and sources for obtaining estimates of new venture performance. The research questions examined were:

1. To what degree does performance information gathered by different methods of data collection produce different results?
2. To what degree is there variation, if any, of performance information across different sources? (1992: 160)

Using a sample of 66 manufacturing new ventures located in Massachusetts, Brush and Vanderwerf found that venture owner/managers preferred to provide information via a short phone interview rather than completing a mail survey. They found high correlations between the data provided by both sources. With respect to the second research question, where summary information is acceptable to the researcher, archival information was useful. Performance data provided by management proved to be reliable by comparison to archival information and had the added benefit of being more detailed. In other words, Brush and Vanderwerf suggest that primary information collected from management is preferable to secondary data sources when depth and context are important to the purposes of a study. However, if such depth and context are not critical to the research, archival information is sufficiently reliable on a summary basis.

Finally, Brush and Vanderwerf conclude by stating that they did not attempt to sort out the problem of which performance measures to use. They note that the fact that 35 different performance measures were used in just 34 studies indicates that more work needs to be done to identify measures that make sense for use across studies.

Robinson's Research

Robinson (1995) examined ten different new venture performance measures to determine which individual measure was the most effective in accurately assessing long-term economic value creation. Each of the performance measures were calculated for the three-year period following the firms' initial public offerings. A sample of 199 new ventures that had issued an initial public offering prospectus between 1980 and 1987 were used as the basis of the analysis. The ten measures studied were: (i) change in sales; (ii) sales level; (iii) return on sales (ROS); (iv) return on invested capital (ROIC); (v) return on equity (ROE); (vi) return on assets (ROA); (vii) net profit; (viii) earnings before interest and taxes (EBIT); (ix) earnings multiples; and (x) shareholder value created. Robinson found strong support for his hypothesis that return to stockholders provided the most power of the ten measures evaluated in corroborating previously established relationships between the influence of new venture strategy and the joint influence of new venture and industry structure on the economic performance of new ventures.

Robinson went on to examine the extent to which differing measures may reasonably be utilized as interchangeable proxies for one another. Specifically, Robinson tested six hypotheses using both parametric and nonparametric methods:

1. There will be strong positive relationships between the sales (level), and net income, ROS, ROA, ROIC and ROE.
2. There will be strong positive relationships among net income, ROS, ROA, ROIC and ROE.
3. There will be weak positive relationships between shareholder value created and both sales and sales changes.
4. Shareholder value created will have a positive relationship with accounting-based profitability measures.
   a. Shareholder value created will have a strong positive relationship with net income.
   b. There will be moderately strong positive relationships between shareholder value created and ROS, ROA, ROIC and ROE (1995: 411–13).

Both parametric and nonparametric tests of these hypotheses were done because the assumptions of normality, equality of variances and linear relationships among dependent variables were significantly violated. While Robinson found that the parametric tests of location were not robust with respect to these violations of data assumptions, he still performed them on his samples because parametric tests are used almost exclusively in new venture performance research. Robinson reported both parametric and nonparametric sets of results in his findings.

The first hypothesis was found to have strong support with the strength of the nonparametric Spearman Rank correlations ranging from 0.59 to 0.64 at a 0.001 level of significance. These results differed significantly from the parametric Pearson product-moment correlations that found sales level to be strongly correlated only with net income with a correlation coefficient of 0.75 at a 0.001 level of significance. The correlations between the sales level and the profitability ratios ranged from 0.05 to 0.20 and were not significant. The nonparametric results corroborate findings of Buzzell and

Gale (1987). However, they are in direct conflict with the parametric findings of Murphy et al. (1993, 1996).

The second hypothesis was found to have strong support with the strength of the nonparametric Spearman Rank correlations ranging from 0.79 to 0.94 at a 0.001 level of significance. These results differed significantly from the parametric Pearson product-moment correlations that found ROIC to be strongly correlated with ROE only with a correlation coefficient of 0.94 at a 0.001 level of significance. The remaining nine correlations were not found to be statistically significant with correlation coefficients ranging from 0.04 to 0.32. These nonparametric findings are once again in direct conflict with the parametric findings of Murphy et al. (1993, 1996).

The third hypothesis was not found to be supported as the nonparametric Spearman Rank correlation coefficient between shareholder value created and sales level was 0.32 at a 0.001 level of significance. The nonparametric Spearman Rank correlation coefficient between shareholder value created and sales change was 0.51 and was also at a 0.001 level of significance. These results indicate that there is a positive and statistically significant relationship between sales as an absolute measure and the change in sales with shareholder value created. However, the parametric Pearson product-moment correlations were –0.04 and –0.01, respectively, at a 0.10 level of statistical significance. The contradictory findings were explained by Robinson as being due to the violations of the parametric test assumptions and the test of association not being robust with respect to these violations.

Both parts of the fourth hypothesis concerning a positive relationship between accounting-based profitability measures and shareholder value created were strongly supported. The nonparametric Spearman Rank correlation coefficients ranged from 0.45 to 0.51 and were significant at the 0.001 level. Robinson noted that these results corroborated the prior findings of Ball and Brown (1968) and Lev and Ohlson (1982). The parametric tests of association did not find any statistically significant relationships at the 0.10 level. The parametric Pearson product-moment correlation coefficients ranged from –0.01 to 0.04.

In summary, all ten performance measures were tested individually for their relationship with multiple independent variables that had been found in prior literature to have positive relationships to new venture performance. The shareholder value created measure was determined to be the most effective measure for differentiating among new venture strategies, the second most effective measure for differentiating among the structures of the new venture's entered industry, and the most effective measure in differentiating among the interactions between new venture strategies and the structure of the industry the new venture entered. The fact that the different performance measures of overall new venture performance resulted in significantly different R-squares implies that the variables do not measure the same things. Since the variables do not measure the same things, yet all are valid dimensions of performance, it holds that performance is a multidimensional construct. Further, Robinson found that the parametric tests of association were not robust with respect to violations or critical assumptions underlying them. Accordingly, nonparametric tests of association were deemed to be more appropriate for investigating new venture performance.

Murphy, Trailer and Hill's Research

Murphy et al. (1996) examined the variables used to measure organizational performance in entrepreneurship research in the years 1987 through 1993. They identified 51 articles published in the *Academy of Management Journal*, the *American Journal of Small Business, Entrepreneurship Theory and Practice*, the *Journal of Business Venturing* and the *Strategic Management Journal* that explicitly used firm performance as a dependent variable. They found, consistent with Brush and Vanderwerf (1992) and Cooper (1993), that there was no consistency in the variables used to measure new venture performance. In total, they identified 71 different dependent variables used to measure performance in their sample. They subsequently categorized these variables into eight separate dimensions of performance. They also found that 75 percent of the sample articles used primary data sources, 29 percent used secondary data sources and only 6 percent used both. The high dependence upon primary data sources is typical in entrepreneurship research, since there are generally no publicly available financial data sources for non-public companies. Another finding was that the performance variables used were primarily financial rather than operational.

Table 2.2 presents the 71 variables summarized by performance dimension. It should be noted that some might dispute some of Murphy et al.'s classifications. For instance, asset, inventory and receivables turnover are generally considered efficiency measures, whereas return on investment, return on equity, return on assets, return on net worth (generally considered the same as return on equity) and internal rate of return are all considered profitability measures, even though Murphy et al. classified them as efficiency measures. Similarly, measures such as return to shareholders, market-to-book value and stock price appreciation are all considered market measures (Brealey et al., 2001) even though Murphy et al. classified them as profit measures. Therefore, while the actual measures and

Table 2.2   *Performance dimensions, measures of dimensions, and*
             frequencies of measures

Dimension	Measure	No.	Measure	No.
Efficiency	Return on investment	13	Average return on assets	2
	Return on equity	9	Net sales to total capital	1
	Return on assets	9	Return on average equity	1
	Return on net worth	6	Internal rate of return	1
	Gross revenue per employee	3	Relative product costs	1
Growth	Change in sales	23	Job generation	1
	Change in employees	5	Company births	1
	Market share growth	2	Change in present value	1
	Change in net income margin	2	Number of acquisitions	1
	Change in CEO compensation	2	Change in pretax profit	1
	Change in labor expense to revenue	1	Loan growth	1
Profit	Return on sales	11	Stock price appreciation	1
	Net profit margin	8	Price to earnings	1
	Gross profit margin	7	Respondent assessment	1
	Net profit level	5	Earnings per share	1
	Net profit from operations	5	Average return on sales	1
	Pretax profit	3	Average net profit margin	1
	Clients' estimate of incremental profits	1	Market to book value	1
Size liquidity	Sales level	13	Number of employees	5
	Cash flow level	6	Cash flow to sales	1
	Ability to fund growth	5	Inventory turnover	1
	Current ratio	2	Accounts receivable turnover	1
	Quick ratio	2	Cash flow to total debt	1
	Total asset turnover	1	Working capital to sales	1
	Cash flow to investment	1		
Success/Fail	Discontinued business	4	Operating under court order	1
	Researcher subjective assessment	1	No new telephone number	1
	Return on net worth	1	Salary of owner	1
	Respondent subjective assessment	1	Change in gross earnings	1
Market share	Respondent assessment	3	PIMS value	1
	Firm to industry product sales	1		

Table 2.2   (continued)

Dimension	Measure	No.	Measure	No.
Leverage	Debt to equity	2	Long-term debt to equity	1
	Times interest earned	1	Stockholders capital to total capital	1
Other	Change in employee turnover	1	Relative quality	1
	Dependence on corporate sponsor	1		

Source: Murphy et al. (1996: 17).

dimensions presented by Murphy et al. are meaningful, their classifications are suspect and may explain why their results of their factor analysis did not conform to the hypothesized dimensions.

Based on these classifications, Murphy et al. then examined 19 financial variables from a sample of 995 public firms with 500 or fewer employees. They found that less than half of the intercorrelations between performance measures were significant, indicating that these variables measured different dimensions of performance. More than 25 percent of the significant correlations of performance measures were negative. Murphy et al. concluded that the 'relationship between a given independent variable and performance is likely to depend upon the particular performance measure used'. They further concluded 'research finding support for an effect on one performance variable cannot justify the assumption that the effect is similar across other measures of performance' (1996: 21). Their study also found that the performance measures tested failed to meet the requirements of convergent and discriminant validity necessary to validate a one-dimensional performance construct (Campbell and Fiske, 1959).

Murphy et al. performed an exploratory factor analysis on the 19 variables, which yielded nine factors that explained over 70 percent of the variance in the performance measures. Table 2.3 presents the variables that comprise each of the nine factors identified.

Testing the conclusions of Murphy, Trailer and Hill
In an attempt to more fully examine the results obtained by Murphy et al., we performed a confirmatory factor analysis of the nine factors identified in their research, using LISREL 8.12 as suggested by Bollen (1989). The covariance data reported in the study, as shown in Table 2.4, was used as the basis for the analysis.

Table 2.3   Factor structure for 19 performance measures

Performance measure	FAC 1	FAC 2	FAC 3	FAC 4	FAC 5	FAC 6	FAC 7	FAC 8	FAC 9
Quick ratio	✓								
Current ratio	✓								
EPS		✓							
Net income		✓							
Times interest earned		✓							
ROA		✓							
ROE			✓						
ROI			✓						
Number of employees				✓					
Sales				✓					
Net sales/ Total capital					✓				
Receivables turnover					✓				
Debt-to-equity ratio					✓				
Sales growth						✓			
Sales/Equity						✓			
Revenue per employee							✓		
Sales/Working capital								✓	
Net profit margin									✓
Net income change									✓

The results of this analysis indicated that the factors determined by Murphy et al. did not fit the data. The model yielded chi-square = 1,292 with 127 degrees of freedom ($p < 0.0001$), Bentler and Bonett normed fit index of 0.727 and a non-normed fit index of 0.657. This indicates that while the variables did load into factors, these factors may not be supported by the data. This is possible since exploratory factor analysis will force variables into the number of factors specified, even though the factors may not have the best possible fit for the data. Even if the data had fit the model, because the analysis was an exploratory factor analysis, there was no theoretical support for the identified constructs. Consequently, the variables within each factor, as determined by the exploratory factor analysis, fail the test for convergent validity using confirmatory factor analysis, and they also did not have any face validity.

Summary of Prior Research on Overall Organizational Performance

It is clear from the prior empirical studies that there has been no consistency in the measures used to represent the construct of overall organizational performance in strategic management or entrepreneurship research. Further, prior empirical research has demonstrated that there are multiple dimensions to the performance construct. While Robinson (1995) found that return to shareholders was the most powerful individual performance with respect to new venture performance among companies that have undergone initial public offerings, these findings cannot be reasonably generalized to studies that use different samples. In short, there continues to be no conclusive research that has identified a 'best' measure of overall organizational performance, nor has a measurement model that accurately represents the construct yet been developed.

OVERALL ORGANIZATIONAL PERFORMANCE MEASURES USED IN RECENT RESEARCH

To assess the current state of performance measurement in entrepreneurship and strategic management research, we examined five years of empirical research from July 1996 through June 2001 published in five journals known for publishing empirical research in these fields, namely the *Academy of Management Journal* (AMJ), the *Strategic Management Journal* (SMJ), the *Journal of Management* (JOM), the *Journal of Business Venturing* (JBV) and *Entrepreneurship Theory & Practice* (ETP).

The objectives of this review were to determine the following:

- How many articles in the journals deal with the ultimate end of management, overall organizational performance?
- How many different measures of performance were used?
- Do the measures of performance actually used in these studies measure the same phenomenon or are authors making claims that are not generalizable beyond the actual measure?

For an article to qualify for inclusion in this tabulation, the author(s) must indicate in their hypotheses that overall organizational performance is their dependent variable. In this review, we made no attempt to judge what an overall organizational performance measure should be. As a consequence, if the author(s) stated that they were seeking to measure overall organizational performance, their study was included together

Table 2.4   Means, standard deviations and correlations of performance measures

Variables	Mean	SD	1	2	3	4	5	6	7
1 Quick ratio	1.42	1.62							
2 Current ratio	2.03	1.96	0.93						
3 EPS	0.57	1.81	−0.01	−0.09					
4 Net income	842.50	6,762	0.08	0.05	0.50				
5 Times interest earned	−18.81	70.58	0.15	0.13	0.23	0.14			
6 ROA	−0.05	0.28	0.17	0.18	0.25	0.29	0.24		
7 ROE	−0.02	2.68	−0.01	−0.02	0.04	0.05	0.04	−0.12	
8 ROI	−0.03	3.23	0.01	0.01	0.05	0.01	0.02	−0.15	0.53
9 No. of employees	171.20	141.80	0.01	0.05	0.04	0.15	−0.08	0.16	0.03
10 Sales	31,681	45,211	0.00	0.00	0.05	0.33	0.03	0.14	0.02
11 Net sales/ Total capital	0.89	0.82	−0.06	0.07	−0.32	−0.10	−0.08	−0.07	−0.05
12 Receivables turn	7.33	13.18	0.03	0.06	−0.18	−0.10	−0.06	−0.07	−0.01
13 Debt to equity	3.79	7.80	−0.10	−0.19	0.29	0.09	0.09	0.11	−0.32
14 Sales growth	12.79	26.95	0.19	0.15	0.03	0.05	0.13	0.09	−0.01
15 Sales/Equity	165,878	113,903	0.04	0.03	0.07	0.17	0.15	0.16	−0.02
16 Gross revenue/ Employment	295.30	764.20	−0.02	−0.04	0.01	0.08	−0.01	0.01	0.04
17 Sales/ Work capital	2.26	17.68	0.02	0.03	−0.03	0.01	0.00	0.02	0.00
18 Net profit margin	−0.29	3.17	0.07	0.08	0.09	0.09	0.06	0.19	−0.15
19 Net income change	0.97	5.18	0.02	0.01	0.08	0.08	−0.01	0.05	0.16

Source: Murphy et al. (1996: 19).

with whatever measures they chose to use to measure overall organizational performance. Further, the article had to be empirical in design and had to clearly define how the dependent measure was calculated. To determine this information, the methods section, hypotheses and conclusions of each article were reviewed. Most articles clearly indicated what measures were used and how they were calculated, but in some cases the description of the dependent variables was inadequate. For example, an article might indicate that return on assets was used as a proxy for organizational performance, but did not reveal whether that measure was an average, or the time period measured, or the actual nature of the calculation of the measure.

8	9	10	11	12	13	14	15	16	17	18
0.01										
0.00	0.49									
−0.09	0.02	0.02								
−0.02	0.01	−0.01	0.20							
−0.24	0.04	0.07	−0.37	−0.19						
−0.16	−0.01	0.07	0.05	−0.03	−0.07					
−0.02	−0.01	0.23	−0.04	−0.03	0.07	0.14				
0.01	−0.17	0.21	0.02	0.03	0.03	0.02	0.04			
0.02	−0.06	0.03	0.10	−0.04	0.03	0.00	−0.05	0.05		
−0.03	0.11	0.07	0.08	0.00	0.04	0.09	0.12	0.03	0.01	
0.16	0.02	0.03	−0.08	0.00	−0.03	−0.01	0.03	0.02	−0.06	0.03

How many Articles in the Journals Deal with the Ultimate End of Management Overall Organizational Performance?

A total of 1,045 articles were examined from the five journals listed above over the five-year period from July 1996 to June 2001. Of these articles, 138 purported to use overall organizational performance as the dependent measure. The remaining 907 used intermediate performance variables that may influence overall organizational performance, and are valuable in their contribution from that standpoint. However, these 907 articles were not reviewed further and were not included in this analysis. Of the 138 studies that used overall organizational performance (as defined by their author(s)) as the primary dependent variable, 64 (46 percent) used only one variable to

Table 2.5   Summary of the number of variables used in prior empirical research to measure overall organizational performance published in AMJ, SMJ, JOM, JBV and ETP

No. of performance variables used	Number of articles	%
One	64	46
Two	35	25
Three	24	18
Four	10	7
Five	2	2
Six	1	1
Seven	0	–
Eight	2	1

represent the performance construct and 35 (25 percent) used two variables. The remaining 39 (29 percent) used between three and eight separate measures of performance. Table 2.5 summarizes the number of variables used.

How many Different Measures of Performance Were Used?

Table 2.6 presents a summary of the different variables used to measure overall organizational performance and the different timeframe variations for each variable. A total of 88 different variables were used and when combined with the different timeframes, 133 distinct measures of overall organizational performance were utilized as dependent variables in these 138 studies. The 88 variables can be grouped into nine primary performance dimensions as found in the prior literature (Helfert, 1994; Higgins, 1995; Brealey et al., 2001; Penman, 2001).

Definitions of the performance dimension categories
Table 2.7 summarizes the mix of variables by primary performance dimension. The profitability dimension includes accounting measures and ratios that incorporate net income or a component of net income such as operating income or earnings before taxes. The operational dimension includes measures of performance that deal with how the organization is developing on non-financial issues, such as market share, patents received and stakeholder performance. Market-based measures of performance include measures and ratios that incorporate the market value of the organization, such as market value added, return to shareholders and Jensen's alpha. The growth dimension includes measures and ratios that include some indication of organizational growth, such as growth in sales or employees. The efficiency dimension includes measures that relate performance to how well

Table 2.6 Summary of dependent variables used to represent overall organizational performance

Description	Type of measure	One point in time	Average for ___ years						Total
			1 year	2	3	4	5	Over 5	
Profitability									
Average monthly net profit for 12 months	Financial	1							1
Earnings before interest and taxes	Financial		1						1
Earnings per share	Financial		1		1				2
Growth rate of profits	Financial				4				4
Net profit	Financial		5		2		1		8
Operating margin – 3-year average standardized (mean 0 SD 1)	Financial				1				1
Operating margin – adjusted for industry averages	Financial	1							1
Operating return on assets	Financial		1						1
Personal income of the entrepreneur	Financial					1			1
Return on assets	Financial		18	3	12	1	6	3	43
Return on assets – adjusted for industry averages	Financial		2	1			1		4
Return on assets – growth rate	Financial				2				2
Return on assets – growth rate of 3-year average adjusted for industry averages	Financial				1				1
Return on assets relative to sales growth	Financial		1						1
Return on equity	Financial		4	1	5	1	1	1	13
Return on equity – average for 4 quarters	Financial		1						1
Return on equity – adjusted for industry averages	Financial		1	3					4
Return on invested capital	Financial		1		1		1		3

Table 2.6 (continued)

Description	Type of measure	One point in time	Average for ___ years						Total
			1 year	2	3	4	5	Over 5	
Return on investment	Financial		1		1	1	1	1	5
Return on investment – adjusted for industry averages	Financial		1						1
Return on sales	Financial		6	1	6		3		16
Return on sales – adjusted for industry averages	Financial				1		1		2
Subjective assessment by top management of profitability	Financial		5						5
Subjective assessment by top managers of overall financial performance	Financial		11						11
Sum of economic value added for 5 years divided by beginning period capital	Financial						1		1
Efficiency									
Employees – net profit per	Financial		1						1
Employees – sales per	Financial		1						1
Employees – turnover rate	Operational		1						1
Return on sales per square foot	Financial		1						1
Sales per square foot	Financial		3						3
Subjective assessment by top management of operating efficiency	Operational		2						2
Subjective assessment by top management of overall efficiency	Operational		1						1

Growth

R&D spending – absolute growth	Financial			1	1
R&D employees – absolute growth	Operational			1	1
Non-R&D employees – absolute growth	Operational			1	1
Total employees – absolute growth	Operational		1	1	2
Growth rate of employees	Operational		3		3
Growth in monthly payroll after 12 months in dollars	Operational			2	2
Absolute growth in sales	Financial	3	1	1	5
Absolute growth in sales – adjusted for industry average	Financial		1		1
Growth rate for sales	Financial	6	1	8	15
Growth rate of sales – adjusted for industry averages	Financial	1		3	4
Growth rate for sales and profit – two-item measure	Financial			1	1
Subjective assessment by top management of sales growth	Financial	6			6

Liquidity

Net cash flow	Financial			1	1
Cash flow taken out by entrepreneurs	Financial		1		1
Cash flow divided by gross capital stock	Financial	1			1
Operating cash flows as a percent of total assets	Financial			1	1
Growth rate of operating cash flow	Financial		1		1
Growth rate of operating cash flow – industry adjusted	Financial		1		1
Subjective assessment by top management of financial stability	Financial			1	1

Table 2.6 (continued)

Description	Type of measure	One point in time	Average for ___ years						Total
			1 year	2	3	4	5	Over 5	
Operational									
Absolute number of patents granted in a year	Operational		1						1
Customer satisfaction index – based on primary survey data	Operational	1							1
Difference between predicted and actual market share	Operational		1						1
Growth in market share	Operational		2		1				3
Growth rate of market share	Operational		1						1
Market share in dollars	Operational		1		1				2
Human resource value	Operational	1							1
Industry-specific measures	Operational		8						8
Subjective assessment by top management of adaptiveness	Operational		1						1
Subjective assessment by top management of customer satisfaction	Operational		2						2
Subjective assessment by top management of future prospects	Operational		3						3
Subjective assessment by top management of market share	Operational		2						2
Subjective assessment by top management of overall effectiveness	Operational		1						1
Subjective assessment by top management of planning performance	Operational		1						1

Measure	Type				
Subjective assessment by top management of R&D performance	Operational				1
Subjective assessment by top managers of innovation performance	Operational				2
Subjective assessment by top managers of market performance	Operational				3
Subjective assessment by top managers of stakeholder performance	Operational				1
Market					
Cumulative abnormal return to shareholders	Market	2			2
Holding period return over 3 years (market price growth of stock ignoring dividends)	Market		1		1
Jensen's alpha	Market	2	1		4
Market-to-book value	Market	1	1		4
Market-to-book value – 2nd year after survey adjusted for industry averages	Market	1			1
Market value added (market value – capital)	Market	1			1
Market value added divided by total invested capital	Market	1			1
Market value added over 5 years divided by beginning period capital	Market			1	1
Perceived market potential – stock price minus book value divided by stock price	Market	1			1
Return to shareholders	Market	3	2	2	7
Return to shareholders relative to sales growth	Market	1			1

Table 2.6 (continued)

Description	Type of measure	One point in time	Average for ___ years						Total
			1 year	2	3	4	5	Over 5	
Stock price at a single point in time – absolute stock price	Market	2							2
Tobin's Q	Market		3						3
Size									
Sales – revenues for one year	Financial		3		1				4
Number of employees	Operational	1							1
Survival									
Business success or failure as compared to industry averages	Financial	2							2
Survival through a point in time	Financial	4							4
Other									
Multidimensional construct with 7 components	Financial		1						1
Subjective assessment by top managers of ideal performance	Financial		10						10

Table 2.7   Summary of variables and articles by performance dimension

Dimension	No. of variables	%	No. of articles	%
Profitability	25	28	96	70
Operational	18	21	25	18
Market based	13	15	24	17
Growth	12	14	37	27
Efficiency	7	8	9	7
Liquidity	7	8	6	4
Size	2	2	4	3
Survival	2	2	6	4
Other	2	2	11	8

organizational resources are utilized, such as sales per square foot, sales per employee and return on sales per square foot. The liquidity dimension measures an organization's ability to meet its financial obligations in a timely manner including measures such as current, quick and cash flow ratios. The size dimension includes measures that represent the size of the organization, such as total sales and number of employees. Survival deals with whether the organization continued in business or not. The final category of performance includes the other measures that researchers have used over time, such as multidimensional constructs or subjective assessments by top managers of ideal performance for the organization.

Clearly, profitability was the primary organizational performance dimension used as a dependent variable. Of the 138 articles, 70 percent included a profitability variable as at least one of the dependent organizational performance measures. Of the profitability measures, return on assets was the most frequently utilized. Growth was the second most common performance dimension used to measure overall organizational performance. In particular, growth was recognized as a critical performance dimension for new ventures.

Market-based measures have become much more popular over the past several years, and were used as a performance dimension in 17 percent of the articles. In the study by Murphy et al. (1996), only three market-based measures were employed (4 percent of the total variables used in the study) while 15 percent of the performance measures in the current study were market-based measures.

The time periods used to measure performance
The time periods for measuring performance ranged from single point in time measures to averages over 15 years. As summarized in Table 2.6, of the

278 performance variables used in the articles, 152 (55 percent) were one-year performance measures, 67 (24 percent) were three-year measures, 16 (6 percent) were single point in time measures, 19 (7 percent) were five-year measures, and the remaining 24 (8 percent) were either two-, four-, or more than five-year measures. Clearly one- and three-year measures were deemed the most appropriate time periods by the researchers for measuring the effects under study. Generally, the choice of the timeframe for measures was defended based on arguments that changes in overall organizational performance would 'lag' changes in the independent variables being measured. Tsai et al. (1991) found empirical support for this argument when they found that strategic initiatives depress return on investment in the early years, but result in improved return on investment after four years.

Do the Measures of Performance Actually Measure the Same Phenomenon or are Authors Making Claims that are Not Generalizable Beyond the Actual Measure?

When examining the issue of whether the variables used in the survey of empirical research actually measure the same phenomenon, that is, overall organizational performance, the heart of the question is whether there is construct validity. In other words, do the empirical variables measured adequately represent the true meaning of the concept under consideration (Babbie, 1998)? Campbell and Fiske summarized this issue when they wrote 'it is valid to assert that a given operation taps a particular construct only if it can be shown that the operation produces results that agree with those achieved with alternative operationalizations of the same construct' (1959: 83).

While at face value, many of the performance measures used in the empirical articles summarized in this analysis would appear to be similar, such as sales growth and profit growth, previous empirical findings have shown that they do not measure the same phenomenon. As mentioned earlier, Venkatraman and Ramanujam (1987) empirically demonstrated that sales growth, profit growth and profitability were different constructs using confirmatory factor analysis.

In other words, even without further empirical confirmation, it is clear that the different measures of overall organizational performance used do not represent the same construct. Our survey indicated that 54 percent of the empirical articles that sought to assess overall organizational performance used multiple 'measures' to assess such performance. Moreover, the reason most commonly cited for using multiple variables was that the different measures produce different results. This clearly indicates that the researchers recognize that their hypotheses are not really affecting overall organizational performance, but rather a single dimension or multiple dimensions of such performance. Therefore, it would seem more appropriate for authors to specifically cite which dimension(s) of performance their study is addressing (profitability, growth, operational performance and so on) rather than claiming to be studying those phenomena that impact organizational performance. Further, in generalizing from prior studies, it would be appropriate only to incorporate works that specifically used the same performance constructs. Since it is apparent from the survey of recent studies that few authors actually are using the same performance constructs in their work, it is also clear that most claims of having made incremental advances in theory building upon prior works are 'exaggerated' at best, and quite possibly spurious (Kuhn, 1970).

Summary of This Review of Prior Research

Our review of five years of articles in the *Academy of Management Journal*, the *Strategic Management Journal*, the *Journal of Management*, the *Journal of Business Venturing*, and *Entrepreneurship Theory & Practice* revealed that 138 of 1,045 (13 percent) of articles published between July 1996 and June 2001, purported to use overall organizational performance as the dependent measure in empirical research. In these 138 articles, 133 distinct measures of overall organizational performance were used. Prior empirical research has shown that these variables measure different and statistically distinct dimensions of performance. Further, no single measure or group of measures of overall organizational performance has emerged as actually representing the construct. This may be because no one-dimensional performance construct is devisable or because no one has adequately identified or described the dimensions on which such a construct could be based. Consequently, claims by authors of having made incremental advances in theory by building upon prior works that do not use the same measures of overall organizational performance would appear to be questionable.

CHAPTER SUMMARY

The conclusions from our survey of the literature confirm the findings by all prior similar studies and indicate that although each of the prior studies called for more scholarly rigor in the selection of measures of overall organizational performance, the problem persists. Although dozens of articles are published each year that test hypotheses of causal relationships between various independent variables and 'organizational performance', there is no consensus with respect to just what 'organizational performance' means.

Overall organizational performance has been both hypothesized and empirically demonstrated to be a multi-dimensional construct in a number of studies. However, there is no agreement on what the different dimensions of overall organizational performance are, or on how they should be measured. The way that many researchers deal with this problem is to create causal models and then test them against several different single-measurement performance constructs, often without any clear theoretical support for why these various performance variables were selected. Unfortunately, the use of so many different variables for measuring organizational performance makes generalization from one study to another dubious at best.

Our test of the dimensions of new venture performance developed by Murphy et al. (1996) does not meet the test for internal validity, leaving the question of what are the appropriate dimensions of new venture performance still unanswered. A similar study aimed at identifying the dimensions of performance for more established firms has not been done to date. Accordingly, the question of what truly constitutes overall organizational performance and how to measure it remains unresolved, since no one has yet successfully developed and tested a multidimensional model of performance that incorporates most of the 'dimensions' of performance identified in the existing research literature.

3. Perspectives of organizational performance and effectiveness

This chapter examines how the concept of overall organizational effectiveness and performance has been characterized and investigated in prior theory and research. The purpose of this chapter is not to propose or examine specific measures of organizational performance, but rather to examine the nature of organizational performance measurement. First, five perspectives of organizational performance are examined: accounting, balanced scorecard, strategic management, entrepreneurship and microeconomics. Next, the general concept of organizational effectiveness and performance is discussed, including an examination of various models of organizational effectiveness and performance. Then, an argument is made for developing a single-constituency model of organizational performance. The chapter concludes by proposing a framework for developing a single-constituency, multidimensional model of organizational performance for for-profit organizations.

FIVE PERSPECTIVES OF ORGANIZATIONAL PERFORMANCE

The nature of organizational performance and its measurement has been a topic for both scholars and practitioners since organizations were first formed. How to determine whether the efforts of the organization are being put to their best use and are achieving the desired outcomes is at the heart of several disciplines. Accountants devote their attention to fairly presenting the historical financial performance of organizations, while the management disciplines focus on how to improve current and future organizational performance. More specifically, for the purposes of management research, and in particular entrepreneurship and strategic management research, *post hoc* performance must be measured to determine the effectiveness of the managerial decisions. The 'balanced scorecard' approach developed by Kaplan (1984) combines both historical accounting perspectives as well as operational measures that capture information about expected future organizational performance. The following sections briefly examine organizational effectiveness and performance from the accounting, balanced scorecard, strategic management, entrepreneurship and microeconomic perspectives.

The Accounting Literature Perspective

In measuring organizational performance, accounting scholars focus on the information content of the organization's financial statements and measures. In fact, the *raison d'être* for the accounting profession is to present the past financial performance of an organization both fairly and consistently. To this end, volumes of accounting rules and procedures have been developed over the years to make the information contained in organizational financial statements both meaningful and comparable over time and across organizations.

One primary stream of research in the accounting literature involves the information content of earnings and their relationship to the valuation of organizations (Ball and Brown, 1968; Beaver, 1968; Lev, 1989). In this context, the focus of accounting research on performance measurement has shifted from its relevance to corporate policies and processes, to the extent to which publicly traded equity security returns are consistent with the information conveyed by earnings (Lev, 1989). It is not the intention of this stream of research to imply causal associations between the information content of financial statements and equity security returns, but rather correlation. Consequently, this stream of inquiry is extremely useful to researchers who are looking for proxies for market returns or shareholder value creation. The higher the correlation between the information content of accounting information and equity security returns, the better proxies for shareholder value creation that can be developed from accounting information. These proxies could be the basis for measures of shareholder value creation for non-publicly traded companies.

Lev reviewed two decades of accounting research on the usefulness of earnings as a proxy for stock returns, or the creation of shareholder value. Two of his findings are critical for the selection of measures of organizational performance.

The correlation between earnings and stock returns is very low, sometimes negligible. Moreover, the nature (parameters) of the returns/earnings relation exhibits considerable instability over time. These findings suggest that the usefulness of quarterly and annual earnings to investors is very limited.

While misspecifications of the return/earnings relation or the existence of investor irrationality ('noise trading') may contribute to the observed weak association between earnings and stock returns, the possibility that the fault lies with the low quality (information content) of reported earnings looms large (1989: 155).

These findings are of particular interest to strategy, entrepreneurship and other researchers who use earnings as a proxy for organizational performance. If stock prices have already anticipated the earnings announcement and do not generally react to the actual announcement of earnings, then stock prices can be deemed to include the information contained in the earnings release, or be considered to be efficient. Therefore, stock prices and the corresponding returns to shareholders over the period being measured can be assumed to include the effects of earnings on overall organizational performance. This is consistent with the findings of Ball and Brown (1968) who indicate that stock prices moved up when earnings increased and moved down when earnings decreased. Further, in an attempt to reproduce the effects found by Beaver (1968), Bamber and Christiansen (2000) found that earnings announcements do not cause market price reactions for the majority of announcements.

One question that should be considered when examining measures of organizational performance is whether the variable selected to represent organizational performance is timely or whether the variable lags the effects of interest. For instance, does return to shareholders coincide with the actions taken by management, or do stock market returns lag the actions, since accounting earnings are not reported until weeks or in some cases months after the quarter or year is over. O'Hanlon (1991), in an empirical test of 20 years of data on 222 UK companies, found that there was a lag effect between stock market and accounting returns. However, the lag went both ways: accounting returns and stock market returns can both be found to lead the other. In other words, assuming a lag effect in a performance measure is not generally going to be appropriate relative to accounting versus market returns.

Several conclusions are suggested, based upon this discussion of some of the accounting research, on the information content of measures. First, the accounting profession, through the application of generally accepted accounting principles (GAAP) consistently applied, produces financial reports that are materially accurate, comparable across organizations in similar industries, and represent the execution on opportunities to date. Second, accounting reports provide important information about value creation that has been realized and retained in the company in the past. However, because of the accounting profession's conservative approach to recognition of gains, these same reports do not capture information about future opportunities that the organization has created but not executed upon. In other words, the accounting perspective of organizational performance is based upon past effects of managerial decision making and specifically excludes the expected future effects. Finally, since the accounting profession develops its rules to provide information for all users of financial statements, including equity providers, creditors and regulatory bodies, it takes a multiconstituency and multidimensional view of performance.

The Balanced Scorecard Perspective

In an attempt to bridge the gap between theory and practice, Kaplan (1984) proposed that effective organizational performance should be measured using a 'balanced scorecard'. He suggested that organizational performance measurement requires measures that are not purely financial in nature, because many of the financial indicators are a result of critical operational measures. For example, accounting measures report only what has happened in the past, and not the investments in future opportunities. Therefore, Kaplan argues that a combination of financial and operational measures is necessary for measuring overall organizational performance. Accordingly, the balanced scorecard is a multidisciplinary view of organizational performance.

Balanced scorecard measures include market share, changes in intangible assets such as patents or human resources skills and abilities, customer satisfaction, product innovation, productivity, quality and stakeholder performance. Most of these measures require primary data from management in the form of their assessment of their own performance, which may lead to questions of the validity of the responses. The primary advantage to using operational measures in conjunction with financial performance measures is when they provide information about opportunities that have been created, but not yet financially realized. Since GAAP do not permit companies to recognize the expected value of new discoveries until the benefits are actually realized, accounting-based measures do not capture this information on organizational performance.

One critical weakness of the balanced scorecard approach is that it utilizes operational measures that are unique to each organization. While practical for implementation by organization insiders, this limits the utility to researchers since it is situationally specific, rather than situationally generic. Accordingly, generalization across companies is only possible when the balanced scorecard variables utilized are applicable to the entire population of interest. However, since a balanced scorecard approach is most effective when it is tailored to the specific circumstances of each organization, it is generally impractical in a research application.

The Strategic Management Perspective

Fundamental to the study of management is an understanding of the goals and objectives of the organization and the processes used to measure their accomplishment (Drucker, 1954; Ansoff, 1965; Hofer and Schendel, 1978; Schendel and Hofer, 1979; Andrews, 1987). Unfortunately, despite all of the scholarly and practitioner attention paid to the subject, the best way to characterize our current understanding of the concept of organizational performance would be to paraphrase the Supreme Court's definition of pornography, that is, 'I can't tell you exactly what it is, but I will know it when I see it'. Thus, even though accountants have developed GAAP for reporting performance, GAAP are constantly changing, in part due to the dynamic nature of organizations, but also as a result of experience with the current state of performance reporting. However, accountants at least have a common set of rules for telling firms how to present organizational performance data. Based on the examination of empirical articles published in the fields of entrepreneurship and strategic management over a recent five-year period presented in Chapter 2, it is clear that for these two disciplines, there is no commonly agreed upon foundation for measuring organizational performance.

Over the years, there have been many conceptualizations of organizational performance in the strategic management literature. Two critical aspects of organizational performance perspectives in the literature are the constituencies for whom the organization performs, and the dimensions which should be measured. The following are several different perspectives on these two issues from the strategic management literature.

Barnard (1938) viewed organizational effectiveness as the accomplishment of organizational purposes, while he defined efficiency as the degree to which individual motives are satisfied. Barnard argued that the primary measure of an effective and efficient organization is its capacity to survive. Clearly, Barnard proposed a multi-constituency, one-dimensional perspective of organizational performance.

Drucker (1954) also argued that the ultimate measure of organizational performance is survival. To this end, Drucker proposed eight different performance dimensions that he felt were essential for the survival and prosperity of a firm: (i) market standing relative to the market potential both now and in the future; (ii) innovation; (iii) productivity; (iv) physical and financial resources; (v) profitability sufficient to cover the risk premium for being in business; (vi) manager performance and development; (vii) worker performance and attitude; and (viii) public responsibility. According to Drucker, these eight dimensions are all necessary for the long-term survival of the organization, which is the ultimate test of performance. Consequently, Drucker's perspective is both multiconstituency and multidimensional.

Ansoff (1965) proposed that the ultimate measure of organizational performance is return on investment. While this was argued to be the aim of the organization, Ansoff acknowledged that the organization was constrained by individual stakeholder objectives. As a consequence, the organization must also have non-economic objectives that lead to maximization of return on investment as limited by stakeholder constraints on organizational flexibility. In contrast to Drucker, Ansoff's perspective can be seen as multiconstituency and one-dimensional. Although Ansoff proposes one primary dimension of performance, he does propose that there are several subdimensions of that construct.

Freeman (1984) proposed that for an organization to accomplish its objectives, it had to utilize its relationships with stakeholders to accomplish both organizational and stakeholder goals. Stakeholders are not considered organizational constraints. Rather, they are a resource to accomplish organizational objectives. This requires satisfying at least the minimal interests of all stakeholders. Freeman's perspective is both multiconstituency and multidimensional.

Porter (1985) argued that the objectives of business units need to be established to reflect the goals of the overall organization. In this context, some business units might be tasked with higher sales growth, while others may be tasked with greater cash generation to finance the sales growth in more productive areas. Porter adopts a multiconstituency, multidimensional perspective of organizational performance.

Venkatraman and Ramanujam (1986) proposed that the domain of organizational effectiveness comprised three primary dimensions: (i) financial performance; (ii) operational performance; and (iii) the influence of stakeholders. According to this model, the financial and operational performance domains are subsets of business performance, which is a subset of organizational effectiveness. Each of these three primary dimensions comprised numerous lower-level dimensions.

Venkatraman and Ramanujam's financial dimension deals with the overall financial performance of the organization, and is the domain of performance generally found in strategy and entrepreneurship research. It may be decomposed into subdimensions such as profitability, growth, efficiency, financial structure, survival, cash flow and resource accumulation. Their operational dimension deals with how the organization is performing on non-financial issues. This operational dimension expands upon the financial dimension, and is more commonly reflected in recent strategy and entrepreneurship research. It may be decomposed into subdimensions, such as market building, organization building, network building, product quality, product and process innovation, quality, and employee and customer satisfaction. Moreover, this list of potential subdimensions is not exhaustive for, as described above, effectiveness is a problem-driven construct, and dimensions of performance can be conceptualized to fit each problem. The third dimension of business performance is related to organizational stakeholders. This dimension captures the multiconstituency model of performance. Consequently, this conceptualization is both multiconstituency and multidimensional.

It is fair to conclude from the perspectives of individual authors, that the strategic management perspective of organizational performance is generally multiconstituency and multidimensional. Any multiconstituency approach to defining organizational performance is problematic, since across companies the perspective of performance will not be uniform. Without a reasonable expectation that perceptions of performance are relatively similar across organizations, researchers will have a difficult time selecting measures of organizational performance that are generalizable. If the interpretation of overall organizational performance is idiosyncratic to each organization, then cross-sectional studies of organizations may not be practical.

The Entrepreneurship Perspective

The same problems that affect the strategic management perspective of organizational performance also affect the entrepreneurship perspective. It can be argued that the goals of the founding entrepreneur are the goals of the organization, a one-dimensional perspective of organizational performance (Bracker and Pearson, 1986; Chandler and Jansen, 1992; Slevin and Covin, 1995). However, it is also clear that entrepreneurship researchers examine other stakeholder perspectives of performance, such as those of venture capitalists, angel investors and family business owners. As with strategic management research, the entrepreneurship researchers adopt a multidimensional view of performance, recognizing that there are inherent tradeoffs between such issues as growth and profitability (Gartner, 1990; Chandler and Hanks, 1993, 1994b; Murphy et al., 1996). Consequently, as with strategic management, the entrepreneurship perspective of performance is both multiconstituency and multidimensional.

The Microeconomic Perspective

Many scholars have argued that owners of productive assets associate in an organization for the purpose of gaining economic advantage (as examples, see Jensen and Meckling, 1976; Simon, 1976; and Barney, 2002). The owners of the assets will contribute them to the organization so long as the return they receive or expect to receive is satisfactory relative to the risk they take. Satisfaction is in part determined by the alternative uses that the owner has for the assets. In other words, the value that an organization creates for the owners of contributed assets must be at least as large as the value expected. When the value created is less than the expected or required return, owners of assets will, if possible, withdraw their support for the organization and put their assets to alternative uses where they can achieve the required return.

Barney (2002) argues that the linkage between the required value sought for the use of assets and the actual value created by the use of these assets is organizational performance. Normal performance is when the value created is exactly equal to the value consumed in using the assets. This does not mean that there is no profit. Quite the contrary is true. At this level of performance, profit is just equal to the organization's weighted average cost of capital. Since the weighted average cost of capital is, by definition, based upon the risk-adjusted returns required by debt and equity providers, the profit of the organization is equal to the value increase necessary to satisfy the demands of equity investors. Above-normal performance occurs when the organization produces more value than that required by those who provide resources. For example, when resource owners cumulatively require a $10 increase in value for providing their resources and the organization produces a $15 increase in value, the organization would produce an 'extra' amount of value other than its expected performance. Below-normal performance occurs when the organization produces less value than that required by resource providers.

The difference between expected and actual value created is known as 'economic rent' (Peteraf, 1993). Above-normal returns result in economic profits, while below-normal returns result in economic losses. Transactional theory, in microeconomics, proposes that under conditions of perfect competition, the value a firm creates is just sufficient to meet the demands of resource providers. Economic profits and losses occur because competition among firms is not perfect. Organizations experiencing economic profits typically have a competitive advantage, while those experiencing economic losses are usually at a competitive disadvantage. Organizations that earn 'normal' returns are in competitive parity with other organizations in their industry. Organizations that persist in earning less than acceptable returns will find that resource providers will withdraw their assets. And, if and when all resources are withdrawn, these organizations will cease to exist. By contrast, organizations that generate more

than acceptable returns will be able to attract additional resources necessary to meet increased demand resulting from their competitive advantage.

THE EVOLUTION OF THE CONCEPT OF ORGANIZATIONAL EFFECTIVENESS

The conceptual issues with organizational effectiveness and performance
have been a topic of academic attention for years. Steers noted:

> The concept of organizational effectiveness is encountered repeatedly in the lit-
> erature on organizations, but there is only a rudimentary understanding of what
> is actually involved in or constitutes the concept. In fact, although effectiveness
> is generally considered a desirable attribute in organizations, few serious
> attempts have been made to explain the construct either theoretically or empir-
> ically. (1975: 546)

Steers proceeded to review the multivariate models of organizational
effectiveness used in 17 different multivariate studies of organizational
effectiveness. These 17 studies used 15 different evaluation criteria to reach
their conclusions. Steers found that the authors of the studies lacked
detailed rationales or empirical defenses for the criteria they selected.
Moreover, while the authors of the studies described the characteristics of
the criteria they used, they did not explain why the model of effectiveness
that they chose should be generalized to other organizations. Steers concluded that an understanding of an organization's functional and environmental uniqueness is a prerequisite to assessing its effectiveness. In his
article, Steers summarized the frequency with which each different evaluation criteria was mentioned or used in the 17 models of organizational
effectiveness that he identified. It should be noted that at the time of his
article, the primary research being conducted was in organizational theory
and not strategic management or entrepreneurship. Table 3.1 summarizes
these results.

Steers found that only one variable was used in more than half the
models. Accordingly, he concluded, 'the effectiveness construct is so
complex as to defy simple attempts at model development. Perhaps more
flexible, comprehensive models are required' (1975: 549).

Cameron (1980) proposed that there are four primary performance
dimensions that prior researchers had used to evaluate effectiveness: (i)
whether the firm accomplishes its goals and objectives; (ii) the acquisition
of critical resources; (iii) whether the firm has effective systems and internal trust; and (iv) whether the firm has satisfied stakeholders. Quinn and
Cameron (1983) further qualified the criteria for effectiveness as being

Table 3.1   Frequency of occurrence of evaluation criteria in 17 models of organizational effectiveness

Evaluation criteria	No. of times mentioned
Adaptability–flexibility	10
Productivity	6
Satisfaction	5
Profitability	3
Resource acquisition	3
Absence of strain	2
Control over environment	2
Development	2
Efficiency	2
Employee retention	2
Growth	2
Integration	2
Open communications	2
Survival	2
All other criteria	1

Source: Steers (1975: 549).

dependent upon the life-cycle stage of the organization being evaluated. For instance, in the early stages of an organization's life, resource acquisition may be more critical than effective systems and internal harmony. In summary, Cameron argued: 'Different models of effectiveness are useful for research in different circumstances. Their usefulness depends on the purposes and constraints placed on the organizational effectiveness investigation. Organizational effectiveness is mainly a problem-driven construct rather than a theory-driven construct' (1986: 541).

Several authors have examined organizational performance from the perspective of organizational life cycles (Hofer and Schendel, 1978; Katz and Kahn, 1978; Quinn and Cameron, 1983; Quinn and Rohrbaugh, 1983). The general consensus of these authors is that it is necessary to have different models of performance at different stages of an organization's life. Cameron and Whetten (1981) empirically found this to be the case in 18 simulated organizations. Quinn and Cameron (1983) found that all of the differing life-cycle models had four primary stages: (i) an entrepreneurial stage in which resource accumulation, creativity and innovation are stressed; (ii) a collectivity stage in which human relationship and team building are stressed; (iii) a formalization stage in which efficiency, goal attainment and internal processes are stressed; and (iv) a formalization stage in which organizational renewal and expansion are emphasized.

Accordingly, they argued that different measures of performance are necessary at different stages of development.

Cameron and Whetten (1983) provided seven critical questions for bounding and assessing organizational effectiveness:

1. From whose perspective is effectiveness being judged?
2. What is the domain for assessment?
3. What level of analysis is being used?
4. Why is effectiveness being assessed?
5. What timeframe is being used for the assessment?
6. What data are being used for the assessment?
7. What is the referent against which effectiveness is being judged?

Cameron and Whetten concluded that the answers to these questions lead to a unique set of effectiveness criteria. The difficulty lies in determining the most appropriate answers for each specific research setting. The key is matching the appropriate model of effectiveness with the existing circumstances. After six years of examining the concept of organizational effectiveness, Cameron (1986) concluded that there is no conceptualization of organizational effectiveness that is comprehensive. Therefore, similar to Hofer (1983), Cameron concluded that performance is a problem-, rather than a theory-driven construct.

In an attempt to summarize the literature on organizational effectiveness, Cameron (1986) identified eight different commonly used models of organizational effectiveness through that point in time. Table 3.2 summarizes these models, which incorporate the life-cycle models as well as other models of effectiveness. Each model has advantages and disadvantages for researchers. The one common trait is that they are not the same and do not measure the same outcomes. Therefore, generalizing between studies that used different models of effectiveness may be inappropriate.

Cameron summarized his findings by observing that researchers do not use much rigor in determining what model of organizational effectiveness they will use in their studies. Specifically, he identified two critical problems with the models of overall organizational effectiveness utilized in research:

1. Evaluators of effectiveness often select models and criteria arbitrarily in their assessments, relying primarily on convenience.
2. 'Indicators of effectiveness selected by researchers are often too narrowly or too broadly defined, or they do not relate to organizational performance . . . determinants of effectiveness often get confused with indicators or effectiveness' (1986: 543).

Table 3.2   Summary of performance models

Model	Definition	When useful
	An organization is effective to the extent that . . .	*The model is most preferred when . . .*
Goal model	It accomplishes its stated goals	Goals are clear, consequential time-bound, measurable
System resource model	It acquires needed resources	A clear connection exists between inputs and performance
Internal process model	It has an absence of internal strain with smooth internal functioning	A clear connection exists between organizational processes and performance
Strategic constituencies model	All strategic constituencies are at least minimally satisfied	Constituencies have powerful influence on the organization, and it has to respond to demands
Competing values model	The emphasis on criteria in the four different quadrants meets constituency preferences	The organization is unclear about its own criteria, or changes in criteria over time are of interest
Legitimacy model	It survives as a result of engaging in legitimate activity	The survival or decline and demise among organizations is of interest
Fault-driven model	It has an absence of faults or traits of ineffectiveness	Criteria of effectiveness are unclear, or strategies for improvement are needed
High performing systems model	It is judged excellent relative to other similar organizations	Comparisons among similar organizations are desired

Source: Cameron (1986: 542).

UNIQUENESS VERSUS THEORY DEVELOPMENT: A SCHOLARLY DILEMMA

If Cameron and Whetten are correct in their assessment of the uniqueness of each organizational situation, then any and all attempts to develop 'universal' management theory are doomed to failure. Theory building refers to making and testing a set of assertions that explain or predict a particular phenomenon that holds true across a broad range of specific instances (Weick, 1989). Accordingly, if performance measurement is inherently situation specific, then generalizations across organizations are impossible.

Where does that leave us? Basically, Cameron and Whetten argued rather convincingly that there can be no universal model of overall organizational effectiveness. However, this conclusion does not preclude the development of a number of situational models. This is consistent with the concepts of the 'contingency theory of business strategy' developed by Hofer (1975). The challenge is to identify a set of factors/variables that apply to a set of common circumstances across many organizations.

In this context, it is the purpose of this research to develop a model of overall organizational performance that is generalizable across a broad group of organizations, although not necessarily all organizations. It has been shown that prior perspectives of overall organizational performance are both multidimensional and multiconstituency. While it is possible to develop a multi-attribute model, building a model that addresses multiple constituencies becomes problematic, since each group may have contradictory objectives. Therefore, a unified perspective of overall organizational performance is necessary to execute this research. The next section discusses the development of this unified perspective by examining the eight models of organizational effectiveness summarized in Table 3.2.

TOWARD THE DEVELOPMENT OF A CONTINGENCY MODEL OF OVERALL ORGANIZATIONAL PERFORMANCE

The eight models of organizational effectiveness identified by Cameron in Table 3.2 are our starting-point for developing a contingency model of overall organizational performance. A closer examination of the eight different models shows that several of them actually describe antecedents to effective performance rather than actual effective performance. Further, several of them can be demonstrated to be subsets of other models. Consequently, the following discussion will demonstrate how the eight models can be reduced to only two.

Eliminating Models that are Antecedents to Performance

Three of the models summarized by Cameron can actually be shown to be antecedents to performance, not performance itself. First, the internal processes model uses the presence or lack of internal strain as a proxy for performance. However, at face value, this is a poor model of organizational performance, since all organizational members could achieve perfect harmony by spending their entire time sitting around watching television without ever accomplishing anything. Accordingly, achieving perfect harmony does not mean that the organization is truly effective. Therefore, it is not surprising that the review of five years of empirical articles summarized in Chapter 2, in which performance was the dependent variable, did not find any uses of this model.

The competing values model of performance obviously cannot be operationalized. If the model is considered applicable in situations when the organization is unclear about what constitutes successful performance, generalization to other organizations is impossible.

The fault-driven model of performance is similarly flawed. The absence of faults or traits of ineffectiveness is not a condition that is generalizable across organizations. Organizations do strive to minimize their weaknesses. However, the absence of weakness does not equate to the presence of competitive advantages that can be capitalized upon to achieve organizational success. Consequently, while the absence of faults or traits of ineffectiveness may be a condition that helps lead to superior organizational performance, it is not a sufficient condition to assume that superior performance occurred. Further, measures of the absence of faults or traits of ineffectiveness would have to be subjective, and at best ordinal. To date, no one has developed a valid operationalization of this approach that is based on an interval or ratio scale. Clearly this model of performance does not provide sufficient information to evaluate overall organizational performance.

Reducing the Five Remaining Models to Three

The remaining five models, identified by Cameron, can be further reduced to three primary constructs, as proposed by Ford and Schellenberg (1982): goal-based, systems and multiple constituency models of measuring organizational performance and effectiveness. From Ford and Schellenberg's perspective, the goal-based model is equivalent to Cameron's goal model, while the systems resource and high performing systems models can be combined into a single classification of systems models. Further, the legitimacy and the strategic constituencies models can be combined into a single classification of multiple constituency models. Each of these three models is discussed individually in the following sections.

The goal-based model of effectiveness
The goal-based approach proposes that a firm is effective when it accomplishes its own unique set of goals (Etzioni, 1960, 1964; Hall, 1972; Steers,

1975). This approach rejects the premise that an organizational effectiveness construct can be universally defined or measured in terms of a static set of measures. The problem with the goal-based approach to effective performance measurement is that the organization's stakeholders may have conflicting sets of goals and objectives for an organization. Where management may be satisfied with a given level of performance, other critical stakeholders, such as owners, may not be satisfied. Whose goals are appropriate for assessing organizational effectiveness and performance? Dess and Robinson (1984) and Venkatraman and Ramanujam (1987) both found statistically significant correlations between primary (information provided by management) and secondary (information retrieved from financial statements and other organization documents) measures of performance. However, in both cases their primary data were provided by only one group of stakeholders: management.

Agency theory proposes that the views of management should by necessity reflect the views of owners, or the managers would be replaced. However, while there may be significant differences in perceptions between the two groups, passive owners are generally slow to make management changes. Therefore, assuming that owners' and managers' goals are aligned is suspect.

Finally, and perhaps more importantly for researchers, different organizations have varied and sometimes contradictory goals, making generalization across firms questionable. For instance, over any given period of time, one group of firms in an industry may seek market-share growth while another group is focused on profitability. Selecting a sample of firms with a homogeneous concept of value creation becomes difficult without information concerning the actual strategic intentions of the organization, which they may be reluctant to share.

The multiple constituency model of performance
In the multiple constituency view of organizational effectiveness, a firm's performance effectiveness is evaluated in the context of its ability to meet the objectives of stakeholders who provide resources to the organization (Pfeffer and Salancik, 1978; Connolly et al., 1980; Freeman, 1984; Barney, 2002). Yuchtman and Seashore's (1967) 'systems resource' approach emphasizes the interests of those that supply vital resources such as the critical evaluative criteria. They argued that because stakeholders provide resources to the organization, they have an interest in how those resources are used. However, because different stakeholders provide different resources with differing utility to the organization, they can have different interests in how the firm is managed. For instance, a labor union will have differing objectives from firm creditors and equity holders. Because different stakeholders have different criteria for evaluating effective organizational performance, it is not always

possible for an organization to completely satisfy all stakeholders. In such situations, the interests of stakeholders who provide more critical resources to the firm will be placed above the interests of other, less critical stakeholders. This was empirically supported by Cameron's 1978 study of higher education institutions. This research demonstrated that with the multiple constituency approach to measuring effective performance, different types of colleges or universities use different criteria to evaluate their effectiveness. In essence, each stakeholder would have a different set of criteria to measure effective performance for the organization. As long as the interests of stakeholders vary, the task of isolating performance measures that account for all of the varied desired outcomes in multiple constituency models is overwhelming. Barney summed up the problem succinctly when he wrote:

> The answer to the question 'Will this strategy improve this firm's performance?' will always be 'Yes and no, depending upon whom you talk to.' In this context, it is necessary for managers and analysts alike to adopt simplified measures of performance, measures that emphasize a few dimensions of performance over others. (2002: 32)

The key to using a multiple constituency approach is to determine what constituencies exist, how each of the constituencies views effectiveness, and the consequences of these assessments. From this evaluation, a set of performance criteria can be derived for each organization. For the purposes of research, the criterion that would be used across organizations would have to be a subjective evaluation of the key stakeholders as to their respective and cumulative level of satisfaction. This would be both subjective and difficult, making results hard to generalize.

The systems model of performance
The systems approach to measuring effective organizational performance considers multiple, generic performance measures (Yuchtman and Seashore, 1967; Steers, 1975; Chakravarthy, 1986; Venkatraman and Ramanujam, 1986). The systems approach suggests that performance is multidimensional, and must be examined using a set of measures simultaneously, which are appropriate to the population and phenomenon of interest, to allow for comparison across organizations. As with the goal-based approach, this model of performance is criticized for failing to adequately account for differences between stakeholder groups' perspectives on performance (Ford and Schellenberg, 1982; Freeman, 1984).

While it can be argued that the use of multiple measures is also appropriate to goal-based models of performance, without specifically connecting performance measures to explicit organizational goals, the use of a system of measures to represent performance is more correctly classified as a systems approach. Based upon the review of recent empirical articles in Chapter 2, entrepreneurship and strategic management researchers typically use multiple performance measures, but without explicit connection to organizational goals. Consequently, it is appropriate to conclude that the systems approach is by far the most commonly used approach in empirical research in recent entrepreneurship and strategic management. Unfortunately, as was also shown in summary empirical articles, there is no agreement as to which measures of performance should be used to represent overall organizational performance.

Some conclusions about models of performance
While Cameron (1986) identified eight models of organizational effectiveness from the strategic management literature, it can be argued that there are actually only three distinct models: the goal-based, multiple constituency and systems models of performance. These models support a multiconstituency, multidimensional view of organizational performance. However, as discussed earlier, the multiconstituency view of organizational performance is problematic for the generalization of findings across companies. Accordingly, the next dilemma to resolve is finding a common perspective for viewing performance that is generalizable across organizations.

IDENTIFYING A GENERALIZABLE, SINGLE CONSTITUENCY VIEW OF PERFORMANCE: THE CASE OF FOR-PROFIT ORGANIZATIONS

It seems quite clear from the preceding discussion that all organizations have multiple constituencies that must at least be satisfied to some degree. However, it also seems clear that using a multiconstituency model of organizational performance is difficult for the development management theory. Therefore, it is important to identify a single constituency view of performance that is common across a large population of organizations.

In for-profit organizations, it can be argued that only one stakeholder group has needs that should be maximized, the common stockholder (Rappaport, 1986; Copeland et al., 2000). The overriding consideration in financial operations of for-profit organizations is satisfying providers of critical resources to the organization. Since shareholders are residual claimants, all other resource providers must be satisfied before they receive a return. Consequently, maximizing returns to shareholders requires balancing the satisfactions to all other stakeholders and meeting at least the minimal requirements of key stakeholders. Shareholders maximize the value of other claims in an attempt to maximize their own value (Freeman, 1984;

Stewart, 1991; Copeland et al., 1996). Gifford summed up the matter from a finance perspective as follows: 'While academics have been busily proving that capital structure can affect shareholder value, few have questioned that shareholder value creation itself is the goal of the corporation' (1998: 76).

Strategic management is concerned with managing an organization for the long term. Therefore, it is appropriate to select a perspective for measuring performance that is compatible. Since common stockholders commit resources to the organization for the longest time period (they get their capital back only after all other claimants against organizational assets are first satisfied), their perspective is closest to the focus of strategic management issues. Common stockholders have long-term interests and must balance short-term satisfactions against long-term benefits. In other words, modern corporations give control over decision making to shareholders (or their agents) because they are the only claimants that require complete information to make decisions in their self-interest.

One final argument in favor of using the common stockholders' perspective is that they are considered to have a relatively homogeneous perspective of performance. Common stock investors can invest in any number of organizations. As a consequence, shareholders require, at a minimum, a risk-adjusted return on their capital that is comparable to similar equity investment opportunities. Shareholder returns for an investment in a specific organization over a given period of time reflect the changes in actual and expected payouts to shareholders as a result of management and market actions (Miller and Modigliani, 1961). Those firms that investors perceive as having created greater opportunity for present and future payouts will have higher returns to common stockholders over the measured timeframe. Therefore, the common referent for shareholder value, across all for-profit organizations, is present and risk-adjusted expectations of future cash flows.

ORGANIZATIONAL PERFORMANCE AS A MULTIDIMENSIONAL CONCEPT

One of the central concepts in the entrepreneurship and strategic management literatures is the idea that performance is a multidimensional construct (Drucker, 1954; Steers, 1975; Cameron, 1980; Chakravarthy, 1986; Venkatraman and Ramanujam, 1986, 1987; Kaplan and Norton, 1992; Murphy et al., 1996). It is well known that companies often sacrifice profitability for growth in order to accelerate the development of new products. Similarly, efficiency may be sacrificed for growth. While it seems clear that organizational performance is multidimensional and that effective performance on one dimension may be at the cost of effective performance in another dimension, exactly what the different dimensions of overall organizational effectiveness are, or should be, is a matter of considerable debate.

The problem identified in the prior literature is the simultaneous measurement of the different dimensions of overall organizational performance and how they interact in the creation of value. One way to conceptualize performance as multidimensional is to treat value creation as an unobservable second-order, hierarchical construct. Using the dimensions proposed by Venkatraman and Ramanujam (1986) as an example, such a construct would be derived from financial, operational and stakeholder first-order constructs. The first-order constructs are measured by specific indicators. For instance, Venkatraman and Ramanujam (1987) demonstrated that the financial construct has at least two subdimensions of profitability and growth. Measures of each would be used in establishing the first-order construct.

Figure 3.1 depicts one structural conceptualization of such a measure following the conceptualization of Venkatraman and Ramanujam (1986). This construct does not include the causal relationships with its antecedents. It is merely a representation of a measure that could provide insight into the inherent tradeoffs in organizational effectiveness.

Each first-order dimension would be operationalized as a set of subconstructs. For instance, the financial dimension might be operationalized using constructs for profitability, growth, efficiency, financial structure, survivability, cash flow and resource accumulation. One or more indicators would measure each of these constructs. An example would be how profitability could be measured by return on equity (ROE), return on invested capital (ROIC) and economic value added (EVA). The growth construct might use indicators such as change in sales, change in number of employees and change in fixed assets. Figure 3.2 is one such representation of how financial performance might be measured.

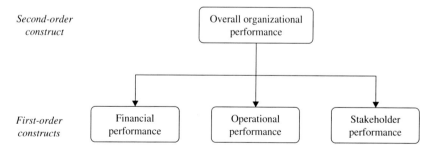

Figure 3.1   Overall organizational performance as a second-order construct

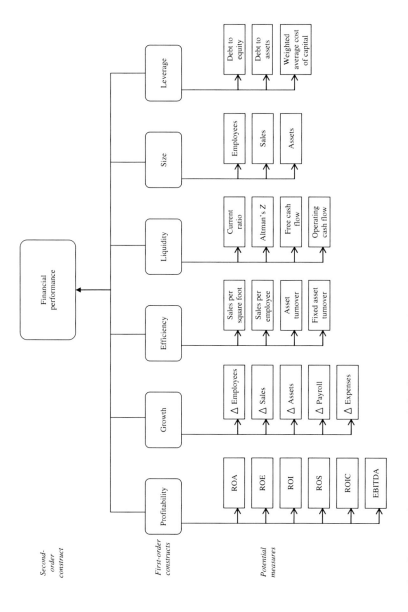

Figure 3.2   Structural representation of the financial performance construct

It should be noted that the models depicted in Figures 3.1 and 3.2 are both measurement models and not causal models. In other words, these models do not propose that the higher-level constructs are a function of the lower-level constructs, but rather, that the former are 'measured' by the latter. A causal model, by contrast, would propose how various independent variables would affect organizational performance. The models proposed in Figures 3.1 and 3.2 measure the dependent variable, overall organizational performance.

As discussed above, this research is adopting a single-constituency view of organizational performance from the perspective of the common stockholder. Given that perspective, there are two critical questions that must be addressed. First, which dimensions of performance are associated with a change in the shareholder value? Second, what are the most appropriate measures that should be used to assess each dimension?

CHAPTER SUMMARY

Chapter 3 reviewed prior literature on the evolution of the concept of organizational effectiveness and performance. This included a review of differing perspectives of organizational performance: the accounting, balanced scorecard, strategic management, entrepreneurship and microeconomic perspectives. Based upon this review, it is clear that there are many schools of thought on how overall organizational effectiveness and performance should be measured. Unfortunately, neither prior research nor prior theory has developed an effective model, much less an effective set of measures, for organizational effectiveness and performance. However, theory development requires that some situational models of performance that can be generalized across a population of organizations, be developed. Accordingly, an argument was proposed for a single-constituency, multidimensional model of performance for for-profit organizations, from the perspective of the common stockholder. The following chapter will address how such a model should be developed.

4.   Categories of performance measures

This chapter discusses the nature of the different categories of performance measures. Since there is no authoritative list of performance categories in the prior literature, the categories of performance measures discussed in this chapter are based upon general classifications of performance measures often found in finance and accounting texts (Helfert, 1994; Higgins, 1995; Brealey et al., 2001; Penman, 2001). Five primary categories are proposed and the nature of the performance measures for each category is discussed.

FIVE CATEGORIES OF PERFORMANCE MEASURES

The primary variables used in research and practice to represent the overall organizational performance construct can be categorized into several distinct groupings. The four primary categories of overall organizational performance variables used in recent empirical research identified in Chapter 2 are: (i) accounting measures; (ii) operational measures; (iii) market-based measures; and (iv) survival measures. In addition, measures of economic value creation are popular in practice but are not frequently used in strategic management or entrepreneurship research.

Although several empirical studies did use size measures to represent organizational performance, most researchers view these measures as control variables to account for variance in other measures as a result of the size of the organization. We found no support in the prior literature for using measures of size to represent overall organizational performance, so that category is not discussed any further in this chapter.

Several of the empirical studies summarized in Chapter 2 utilized subjective assessments by top management of overall organizational performance. The use of such subjective assessments can be viewed as an attempt to address the multiple dimensions of performance for the organization. However, although management is one stakeholder group in an organization, their satisfaction may not necessarily be equated into satisfaction by the owners of the organization, or any other stakeholder group for that matter. The validity of managerial satisfaction as a measure of overall organizational performance has never been established and is beyond the scope of this research. Accordingly, these subjective assessments are not discussed any further in this chapter.

Accounting Measures

Accounting measures are those that rely upon financial information reported in income statements, balance sheets and statements of cash flows. Accounting measures can be further subcategorized into profitability measures, growth measures, leverage, liquidity and cash flow measures, and efficiency measures.

Profitability measures

Profitability measures include values and ratios that incorporate net income or a component of net income such as operating income or earnings before taxes. It is through the generation of a profit that an organization is able to provide a return to providers of equity capital, once the profits have been converted into liquid assets. In the absence of profits or the likely prospect for profits, equity capital providers will withdraw their resources from an organization and redeploy them to alternative investments where a positive return can be realized.

Growth measures

Growth measures include values and ratios that present some indication of organizational growth. Growth has been conceptualized both in the context of resources and from a business operations perspective. Typical accounting-based growth measures include absolute or percentage change in total assets, operating assets, sales, total expenses and operating expenses. Measures of organizational size can be conceptualized as being part of the growth construct since size generally is measured in absolute terms of a growth variable of interest, where growth is the change in the variable. Size in absolute terms is typically used as a control variable and not an outcome variable. In Chapter 2, it was noted that some empirical studies did use size measures as dependent variables, but the number of these studies was very small.

Leverage, liquidity and cash flow measures

Leverage, liquidity and cash flow measures include values and ratios that represent the organization's ability to meet its financial obligations in a timely manner and provide a cash return to capital providers. The ability to meet financial obligations can be measured both by the ratio of liquid assets to liabilities, and/or by the organization's ability to generate sufficient cash flow to meet outstanding liabilities.

Efficiency measures
Efficiency measures include values and ratios that represent how well the organization utilizes its resources. Typical efficiency ratios include asset turnover, net profit per employee, net profit per square foot, sales per employee and sales per square foot. Clearly, most efficiency ratios require information that comes from outside the three basic financial statements.

Operational Measures

Operational measures include variables that represent how the organization is performing on non-financial issues. Measuring performance on non-financial dimensions has received renewed attention over the past many years as corporations have adopted a 'balanced scorecard' approach for the integration of strategy and performance measurement (Kaplan, 1984; Kaplan and Norton, 1992). These variables include market share, changes in intangible assets such as patents or human resources, customer satisfaction and stakeholder performance. Most of the measures in this category require primary data from management in the form of their assessment of their own performance, which may lead to questions of the validity of the responses.

Market-based Measures

Market-based measures of performance include ratios or rates of change that incorporate the market value of the organization. These variables include return to shareholders, market value added, holding period returns, Jensen's alpha and Tobin's *Q*. The calculation of these variables requires a market valuation for the company and is generally only available for publicly traded companies.

Survival Measures

Survival measures of performance simply indicate whether the organization remained in business over the time period of interest. Barnard (1938) and Drucker (1954) proposed that survival is the ultimate measure of long-term performance. However, since most empirical research in entrepreneurship and strategic management addresses time horizons of five years and less, survival is rarely used as a measure of overall organizational performance, as indicated in the summary of recent empirical research studies in Chapter 2.

Economic Value Measures

Economic value measures of performance are adjusted accounting measures that take into consideration the cost of capital and some of the influences of external financial reporting rules. These measures have rarely been used by researchers in strategic management or entrepreneurship empirical studies because the values are not generally reported and most companies do not even calculate them internally. Typical economic value measures include residual income, economic value added and cash flow return on investment.

There are advantages and disadvantages to the use of measures in each of the categories proposed above. While each category of measurement addresses performance from a unique perspective, not all organizations can be measured in all categories. It is incumbent upon each researcher to select a set of measures that capture the essence of organizational performance given the environmental circumstance of the individual study. The following sections address the relevant considerations with respect to each category of performance measures.

ACCOUNTING MEASURES

Accounting measures refer to variables that can be derived from the three basic financial statements of all businesses, namely balance sheets, income statements and statements of cash flows. Most accounting measures are generally expressed as values, ratios or percentages. The calculation of the amounts presented in reporting companies' (those companies required to file periodic reports with the Securities and Exchange Commission) financial statements in the United States is based upon generally accepted accounting principles (GAAP) consistently applied both over time and across companies. While it would seem that following a common set of rules for reporting financial results would produce uniformity in presentation among similar companies, there is sufficient variation both in the nature of financial transactions and interpretation by those applying GAAP, to result in significant variation in the way companies present their financial information, often making comparison across companies difficult.

The heart of the issue of using accounting measures for entrepreneurship and strategic management research is whether a company's financial statements, as presented, actually measure the economic value of the firm. Both strategy and entrepreneurship, by their nature, are concerned with the future, not the past. The focus of financial reporting is to present the historical actions of the company, and financial statements measure investments only at book value and reflect only the execution on existing opportunities. In other words, they do not fully incorporate the future value of investments and the opportunities they create.

For example, research and development (R&D) expenditures are written off in the period incurred, even though they may well be creating new products that will reap large benefits in the future. In the current period, R&D expenditures reduce both profitability and the net worth of the company. This accounting treatment results in much higher returns on investment in the future as a result of the revenues being realized with the corresponding R&D expenses already written off. Beyond the mismatching of revenues and expenses, the lowered net worth of the company becomes the denominator for return on equity calculations, thereby further increasing the calculated returns (Rappaport, 1986; Stewart, 1991; Copeland et al., 1995).

From a management accounting perspective, in a 1996 survey the Institute of Management Accounting addressed the question of whether financial measures support top management business objectives. Only 15 percent of the respondents reported that their financial measures actually supported top management's business objectives well, while 43 percent reported their systems were less than adequate or poor (Ittner and Larcker, 1998). A 1996 survey of 203 executives by William Schiemann and Associates on the quality, uses and perceived importance of various financial and non-financial performance measures found that only 61 percent of the respondents were willing to bet their jobs on the quality of their financial performance information, and only 41 percent on the quality of their operating efficiency measures (Lingle and Schiemann, 1996). Yet, it is these same accounting measures that investors and researchers rely upon to evaluate the performance of organizations.

As a result of perceived inadequacies of traditional accounting-based performance measures, numerous new financial metrics such as 'economic value' measures, including economic value added (EVA®) and cash flow return on investment (CFROI) have become popular (Birchard, 1999). Unfortunately, many of these economic value metrics are not easily calculated and are not freely published by companies. Accordingly, they are rarely available to researchers without considerable effort.

Even though there are significant challenges in using accounting measures, they are the most readily accessible for researchers from both secondary and primary sources. Further, although there are variations in how GAAP are applied, there is a common basis for the presentation of accounting data across organizations. Additionally, financial statements of publicly traded companies are subjected to audit by independent certified public accountants and are reviewed by the Securities and Exchange

Commission with significant penalties for purposefully misstating results. Non-reporting companies may or may not be audited by independent accountants, but are subject to audit by the Internal Revenue Service, as well as private financing institutions such as banks, again with significant penalties for material misstatement. Consequently, although there may be questions about the content of accounting measures, they are generally reliably and consistently reported.

Common Adjustments to Accounting Measures

When comparing financial performance across companies, it is incumbent upon the observer to control for influences on the dependent measures that are not part of the phenomenon of interest of the study, but that do cause variation in the performance of the sample. Two primary influences on performance outcomes that have been shown to be significant in prior studies are industry membership and the time lag between action and outcome, as the effects of some decisions being studied may take many years to manifest, while other effects may manifest in relatively short periods of time. Each of these moderators of performance warrant separate discussion.

Adjusting for industry effects

The industry in which companies compete may significantly influence results based upon its competitive attractiveness or the structural nature of the industry (Porter, 1980). Numerous studies have examined the effects of different elements of industry structure on performance, and they have consistently found industry structure to have a significant impact on organizational performance (see Bain, 1959; Caves, 1972; McDougall et al., 1992; and Robinson, 1998 as examples). Consequently, when organizational performance is the outcome being affected, it is incumbent upon the observer to control or account for the effects of industry membership.

Another industry-related issue is the significant differences between the characteristics of industries, such as the average amount of total assets of their members. It is appropriate to statistically address the associated variance in performance measures. This can be accomplished by using a control variable for industry membership or adjusting accounting measures for industry averages (Dess et al., 1990).

Normalizing organizational performance around the industry mean is certainly appropriate when there is a significant industry effect on performance that is unrelated to the actions of management. Performance is, in essence, benchmarked to the industry norm for comparison (Wesphal, 1999). The primary advantage to this approach for controlling for industry effects is that it does not use up the, all too often, limited degrees of freedom in the statistical tests. The problem with this approach is that performance is measured as a variance from an industry mean, and the magnitude of the standard deviation from the industry mean may vary considerably across industries. Theoretically, in industries where there is competitive parity, variance from the mean may be much smaller than in industries where competition is less intense or where demand exceeds supply. This makes comparison across industries less meaningful with respect to managerial actions that do not involve industry choice.

Conversely, using a control variable to account for the variance in the dependent measure resulting from industry membership requires a nominal measure. This is accomplished by creating a separate variable for each industry represented, and assigning a value of 1 for industry membership or a value of 0 for non-membership. However, when there are a significant number of industries in the sample, this coding approach will use up considerable degrees of freedom in the analysis and result in reduced power of the statistical tests. This reduction in power may obfuscate relationships that might otherwise be significant.

The question of time
When selecting measures, or a set of measures, to represent organizational performance, it is necessary to consider the time lag between the action taken in the causal variables and the effects generated in the dependent measures. It should be kept in mind that short-term manipulation of accounting numbers though adjustments of reserves, revenue recognition policies, capitalization policies, investments to create future products, and deferred maintenance is not only possible, but has been known to occur relatively frequently in practice.

It is much more difficult for management to manipulate long-term performance measures. Over time, true performance becomes more apparent. It is up to the researcher to decide whether the reliability of the short-term measures is sufficient. One primary weakness of long-term measures is that intervening events, not included in the study, can obfuscate the effects of interest. The longer the time lags between cause and effect, the greater the risk of intervening events causing variation in the dependent measures.

Based upon the survey of empirical articles discussed in Chapter 2, researchers overwhelmingly used one-year measures of performance, while three-year measures were the second most frequently used. In general, the reason cited by authors for the timeframe used in the study was the expected lag between the causes represented by the independent variables and the corresponding effects reflected in the variations of the dependent variables.

Profitability Measures

The ability for a company to consistently make a profit, or a surplus of revenues over expenses is critical to the survival of an organization (Drucker, 1954). In particular, an organization must earn greater profits over time than its cost of capital in order to continue to attract and retain essential resources. Accordingly, measures of profitability are among the most commonly used to represent organizational performance. The key question researchers must ask in using profitability measures as dependent variables for empirical research is whether earnings can reliably be used as a proxy for the change in the present value of a company (Rappaport, 1986).

Five primary limitations of profitability measures
Rappaport (1986) identified five key reasons why reported accounting measures of profitability fail to fully account for changes in the economic value of an organization:

1. Alternative accounting methods may be employed.
2. Risk is excluded.
3. Investment requirements are excluded.
4. Dividend policy is not considered.
5. The time value of money is ignored.

Each of these concerns will now be briefly addressed.

Alternative accounting methods may be employed   GAAP allow for equally acceptable, but different, methods of accounting for similar transactions. The only stipulation is that once an accounting method is adopted, it must be consistently applied for all accounting periods. Common examples that can create material differences in accounting earnings across companies include first-in, first-out (FIFO) versus last-in, first-out (LIFO) approaches to valuing inventory consumed as a cost of sales, accelerated versus straight-line depreciation methods, pooling-of-interests versus purchase accounting for acquisitions, and the capitalization policies used for research and development expenses. This list is hardly exhaustive, and any one of the different accounting method differences can cause material variances in earnings across companies.

In addition to different accounting methods, managerial estimates play a critical role in accounting measures of performance. For instance, management estimates of various reserve accounts can dramatically impact reported earnings. Typical reserves estimated by management include reserves for bad debts, reserves for obsolete inventories, reserves for prepayments, and impairment of asset reserves, including goodwill and other intangible assets.

Risk is excluded   Risk is one of the critical elements in determining the economic value of an asset. Inherent in the discount rate used in present-value calculations is a premium for risk. This risk premium is based upon the expected variance of projected outcomes from the mean expectation (Bromiley, 1990; Ruefli et al., 1999). Overall risk is a combination of business and financial risks.

Business risk arises from the fact that a chosen strategy may lead to different possible outcomes, each of which may have a different probability of occurrence. Thus, managers often must make a choice between high risk/high reward and moderate risk/moderate reward strategies. Moreover, even when the probability-adjusted returns of each strategy are equivalent, the distribution of earnings performance can be considerably different.

Financial risk derives from the variability of the firm's cash flows and the firm's debt-to-equity ratio. Thus, the greater the variance in a firm's cash flow, the greater the shareowners' risk associated with large amounts of debt. As a result, industries with lower cash flow uncertainties tend to have much higher debt-to-equity ratios and, accordingly, lower cost of capital than industries with greater cash flow uncertainties. The reason for this is that the latter industries are at greater risk of not being able to make their fixed debt service obligations, thus they tend to carry lower debt-to-equity ratios with higher costs of capital. A firm may attempt to achieve above-normal returns from a lower weighted average cost of capital relative to its industry by carrying more debt than other firms in the industry. If successful, such a firm's lower cost of capital can result in greater returns on equity. If unsuccessful, the greater risk of carrying excess debt can result in bankruptcy. Consequently, the economic value of a firm may not change because of increased earnings from accepting greater financial risk, since investors may require a higher return on investment due to the greater risks.

Ruefli et al. summed up the issue of the consideration of risk in strategic management studies:

> It might be argued that strategic management researchers do not give as much prominence to risk as do strategy practitioners since there are numerous strategic management studies that do not measure (or even mention) risk, while there are precious few strategic decisions in which risk is not considered. (1999: 181)

Investment requirements are excluded   Economic value is created by a firm earning a cash-based return on investment in excess of the cost of capital required to finance the investment. Therefore, economic value creation is not solely tied to earnings, because additional investment may be required as a firm grows. If earnings increase proportionately to sales, organizations will generally require greater investments in working capital and, more than likely, in fixed assets, especially if significant growth exists. As a result, free cash flow generally will grow at a much slower rate, or may even be negative, if sales grow rapidly. The economic value of the organization should only increase by the impact that sales growth has on expected future cash flows to investors, discounted by the investors' required rate of return over time. Accordingly, profitability measures that do not consider the cost of non-interest-bearing investments, such as in increased accounts receivable and inventory that accompany increased sales levels, do not adequately reflect true economic value creation.

Dividend policy is not considered   The payment of dividends reduces the economic value of the organization. However, the reduction in economic value is, in theory, exactly offset by the returns received by shareholders. To avoid destroying economic value, organizations should pay out surplus capital to shareholders unless the organization can earn a greater return on investment than its cost of equity. This is contrary to a goal of maximizing profitability since any return on investment would increase absolute earnings, and therefore profitability.

The time value of money is ignored   The earnings calculation also does not take into account the time value of money. Economic value is created only when the amount earned exceeds the discount rate that must include compensation not only for inflation but also for the specific risk of the enterprise. Thus, the longer the time between management's action and the resulting free cash flow, the less valuable the action in present dollars. Performance measures that value cash flow equally regardless of when it occurs are misleading (Copeland et al., 2000; Brealey et al., 2001).

The effects of GAAP on the economic reality of intangible assets
In addition to the five limitations developed by Rappaport, another key consideration is inherent problems with generally accepted accounting principles themselves. For instance, a firm's intangible assets are hard to both measure and observe. GAAP require conservative procedures for the capitalization of intangible assets such as goodwill, intellectual property, and even for the appreciation of the underlying value of physical assets such as buildings and land. The unrecognized value of intangible assets can be observed by looking at the market-to-book value ratio for a company. For instance, The Coca-Cola Company at the end of 2002 was trading at a market-to-book ratio of a little over 8.0. Coke's market capitalization of approximately $96 billion exceeded its book value of $12 billion by

$84 billion. The implication is that $84 billon of intangible assets and unrecognized appreciation of tangible assets for The Coca-Cola Company was omitted from the balance sheet. Certainly, the performance of the company based upon profitability measures, such as return on assets, would be significantly different if the value of intangible assets were included in the calculations.

Growth Measures

Growth has long been considered a critical and distinct component of organizational financial performance (see Drucker, 1954; Cameron, 1986; Venkatraman and Ramanujam, 1987; Tsai et al., 1991; Brush and Vanderwerf, 1992; Murphy et al., 1996 as examples). Capon et al. (1990) found, using a meta-analysis of performance-related studies, that sales growth rate was a generally accepted performance indicator. They found that sales growth is positively and robustly associated with other measures of firm financial performance. Castrogiovanni (1991) argued that in benign environments, a firm's ability to exploit product-market opportunities is measured by its sales growth rate. Following Castrogiovanni, Edelstein (1992) argued that a firm's ability to maintain or increase its sales level and market share in hostile environments, where there is increasing competition from both domestic and foreign firms, is a generally accepted performance indicator of short-term survival and adjustment.

It is understandable on the face of it, that growth is a commonly used performance indicator, since growth is a critical variable in determining the value of a company. For instance, in the constant-growth dividend discount model (Brealey et al., 2001), growth rate reduces the required rate of return in the divisor of the formula:

$$\text{Present value of investment} = \frac{\text{Cash flow in the next year rate}}{\text{Required of return} - \text{growth rate}}.$$

This is a reasonable assumption if one accepts that the organization will be able to earn the same return on sales in the future as in the present. The faster sales grow, the faster profits grow, and the greater the projected return to shareholders, the more valuable the organization is to resource providers.

Growth is considered a particularly important performance dimension for new ventures, since sales growth indicates market acceptance of the venture's products and the establishment of legitimacy of the venture (Tsai et al., 1991; Brush and Vanderwerf, 1992; Chandler and Hanks, 1993). Accordingly, firms often trade off profitability for growth. New venture researchers, in recognition of these issues, frequently use both profitability and growth measures (calculated in both absolute and percentage terms) to describe an organization's financial performance (see, for example, Cooper, 1993; Shrader and Simon, 1997; Zahra and Bogner, 2000).

While sales growth is the primary measure of growth used in the empirical studies summarized in Chapter 2, several other measures were also used. These include growth in employees, growth in R&D expenditures, growth in payroll expenses and growth in profit. Drucker (1954) included the ability of an organization to continue to attract capital as a critical performance dimension. It follows that growth in total assets could be considered a measure of organizational effectiveness. However, neither growth in operating assets nor growth in total assets was used as a measure in the empirical articles surveyed in Chapter 2. The use of growth measures other than sales was generally defended based on the independent measures being studied and the phenomenon of interest. No researcher attempted to demonstrate the validity of such other growth measures either internally or externally. The only empirical tests of growth as a measure of organizational performance have used sales growth (see Venkatraman and Ramanujam, 1987; Chandler and Hanks, 1993; Murphy et al., 1996; Robinson, 1998 as examples). Consequently, it remains to be demonstrated whether other measures of growth are valid descriptions of organizational performance, or whether growth is a valid dimension of the organizational performance construct.

Leverage, Liquidity and Cash Flow

Leverage, liquidity and cash flow measures deal with the financial structure of an organization and the ability of the organization to pay its liabilities in a timely fashion. Each of the three categories of measures relate to a separate component of this aspect of company performance. Leverage measures describe the financial structure of the organization and include such measures as debt to equity, debt to total assets and times interest earned. Liquidity measures describe the ability of the organization to convert assets into cash and include such measures as current ratio, quick ratio and the interval measure. Finally, cash flow measures describe the amount of cash an organization has generated and the sources of that cash, relative to the organization's demands for cash, and include such measures as cash flow to equity and cash flow to assets. The following subsections discuss each of these categories in more detail.

Leverage measures
Leverage measures deal with the financial structure of the organization. Financial leverage can be defined as the degree to which operating assets

are financed with debt versus equity (Penman, 2001). Debt obligations generally require mandatory calls on the firm's cash through the payment of interest and repayment of principal on a periodic basis. Common equity, on the other hand, does not have a mandatory call on cash either for period returns to capital providers or for retirement of equity holders' capital investment in the firm. Thus, debt holders receive a fixed payment while equity holders receive the residual after all other claimants have been satisfied. Accordingly, if a firm is able to earn profits in excess of the cost of borrowed capital, the spread of those profits in excess of the cost of the borrowed capital becomes additional profits for the equity holders. If a firm is unable to earn profits in excess of the cost of its borrowed capital, the equity holders take a loss to the extent of that spread while the debt holders continue to earn a return. The greater the ratio of capital provided by debt to the capital provided by equity, the higher the potential gains and losses for equity holders. This relationship is often referred to as the risk–reward tradeoff. The greater a firm's leverage, the greater the bankruptcy risk in poor times, and conversely, the greater the profits in good times, for equity capital providers.

Brush et al. (1999) found that the strategic choices available to managers may be limited in highly leveraged firms because of the inability to raise additional debt capital or by being forced to use more costly equity capital. As a consequence, leverage may be used as a control variable in strategic management studies (see Lubatkin and Chatterjee, 1991; Hoskisson et al., 1993 as examples). Although leverage may be used as a control variable, our review of dependent measures used to represent the overall organizational performance construct in Chapter 2 did not identify any studies that used leverage measures.

Liquidity measures
Liquidity refers to the ability of a firm to meet its financial obligations in a timely manner. In essence, the assets owned by a company are liquid if they can quickly and cheaply be converted to cash (Brealey et al., 2001). The critical performance issue relative to liquidity is whether the organization has or is developing enough readily accessible capital to continue to operate. Accordingly, liquidity measures represent one aspect of a dimension of overall organizational performance, but are not sufficient measures by themselves to represent the entire construct.

Liquidity can be measured in both absolute and percentage terms. An example of an absolute measure of organizational liquidity is working capital, or the excess of current assets over current liabilities. Another absolute measure of liquidity is the interval measure, which represents the length of time the organization can continue to operate using its liquid assets, without making any further sales. Examples of percentage measures of liquidity include change in working capital, current ratio and quick ratio.

One critical weakness of liquidity measures calculated from financial statements is that they do not include the organization's ready access to capital through existing lines of credit and other revolving debt agreements. Since loans usually have a higher cost of capital than can be earned on short-term investments, prudent business practice would be to use all surplus cash to reduce short-term interest-bearing liabilities, so long as the capital can be quickly replaced under existing borrowing arrangements. The access to capital under existing borrowing agreements provides an organization with extra liquidity that is not reported in the organization's financial statements, thereby underreporting the actual liquidity of the organization.

Cash flow measures
Cash flow is not only critical for meeting current obligations but is also a measure of the firm's ability to actually pay a return to resource providers. Ultimately, the availability of cash payouts to resource providers determines the financial benefit, or value, that they realize from an organization. Typical business valuation methods are based upon projected available cash flows and the timing of the cash payouts to investors (West and Jones, 1999; Copeland et al., 2000). As an example, in the constant-growth dividend discount model presented previously, cash flow is the numerator used in determining the current value of an organization. Accordingly, it is appropriate to measure cash flow available to investors as a component of organizational performance. The pertinent issue for researchers is over what time should cash flow be measured, since the sources and uses of cash can vary significantly year to year based upon growth rates and investment opportunities.

Examples of cash flow measures identified in our review of recent empirical studies include net cash flow from operations, cash flow as a percentage of capital stock (cash flow return on equity), operating cash flows as a percentage of total assets (cash flow return on assets), and the growth rate of operating cash flows. Each of these measures deals with the cash available to the organization to meet its calls on capital for investment and financing activities.

Efficiency Measures

Efficiency measures how well organizations utilize their resources. These resources include physical, financial and human resources. Examples of efficiency measures include turnover ratios for total assets, receivables, inventory and fixed assets. Industry specific efficiency ratios include measures such as net profit per employee, net profit per square foot, employee and equipment utilization percentages, sales per employee and sales per square foot. Obviously, efficiency ratios can include both accounting and non-accounting information.

Many authors have used efficiency as a primary dimension of performance (see Drucker, 1954; Cameron, 1986; Venkatraman and Ramanujam, 1986; and Murphy et al., 1996 as examples). While efficiency is a critical dimension of performance, Porter (1996) points out that it is not a sufficient condition for organizational performance. Porter argues that market advantages gained through efficiency are diminished over time through imitation and appropriation of critical resources and processes. Firms must not only be efficient, they must also create competitive advantage, based upon differences from their competition that are valuable to customers, to be successful.

One of the critical issues with efficiency measures is comparability across industries and even across companies within industries. For instance, sales per square foot is a critical measure for retail industry performance yet is meaningless for most consulting firms. Another example is trying to compare sales per employee. The value for automotive companies will be quite different from that for temporary employment businesses. Even within the same industry, efficiency can mean different things by company. For instance, sales per employee in construction firms that outsource most of their site work will be quite different from construction firms that use their own crews to do site work.

Turnover ratios (typically calculated as revenues divided by the statistic of interest such as receivables, inventory, fixed assets and so on) are also subject to industry and firm-to-firm differences. Inventory turnover can differ significantly based on industry. Inventory in the produce industry typically turns over daily while inventory in the high-end jewelry industry is lucky to turn over once per year.

The use of efficiency measures as a dependent measure in research requires that the population of interest has a homogeneous interpretation of what efficiency actually is. It can be argued that companies pursuing a low cost strategy will have very different efficiency measures from those pursuing differentiation strategies (Porter, 1996). Controlling for the variance in efficiency measures for all of these factors becomes problematic in operationalization. Accordingly, a researcher who uses efficiency as a measure of organizational performance must take great care in research design. Consequently, only ten studies in our review of recent empirical studies summarized in Chapter 2 used an efficiency measure to represent overall organizational performance.

OPERATIONAL MEASURES

Operational measures represent the non-financial performance of an organization. The popularity of performance measurement systems such as the 'balanced scorecard' that represent the integration of strategy and performance measurement have placed renewed emphasis on these non-financial measures (Kaplan, 1984; Kaplan and Norton, 1992). Examples of non-financial measures include market share, changes in intangible assets such as patents or human resources skills and abilities, customer satisfaction, product innovation, productivity, quality and stakeholder performance. Non-financial measures often include qualitative assessments by management rather than objective, quantitative measurement. Consequently, the validity of the measures may be questionable and may require additional validation from outside parties.

One critical question that researchers must answer in using operational measures of performance is whether the measures are antecedents to performance or represent actual performance. For instance, an organization can obtain patents on lots of new products, but if there is no market for the products, then the increase in the number of patents held by the organization actually can represent poor performance. In other words, if marginal cost exceeds marginal revenue, an organization cannot improve financial performance by increasing sales. Another example is measuring performance on customer satisfaction scores. There is a point at which the cost of increasing customer satisfaction can exceed the benefits derived. From an overall organizational perspective of the for-profit company, improving customer satisfaction only matters if it translates into wealth creation for owners.

The primary advantage to using operational measures in conjunction with financial performance measures is when they provide information about opportunities that have been created, but not yet financially realized. For instance, a pharmaceutical company may create significant shareholder value when they first receive FDA (Food and Drug Administration) approval for a new drug, even though the actual realization of the cash flows underlying that wealth creation may not happen for quite some time. Another example is an oil and gas exploration company. Significant shareholder value can be created upon the discovery of a new oilfield, but the financial benefits to the company will not actually be realized until the newly discovered oil reserves are pumped out of the ground.

Since GAAP do not permit companies to recognize the expected value of new discoveries until the benefits are actually realized, accounting-based measures do not capture this information on organizational performance. On the other hand, market-based measures of overall organizational performance do react when the market becomes aware of operational information that is not included in financial results. Unfortunately, market-based measures are not available for privately owned companies, so in those instances a combination of operational and accounting-based measures may be necessary to represent the overall performance construct. However, researchers are yet to determine which operational measures to use and it may well be the case that appropriate operational measures are unique to each industry, making generalization across industries impractical.

MARKET-BASED MEASURES

Market-based measures of performance incorporate the market value of the organization in ratios or rates of change. Accordingly, these measures are only available where observable markets or market value estimates exist for companies such as publicly traded companies, portfolio companies of private equity firms, or companies sold through intermediaries that make the transaction values available to researchers. Examples of these measures include returns to shareholders, market value added, holding period returns, Jensen's alpha and Tobin's Q.

Since there are rarely publicly available market values for privately owned firms, the use of market-based measures for entrepreneurship research is problematic.

Market-based measures have been hailed as the best possible measures of organizational economic performance (see Rappaport, 1986; Robinson, 1995; Copeland et al., 2000 as examples). They have also been criticized (see Bromiley, 1986, 1990 as examples). There are several key arguments in favor of market-based measures. First, they include the value created by both the execution on existing opportunities, as well as the risk-adjusted expected value of future opportunities that have yet to be realized. Second, and perhaps more important, the issues with accounting-based measures do not affect stockholder returns (Brush et al., 2000), since accounting measures are subject to manipulation by management while a well-regulated market is generally not subject to manipulation. Third, if one accepts the assumption that markets are relatively efficient (and this is still a matter of considerable scholarly debate), market-based measures quickly reflect management actions and changes in the economic value of the organization. Also, since the value of past actions is quickly incorporated into the market value of the organization, the change in market value during a given period can be assumed to reflect the actions taken by management and changes in general market conditions during that specific time. In contrast, changes in accounting-based measures may lag managerial actions by considerable periods, which introduces problems for researchers since intervening events with shorter time lags between action and effect may also act on accounting-based measures during the lag period in question.

Criticisms of using market-based measures are also numerous. First, under efficient market theories, changes in returns to capital providers in excess of the weighted average cost of capital of the organization are considered surprises to the market. If the market anticipates an organization's sales and profit growth correctly, then the risk-adjusted present value of these expectations is already incorporated into the market value of the organization (Bromiley, 1990). While this assertion is true, it seems intuitive that entrepreneurship and strategic management researchers are looking for exactly this information. Specifically, the changes in market value that researchers are interested in are those that are created by the new actions of management. The only way the market could anticipate sales and profitability growth is if there already existed information, based upon actions already taken by the organization's management, which is incorporated in the beginning market value of the organization. Therefore, market 'surprises' must result from new information that becomes available to the market. Under efficient market theories, this new information must come from (i) a more complete understanding about the consequences of past management actions, (ii) new actions taken by the organization, or (iii) changes in the organization's operating environment. Controlling for the external changes in the organization's operating environment should result in capturing the effects of firm-specific actions in the market-based measure. In finance terms, entrepreneurship and strategic management researchers are interested in unsystematic risk, or the variance in the price of an individual stock that results from the unique circumstances of the company, not the market as a whole (Brealey et al., 2001).

Bromiley (1990) argues that strategic managers do not manage stock prices. Managers attempt to influence sales, profits, capital structure and so on. Since the relationship between these individual measures and changes in stock prices is only partially understood, the use of changes in stock prices and the associated concepts of risk are difficult to apply to strategic management research.

Bromiley further argues that stock market returns focus only on the objectives of shareholders. Many strategic management theorists believe that corporations have multiple goals (see Cyert and March, 1963; Freeman, 1984 as examples). Conversely, finance theory proposes that the market for corporate control results in management being replaced if they do not act in the best interest of shareholders. Accordingly, shareholder goals become primary in the management of for-profit firms, and managers must make decisions guided by this principle or risk being replaced. Therefore, maximizing shareholder value, however shareholders define value, becomes the primary aim of managers.

SURVIVAL MEASURES

Survival measures of performance indicate whether the organization remained in business over the time period of interest or the likelihood that the organization will continue in business in the future. However, since most empirical research in entrepreneurship and strategic management addresses time horizons five years and less, survival is rarely used as a measure of overall organizational performance. Only six studies in the survey of recent empirical research studies in Chapter 2 used an organizational survival measure.

Drucker (1954) proposed that survival is the ultimate measure of long-term performance. To survive in the long term, organizations must satisfy the demands of all critical resource providers and provide a satisfactory risk-adjusted return to shareholders. The ability of the organization's management to adapt to changing environmental circumstances determines survival. Those that are adept at managing both in the present and for the future are the superior organizations.

This Darwinian approach to performance measurement, survival of the fittest, has a number of drawbacks in addition to the appropriateness of time periods. First and foremost, some organizations that do not survive can be viewed as extremely successful from the perspective of primary constituents. For instance, a company that is purchased at a significant premium to market value, as well as invested capital, can be perceived by shareholders as a success. A not-for-profit firm can also be successful even though it does not survive. Take the example of Hemophilia of Georgia, Inc., an organization that serves the needs of the bleeding disorder community in Georgia. If a cure for hemophilia is discovered, the organization's purpose of seeking a cure and providing clotting factor and medical services to individuals with the disorder, will become unnecessary. At such a time, the board of directors of the organization could decide that the organization has accomplished its mission and disband Hemophilia of Georgia, Inc. That would not mean that the organization had performed poorly. Quite the contrary would be true. Under the described circumstances, the demise of the organization would be heralded as a resounding success.

The question of survival as a measure of success is dependent upon the goals and objectives of the stakeholders of an organization. If one of the primary aims of the organization is to provide employment for a certain group of workers, such as goodwill industries, survival would be a paramount goal. However, for-profit companies that seek to maximize return to shareholders will view survival as secondary to shareholder wealth creation. If greater wealth can be created by liquidating the assets of the organization rather than continuing to operate the business, then survival is not a good measure of organizational success. In essence, in the absence of knowing the goals and objectives of the primary stakeholders of an organization, survival as a measure of performance becomes questionable.

One alternative to using survival as an absolute measure is to use a measure of the financial likelihood of organizational survival. The most commonly used measure is Altman's Z-score. Beaver (1968) was one of the first researchers to develop a univariate analysis of financial ratios to discriminate between firms that go bankrupt and those that do not. He found that cash flow divided by total debt was the single best measure in predicting bankruptcy. Altman (1968, 1993) was the first to use multiple discriminate analysis to predict bankruptcy, known as the Altman Z-score model (discussed in detail in the next chapter). The use of a measure of the likelihood of financial survival, such as the Z-score, is intuitively appropriate since it solves the problems of using an absolute measure subject to the limitations discussed above. The Z-score addresses financial solvency, which is the heart of the 'survival' construct, rather than survival itself. Unfortunately, none of the empirical articles in the survey summarized in Chapter 2 used the Z-score as a measure of overall organizational performance.

ECONOMIC VALUE MEASURES

Economic value measures are adjusted accounting measures that take into consideration the cost of capital and some of the influences of external financial reporting rules. These measures have their foundations in the residual income and internal rate of return concepts developed in the 1950s and 1960s (Ittner and Larcker, 1998). The most common economic value methods utilized in practice are: (i) residual income, originally developed and used by General Electric and popularized by McKinsey & Company as economic profit, (ii) Stern Stewart & Company's EVA®, and (iii) CFROI supported by HOLT Value Associates and Braxton Associates. Of these measures, EVA® has received almost all of the scholarly attention.

Advocates of economic value measures claim that they are superior measures of organization performance, since they examine returns to an organization after the associated costs of capital have been deducted, approximating shareholder value creation. Several studies, primarily in accounting research, examined these claims by testing the association between economic value measures and stock market returns. An examination of the computer server industry by Milunovich and Tseui (1996) found that EVA® was more highly correlated with market-value added between 1990 and 1995 than with earnings per share, earnings per share growth, return on equity, free cash flow or free cash flow growth. Also, a study by Lehn and Makhija (1997) found EVA® to be more highly correlated with stock returns over a ten-year period than with average return on assets, return on sales or return on equity. In another study, Chen and Dodd (1997) compared the explanatory power of EVA®, ROE, ROA, EPS and residual income with respect to stock returns. They found that EVA® outperformed the accounting measures (ROE, ROA and EPS) and was marginally better than residual income.

However, more recent research provided contradictory findings about the association of EVA® and stock returns. Biddle et al. (1998) performed individual regressions of EVA®, residual income (RI), operating cash flow (CFO) and net income before extraordinary items (NI) for a sample of 6,174 individual firm-years and found that NI is significantly more highly associated with market-adjusted annual stock returns ($R^2 = 13$ percent) than RI ($R^2 = 7$ percent), EVA® ($R^2 = 6$ percent), or CFO ($R^2 = 3$ percent). Their data suggest that realized earnings is a better predictor of future EVA® than realized EVA® itself. Similarly, Chen and Dodd (2001) found that the statistical association between annual stock returns and EVA® was less than that of both operating income and residual income measures. The greater explanatory power of operating income in this study was suggested to be due to the market placing higher reliance on audited accounting earnings than on consultant constructed measures that are not publicly reported. Chen and Dodd also found that over 90 percent of the variation in stock returns was not explained by accounting-based numbers. They concluded that their data suggest that stock returns are more closely aligned with organizational metrics other than earnings.

In short, the question as to what measures provide a better association with stock returns remains unresolved in the research conducted to date. Proponents of economic value measures find fault with the methodology of those that criticize their measures (see O'Byrne, 1999 as an example). Thus, most researchers agree that the cost of equity should be included in the evaluation of organizational economic performance, but how to include the measure is still a matter of debate.

CHAPTER SUMMARY

This chapter has examined the strengths and weakness of different categories of overall performance measures. Each category of measures has advantages and disadvantages for use in evaluating overall organizational performance, but no category individually has been demonstrated to actually represent the construct adequately. What is clear from prior research is that no individual category of performance measures is commonly accepted as the 'best' proxy for overall performance measurement and that further work needs to be done to identify which categories, either individually or in combination, provide the most complete information about construct.

The categories of performance measures that appear at face value to hold the most promise for generalizable entrepreneurship and strategic management research, specifically addressing for-profit organizations, are: (i) profitability, cash flow and growth accounting-based measures; (ii) likelihood of survival measures (rather than survival itself); (iii) market-based measures; and (iv) economic value measures. Measures of size should primarily be used as control variables to explain variance in other performance measures, while operational and efficiency measures are often unique to specific industries, making their use in cross-industry studies questionable. Of these categories, accounting-based measures are clearly the most frequently used in empirical research due to their common foundation in GAAP, and because they are generally available both from primary and secondary sources. The following chapter discusses the strengths and weaknesses of individual measures within each of these categories in detail.

5. Performance measures used in research and practice

This chapter discusses the strengths and weaknesses of different performance measures that have been used most frequently in research and practice. Each of these measures is defined and samples of the arguments for them, as put forth by authors who have utilized the variables in empirical studies, are discussed. In addition, the validity of the arguments in favor of using these variables is examined and discussed. They include traditional accounting-based measures of performance, likelihood of financial survival measures, market-based measures and economic value measures.

ACCOUNTING MEASURES

As discussed in Chapter 4, accounting measures are those that rely upon financial information reported in income statements, balance sheets and the statement of cash flows. These accounting measures can be further subcategorized into profitability measures, growth measures, and leverage, liquidity and cash flow measures. Table 5.1 summarizes the findings from the survey of recent empirical articles presented in Chapter 2 with respect to the use of the most frequently used individual accounting measures.

The following is a discussion of the most frequently used accounting measures in entrepreneurship and strategic management studies. Each measure will be defined and examined for its strengths and limitations as a measure of organizational financial performance.

Profitability Measures

Profitability measures include values and ratios that incorporate net income or a component of net income such as operating income or earnings before taxes. In Chapter 4, the strengths and limitations of this category of performance measures were discussed. The following discussion addresses the strengths and weaknesses of each individual measure.

Table 5.1 Summary of accounting measures used in recent empirical studies

Measure	Frequency
Profitability	
Return on assets	52
Return on equity	18
Return on sales	18
Net income	13
Return on investment	9
Growth	
Sales growth rate	32
Employee growth	7
Leverage, Liquidity and Cash Flow	
Growth rate of operating cash flow	2
Cash flow return on equity	1
Cash flow return on assets	1

Net income (NI)

Because net income is the numerator in each of the following profitability measures that will be discussed, it is addressed first. Net income measures the difference between sales and expenses. NI is defined by the following formula:

$$\text{Net income} = \text{Revenues} - \text{Expenses}.$$

As discussed in Chapter 4, there are six primary problems with using NI as a measure of organizational financial performance. To review, these questions are: (i) the use of alternative accounting methods; (ii) issues of risk are excluded; (iii) investment requirements and financial structure are excluded; (iv) the effect of dividends is excluded; (v) the time value of money is ignored; and (vi) conservative accounting for intangible assets required by generally accepted accounting policies (GAAP) understate total assets and net worth. Since each of the following four measures includes net income in the numerator, they are all subject to the same issues.

As a stand-alone measure, NI is further subject to the issues of size discussed in Chapter 4. Without controlling for the size of the organization, NI is not comparable across firms. An increase of $1,000,000 in net income for a General Motors is not comparable to a similar increase in net income for a small business. Using NI only is appropriate if the independent measures are on a similar scale or if size is controlled for in the study.

Using NI as a change score also has two primary problems inherent with all change scores (Cronbach and Furby, 1970; Cohen and Cohen, 1983; Allison, 1990). First is the problem of 'floor/ceiling' effects, which relate to the magnitude of the change. A startup or early-stage company can exhibit significant sales growth simply because the starting sales level is either zero or very small. The second problem with change scores is that the pre-change value is generally correlated with the post-change value. Accordingly, it is often appropriate to use the pre-change value as control variable as suggested by Cohen and Cohen (1983).

Return on assets (ROA)
ROA measures the organization's ability to utilize its assets to create profits. It is defined by the formula:

$$\text{Return on assets} = \frac{\text{Net income}}{\text{Average total assets}}.$$

The primary reason cited by authors in the survey of recent empirical articles in Chapter 2 for selecting this measure was that it was widely used in previous studies (see Agle and Mitchell, 1999; Berman and Wicks, 1999; Miller and Lee, 2001 as recent examples).

Hitt, Hoskisson and Kim (1997) chose ROA rather than ROE, because ROE is more sensitive to capital structure. However, ROA varies significantly across industries as a result of differing capital intensity, financial structures and accounting policies. To adjust ROA to make it comparable across companies with different capital structures, Brealey et al. (2001) suggest adjusting the ROA calculation to eliminate the effect of interest expense and the related tax shield from the numerator. The adjusted formula is:

$$\text{Adjusted return on assets} = \frac{\text{Net income} + \text{Interest expense} - \text{Interest tax shield}}{\text{Average total assets}}.$$

The result of this proposed adjustment is to use a proxy for income as if the firm was financed solely with equity. While this adjustment approximates that affect, it does not take into account the increase in the cost of equity that a firm with high leverage ratios typically experiences or higher operating expenses resulting from compliance with debt covenants.

Generally, most entrepreneurship and strategic management researchers are interested in the effects of managerial decisions on operating income. Companies with significant non-operating assets may have significant non-operating income. Although it is a managerial decision to maintain significant investments in non-operating assets, generally researchers are interested in phenomena that impact operations. Accordingly, it may be appropriate to exclude non-operating income from profitability measures. One such adjustment is to use operating return on assets rather than overall return on assets. This adjusted formula is:

$$\text{Operating return on assets} = \frac{\text{Net operating profit} - \text{Assumed taxes}^1}{\text{Average operating assets}}.$$

Because of the significant differences across industries in the average amount of total assets of their members, it is appropriate to statistically address the associated variance. This can be accomplished by using a control variable for industry membership or by adjusting reported ROA for industry averages. As noted in Chapter 4, if the study includes organizations in many industries, the use of control variables becomes problematic due to the large numbers that would be required and the corresponding loss of degrees of freedom for statistical tests. The problem with the latter approach is that performance is measured as variances from an industry mean, which may be considerably different across industries. Also, it does not account for the full effects of industry membership. In industries where there is competitive parity, variance from the mean theoretically may be much smaller than in industries where competition is less intense or where demand exceeds supply. Consequently, these problems associated with industry effects make the use of ROA challenging when many industries are represented in the sample.

Return on equity (ROE)
ROE measures the income available to common stockholders (residual claimants) as a percentage of the book value of their investment in the organization. ROE is defined by the formula:

$$\text{Return on equity} = \frac{\text{Net income available to common shareholders}}{\text{Common stockholders' equity}}.$$

Normally, common stockholders earn a return on their investment only after all other resource providers to the organization, including employees, vendors, lenders, preferred stockholders and the government have been compensated, thereby making the common stockholders residual claimants. Since common stock investors can choose to invest in many assets, they must be sufficiently compensated both for the type of investment involved (common stock) and the inherent risk for the specific organization involved, in order to continue to hold their stock or to provide further capital to the organization. Those providing the capital will only commit it to the organization so long as they are satisfied with the value they receive in exchange, relative to their alternative uses of the capital (Alchian and Demsetz, 1972; Jensen and Meckling, 1976; Simon, 1976; Barney, 2002). From this standpoint, ROE is an attractive performance measure since it can be employed in many different industries and the risk-adjusted required rate of return on equity capital should be similar.

As a construct, ROE can be decomposed into several lower-order constructs. The well-known DuPont analysis expresses ROE as the product of profit margin, asset turnover and leverage as shown in the following formula:

$$\text{Return on Equity} = \underbrace{\frac{\text{Net income}}{\text{Sales}}}_{\substack{\textit{Profit} \\ \textit{margin}}} \times \underbrace{\frac{\text{Sales}}{\text{Assets}}}_{\substack{\textit{Asset} \\ \textit{turnover}}} \times \underbrace{\frac{\text{Assets}}{\text{Common equity}}}_{\textit{Leverage}}$$

Each of these lower-order constructs individually represents separate dimensions of performance. Deconstructing a higher-order performance construct into separate lower-order constructs is informative about which dimension(s) of performance actually contributed, and to what degree, to overall organizational performance in the given circumstances. However, if the construct of interest is actually the higher-order construct of overall organizational performance, the extra information may not serve a purpose. Examining the impact of the lower-order performance constructs can be done by examining the effects on each variable individually, as was done in 54 percent of the empirical research articles, which utilized two or more dependent measures of organizational performance, summarized in Table 2.6. However, in most cases, these studies did not examine the actual tradeoffs between the lower-order constructs. They simply reported that results varied significantly across measures.

ROE is subject to the same issues as all profitability measures with respect to its numerator, net income. It is further complicated by accounting issues associated with the denominator, common stockholders' equity. Anything that impacts reported net income has an accumulating effect on retained earnings. Net income carries the impact of one year's worth of investment in intangible assets through advertising and research and development while retained earnings carries the accumulated effects of what may be years of investing in creating intangible assets. At the point in time when those investments begin to have a positive affect on earnings, equity has reached its lowest level due to the write-off of all of the expenditures in intangible assets made to date.

Consider, for example, a pharmaceutical company that invests $20 million a year for five years to develop and make ready for market a new drug. Each year the research and development expense associated with the new drug is written off against earnings until, after five years, the full $100 million invested has been expensed and retained earnings reduced accordingly. The drug will be priced to yield a high margin when it is brought to market in order to recover the amounts previously expensed for its development. Since there is no continuing expense for development, this component of the price of the drug becomes profit in the company's accounting records. The calculation of ROE will then reflect the high margin in the numerator while the denominator does not include the investment made to create this profit. As a consequence, the company's ROE will be extremely high by comparison to its prior ROE ratios while the drug was in development. In reality, most of the value was created for the company at the point in time when the drug became a viable product. During the period when sales are being realized, the valuation of the business will be affected only to the extent that realized sales margins from the drugs meet or differ from expectations. Yet, the company's ROE reflects just the opposite over those same time periods.

Return on sales (ROS)
ROS measures the percentage of sales retained as profits, and is also known as net profit margin. It is defined by the formula:

$$\text{Return on sales} = \frac{\text{Net income}}{\text{Sales}}.$$

ROS is influenced by the financial structure of the organization since net income is calculated after interest expense. Those firms that are more highly leveraged relative to their peer group, all other circumstances being equal, will have lower ROS simply because of higher interest expense. Since debt is generally less expensive than equity capital, firms that employ a mix of debt and equity in their financial structure will generally have a lower weighted average cost of capital (Brealey et al., 2001). Consequently, these same firms will have a lower ROS because the cost of their debt will be subtracted from the firm's net income in calculating the numerator of the ROS ratio, while the cost of their equity is excluded from the ratio. An adjustment to ROS can be made to eliminate the effect of financial structure and the associated tax shield as follows:

$$\text{Operating return on sales} = \frac{\text{Net income} + \text{Interest expense} - \text{Interest tax shield}}{\text{Sales}}.$$

ROS is subject to the same accounting method limitations as all profitability measures. Further, the strategy of the organization influences the ratio. For instance, a high-price, high-gross-margin strategy of a branded pharmaceutical company generally results in lower sales relative to a low-price, low-gross-margin strategy of a generic pharmaceutical company. The two strategies may ultimately result in exactly equal net income, yet the high-price, high-gross-margin strategy will have lower sales. The result is a higher ROS. Shareholder value created may be exactly equal between the organizations, yet using ROS as a dependent measure in empirical research would indicate that the high-price, high-gross-margin firm had superior 'performance'.

Return on investment (ROI)

ROI measures the return available to providers of long-term capital to the organization, including both debt and equity capital. It is defined by the following formula:

$$\text{Return on investment} = \frac{\text{Net income}}{\text{Long-term liabilities} + \text{Equity}}.$$

This measure of organizational performance is subject to all of the limitations previously discussed concerning the calculations of both net income and equity. In addition, the intention of this calculation is to examine the return available to *all* capital providers, so it is generally inappropriate to use net income after the effects of interest expense. Accordingly, the ratio is generally adjusted to be return on invested capital (ROIC) to focus on the return earned on operating assets as follows:

$$\text{Return on invested capital} = \frac{\text{Net operating profits less assumed taxes[2]}}{\text{Invested capital}}.$$

There are many different approaches to the adjustments for this calculation. The simplest approach is net operating profits less assumed taxes (NOPLAT) as:

$$\text{NOPLAT} = \text{EBIT} - \text{Taxes on EBIT} + \text{Changes in deferred taxes,}$$

and invested capital as the amount of money a firm has invested in the operating assets of its business calculated as:

$$\text{Invested capital} = \text{Stockholders' equity} + \text{Interest-bearing debt.[3]}$$

One advantage to ROIC is that it is not subject to manipulation based upon the mix of debt and equity used to capitalize the firm. This is in contrast to ROE which has leverage as a primary component as described previously (in other words, ROE includes interest expense in the numerator). Conversely, capital structure does limit strategic choice. Accordingly, information about the overall performance of the organization could be considered lost by using an unleveraged, and therefore, risk-free measure of performance.

There are several disadvantages to using ROI as an organizational performance measure. First, underinvestment can result in improved short-term gains but long-term declines, since ROI ignores events beyond the current period. Second, ROI can be influenced by prior investments that have not been fully depreciated or amortized, thereby obscuring the impact of current period actions. Third, ROI ignores the terminal value of actions for unrealized opportunity gains. Finally, prior performance measurement research has found that ROI was not a reliable estimate for the discounted cash flow rate of return, both for individual and complete collections of company projects (Ittner and Larcker, 1998). As discussed previously, finance theory posits that the best way to value a company is as the sum of the discounted, future cash flow to investors. Therefore, if organizational financial performance is measured by change in the value of the economic value of the organization, then information is lost by using only a historical measure, such as ROI.

Growth Measures

Growth measures include values and ratios that present some indication of organizational growth. Growth has been conceptualized both in the context of resources and from a business operations perspective. Typical accounting-based growth measures include absolute or percentage change in total assets, operating assets, sales, total expenses and operating expenses. Table 5.1 lists the most frequently used growth measures used in the empirical studies summarized in Chapter 2. The following is a discussion of the strengths and weaknesses of these two growth measures as well as some alternative measures of growth. All growth variables can be stated either as a value change between two points in time or as a percentage change between two points in time.

As with net income, using growth as an absolute value is subject to all of the problems associated with size. Further, the issues of 'floor/ceiling' effects and correlation of pre- and post-change value are problems. On the other hand, as discussed in Chapter 4, growth is generally accepted as a separate and important dimension of organizational financial performance so it is appropriate to include organizational growth in any analysis of overall organizational performance.

Sales growth

Sales growth is the primary measure of growth used in the empirical studies summarized in Chapter 2. The majority of these studies, 81 percent, used the change score for growth rate of sales as the measure. The remaining 19 percent used the value representing the actual dollar change in sales.

The only empirical tests of growth as a measure of organizational performance used sales growth (see Venkatraman and Ramanujam, 1987; Chandler and Hanks, 1993; Murphy et al., 1996; Robinson, 1998 as examples). Sales growth was consistently found to represent a distinct dimension of performance from profitability. As discussed in Chapter 4, growth is a critical component of the constant-growth dividend discount model of financial valuation. However, the growth rate used in this model assumes that cash flow available to stockholders increases proportionately with sales growth (Brealey et al., 2001). Sales growth in the absence of profitability growth will not yield the change in economic value sought by shareholders. Therefore, the correlation of sales growth with future profitability and cash flow is critical for the measure to be useful in representing organizational financial performance.

Employee growth

Employee growth represents the change in the number of people employed by an organization between two time periods. This measure was the second most frequently used measure in the summary of empirical articles in Chapter 2. Murphy et al. (1996) also found that employee growth was used as a performance indicator, second to the use of sales growth.

The growth in employees can be viewed as a proxy for several performance indicators. First, companies add employees in anticipation of, or coincident with, sales growth. Second, employee growth can indicate that the organization is adding critical resources necessary for growth. In this regard, growth in research and development employment, representing the addition of critical knowledge, has been used as a measure of performance (Baum et al., 2000).

Total asset growth

Drucker (1954) included the ability of an organization to continue to attract capital as a critical performance dimension. It follows that growth in total assets could be considered a measure of organizational effectiveness. However, neither growth in operating assets nor growth in total assets was used as a measure in the empirical articles surveyed in Chapter 2. As total asset growth is an intuitively attractive measure of organizational growth, examination of the information content of this variable relative to organizational financial performance is warranted.

Leverage, Liquidity and Cash Flow

Leverage, liquidity and cash flow measures deal with the financial structure of an organization and the ability of the organization to pay its liabilities in a timely fashion. Each of the three categories of measures relates to a separate component of this aspect of company performance. Leverage measures describe the financial structure of the organization. Liquidity measures describe the ability of the organization to convert assets into cash. Finally, cash flow measures describe the amount of cash an organization generated, and the sources of that cash, relative to the organization's demands for cash.

The ability to meet financial obligations can be measured both by the ratio of liquid assets to liabilities, and/or by the organization's ability to generate sufficient cash flow to meet outstanding liabilities. Table 5.2 presents examples of common leverage, liquidity and cash flow measures. The following subsections discuss these measures in more detail.

Table 5.2   Examples of leverage, liquidity and cash flow measures

Measures	
Leverage	
Debt-to-equity ratio	$\dfrac{\text{Long-term dept}}{\text{Equity}}$
Debt-to-total assets ratio	$\dfrac{\text{Total liabilities}}{\text{Total assets}}$
Times interest earned	$\dfrac{\text{EBIT}}{\text{Interest payments}}$
Liquidity	
Working capital	Current assets – Current liabilities
Current ratio	$\dfrac{\text{Current assets}}{\text{Current liabilities}}$
Quick ratio	$\dfrac{\text{Current assets – Inventory}}{\text{Current liabilities}}$
Interval measure	$\dfrac{\text{Cash + Marketable securities + Receivables}}{\text{Average daily operations expenditures}}$
Cash flow	
Cash flow return on equity	$\dfrac{\text{Cash flow}}{\text{Equity}}$
Cash flow return on total assets	$\dfrac{\text{Cash flow}}{\text{Equity}}$

Leverage measures

Leverage measures specifically address the capital structure of the organization. As discussed earlier, leverage is a component of return on equity, as well as other profitability measures. Further, leverage is a component of Altman's Z-score calculation. As the information provided by these variables is contained in other measures of organizational performance, these measures should only be used as a measure of organizational financial performance if the other measures are not used. If measures that already include leverage as a component are used in research, then there may be significant covariation between measures, raising questions about the discriminant validity between the measures.

Liquidity measures

Liquidity refers to the ability of a firm to meet its financial obligations in a timely manner. In essence, the assets owned by a company are liquid if they can quickly and cheaply be converted to cash (Brealey et al., 2001). The critical performance issue relative to liquidity is whether the organization has or is developing enough readily accessible capital to continue to operate. Accordingly, liquidity measures represent one aspect of a dimension of overall organizational performance, but are not sufficient measures by themselves to represent the entire construct.

Liquidity measures are driven by the balance sheet of an organization. As previously argued, organizational financial performance relates to the change in state over a period of time. Since the balance sheet represents a snapshot of an organization as of a single point in time, balance sheet measures as reported, and the ratios calculated from them, are not appropriate for representing performance over a period of time. Further, while it can be argued that changes in liquidity measures represent one aspect of organizational financial performance, since accounting-based liquidity measures ignore the organization's ready access to capital through established financing agreements, it can also be argued that accounting-based liquidity measures do not fully represent the organization's ability to meet its financial obligations in a timely manner. The amount of borrowing capability of an organization is not generally available information to researchers. Accordingly, liquidity measures as a component of organizational financial performance should be used with great circumspection.

Cash flow measures

Cash flow is not only critical for meeting current obligations but is also a measure of the firm's ability to actually pay a return to resource providers. Ultimately, the availability of cash payouts to resource providers determines the financial benefit, or value, that they realize from an organization. Typical business valuation methods are based upon projected available cash flows and the timing of the cash payouts to investors (West and Jones, 1999; Copeland et al., 2000). As discussed in Chapter 4, in the constant-growth dividend discount model, cash flow is the numerator used in determining the current value of an organization. Accordingly, it is appropriate to measure cash flow available to investors as a component of organizational performance.

Cash flow return on equity   The ratio of cash flow from operations to total equity is a measure of the cash return available to equity investors, provided there are no capital calls by debt holders. Since cash flow from operations includes the carrying cost of debt, in the form of interest expense, the use of this cash is at the discretion of management. The cash can be reinvested in the organization in the form of capital expenditures; it can be used to reduce debt; or cash can be paid out to equity holders. The use of net cash flow from operations in the numerator inherently assumes that management will only choose to make capital investments in positive net present value opportunities. If no such investments are available, management will use cash to pay a return to capital providers. Of course, if cash flow from operations is negative, the organization will have to acquire additional capital from creditors, from the liquidation of capitalized assets, or from equity investors.

Free cash flow (net cash flow from operations and net cash flow from investing activities) is often used in place of net cash flow from operations as the numerator. This is intuitively attractive since the sum of the cash flows from all sources, except financing sources, is the amount available to distribute to capital providers. It should be noted that changes in working capital accounts are accounted for in net operating cash flows. However, since capital investments are removed from the numerator, the ratio of free cash flow to total equity does not capture the net present value from the investments to be realized as cash flow in the future. This can distort actual performance in short-term studies.

Cash flow return on assets   Cash flow return on assets is similar in purpose to cash flow return on equity, with the exception that it measures the cash return relative to the total capital deployed by the corporation. As with return on assets, this measure is subject to significant differences across industries. Accordingly, researchers must control for industry effects in their samples.

SURVIVAL MEASURES

Survival measures of performance either indicate whether a company stayed in business over a specified period or the likelihood that the organization will continue in business. Survival is rarely used in entrepreneurship and strategic management research since typical timeframes used in these fields are five years or less. However, for longitudinal research, survival measures may be particularly useful. As discussed in the previous chapter, although actual survival is generally not an appropriate measure of organizational financial performance, the likelihood of survival can be viewed as a relevant measure of one dimension of organizational financial performance. The most commonly used measure of the likeliness of financial survival is Altman's Z-score.

Altman's Z-score

Altman's Z-score is the most commonly used measure of the financial likelihood of organizational survival. Altman (1968, 1993) was the first to use multiple discriminate analysis to predict bankruptcy, known as Altman's Z-score model. The model yields a Z-score based upon the discriminant function:

$$Z = 1.2X_1 + 1.4X_2 + 3.3X_3 + 0.6X_4 + 1.0X_5,$$

where:

X_1 = working capital / total assets,
X_2 = retained earnings / total assets,
X_3 = earnings before interest and taxes / total assets,
X_4 = market value of equity / book value of total liabilities, and
X_5 = sales / total assets.

Altman found that firms with a Z-score greater than 2.99 were clearly in the non-bankruptcy category, while those firms with a Z-score less than 1.81 were clearly in the bankrupt category. Firms between these two values were deemed to be in danger of going bankrupt, although they were not yet bankrupt (in the 'grey zone'). This formula was subsequently revised to drop the X_5 coefficient to minimize potential industry effects relating to asset turnover, primarily in non-manufacturing firms. The revised formula for non-publicly traded, non-manufacturing firms was:

$$Z = 6.56X_1 + 3.26X_2 + 6.72X_3 + 1.05X_4,$$

where:

X_1 = working capital / total assets,
X_2 = retained earnings / total assets,
X_3 = earnings before interest and taxes / total assets, and
X_4 = net worth / total liabilities.

In the revised formula, Altman found that firms with a Z-score greater than 2.60 were clearly in the non-bankruptcy category, while those firms with a Z-score less than 1.10 were clearly in the bankrupt category. Firms between these two values were deemed to be in the grey zone. The use of a measure such as the Z-score is intuitively appropriate, since it solves the problem of using an absolute measure subject to the limitations discussed above. The Z-score addresses financial solvency, which is the heart of the 'survival' construct, rather than survival itself. Unfortunately, none of the empirical articles in the survey summarized in Chapter 2 used the Z-score as a measure of overall organizational performance.

MARKET-BASED MEASURES

Market-based measures of performance include ratios or rates of change that incorporate the market value of the organization. These variables include: (i) return to shareholders; (ii) market value added; (iii) holding period returns; (iv) Jensen's alpha; and (v) Tobin's Q. The calculation of these variables requires a market valuation for the company and is generally available only for publicly traded companies. As there are no publicly available market valuations for privately held companies, the use of market-based measures for entrepreneurship research is problematic.

The following is a discussion of the market-based measures most frequently used in practice. Based upon the review of recent empirical studies in Chapter 2, these measures were used in over 10 percent of the empirical studies summarized. The most commonly used market-based measures will be defined and examined for their strengths and limitations as measures of organizational financial performance.

Return to Shareholders (RTS)

Return to shareholders is a measure that represents the total financial value created for shareholders over the time period of interest. RTS includes both the appreciation of common stock plus distributions to shareholders in the form of dividends. The formula for this measure is:

Return to shareholders = Holding period return + Dividend yield,

where:

$$\text{Holding period return} = \frac{\text{Beginning} - \text{Ending stock price}}{\text{Beginning stock price}}.$$

Robinson (1995) found that RTS provided the most power among 10 variables tested for measuring new venture performance. Unfortunately, Robinson did not measure RTS over the same time period for each company in his sample nor did he adjust RTS for market returns for the period actually measured. As a result, the values for RTS include both firm-specific performance effects as well as general market performance effects. Since the market effects are not equivalent over the different time periods, the confounding effects of these returns on Robinson's results cannot be determined. Consequently, the overall conclusions of his study concerning RTS may be open to question. Further research to confirm Robinson's findings is necessary.

An advantage of using RTS as a performance measure in empirical research is that the information is readily available for public companies. Not surprisingly, our survey of empirical studies indicated that RTS was the most commonly used market-based performance measure. The other advantages of using market-based measures, discussed in Chapter 4, apply to RTS as well. To review these advantages, market-based measures include:

- The value created by both the execution on existing opportunities, as well as the risk-adjusted expected value of future opportunities that have yet to be realized.
- Stockholder returns, in a well-regulated and open market, are not subject to manipulation by management, while accounting-based measures can be manipulated.
- Market-based measures quickly reflect management actions and changes in the economic value of the organization in an efficient market.
- Since the value of past actions is quickly incorporated into the market value of the organization, the change in market value of the organization during a given period can be assumed to reflect the actions taken by management and changes in general market conditions during that specific time.

The primary disadvantage for using RTS as a performance measure is that the information is not readily available for privately held companies.

Therefore, generalization of findings from populations of public companies to the population of all companies is problematic.

Market Value Added (MVA)

MVA is a measure of the long-term economic profit creation of a firm (Barney, 2002). It is calculated as the firm enterprise value (market value of equity plus the market value of debt) less the economic book value of the organization (book value of equity plus the book value of debt).

The formula for MVA is:

Market value added = Enterprise value – Economic book value,

where:

Enterprise value = Market value of common stock
+ Market value of preferred stock
+ Market value of a firm's short-term debt
+ Market value of a firm's long-term debt,

and:

Economic book value = Book value of equity + Book value of debt.

In essence, MVA is the sum of the annual economic profit performance over the life of the firm. The change in MVA, over any given period, is the sum of the economic profit earned over the time period of interest. Firms that consistently earn positive economic profits will, over time, accumulate significant MVA, while firms that earn negative economic profits will actually have enterprise values below their economic book values.

There are two primary problems with the use of MVA as a measure for researchers. First, if the population of interest is not public companies, market value is generally not available for individual observations. This is particularly problematic for entrepreneurship research where most companies being studied are not publicly traded. The second problem is that economic book value is based upon the amount that has been invested in the firm since inception. The adjustments to book value of a firm for MVA calculations are similar to those for EVA® (detailed in the discussion of EVA® below). The consulting firm Stern Stewart publishes EVA® and MVA for the 1,000 largest publicly owned US firms annually but the information is not generally available for any other population of organizations (Barney, 2002). Not surprisingly, our survey of empirical research found only three studies that used variations of MVA.

Jensen's Alpha

Jensen's alpha is a risk-adjusted performance measure that is calculated as
the average return to shareholders for a company in excess of its cost of
equity capital as determined using the capital asset pricing model (CAPM).
The measure is defined by the formula:

$$\alpha_p = \bar{r}_p - [r_f + \beta_p(\bar{r}_m - r_f)],$$

where:

$\bar{r}_p$ = Expected total portfolio or company return,
r_f = Risk-free rate,
β_p = Beta of the portfolio or single company, and
$\bar{r}_m$ = Expected market return.

For calculation purposes for researchers, the expected return is the actual
return over the measurement period. The risk-free rate is the appropriate US
government borrowing rate, typically the 20-year T-bill rate (Brealey et al.,
2001). The beta is the covariance of the returns for the company during
the measurement period with the overall market returns. In finance theory,
beta is considered a measure of the risk of an investment in an individual
company relative to the market or its systematic risk. The expected market
return is operationalized as the average return earned by the overall market
for the period of interest. The difference between the expected market return
and the risk-free rate is referred to as the market risk premium.

There are many problems in using Jensen's alpha in empirical research.
First, like other market-based measures, it can only be calculated for
public companies due the lack of market valuations of privately held companies. Second, although the CAPM is the most frequently used method
for estimating the cost of equity, it has been criticized by many finance
scholars, primarily because it uses historical returns or risk premiums as
predictors of future returns (see Brealey et al., 2001 and Penman, 2001
for discussions of the CAPM). Bettis (1983) as well as Bromiley (1990)
criticized the use of beta as a measure of risk in strategy research. Beta is
a finance theory approach to risk that proposes risk as a symmetric
distribution around a mean return with normal distribution. Strategic
conceptions of risk are asymmetrical, since the danger of loss is perceived
as a risk while achieving gains in excess of expectations is not. In essence,
the CAPM uses a market approach to estimating risk, while entrepreneurship and strategic management researchers are more interested in
operational or accounting risks. Total corporate risk including both firm-

specific and market risks are important to strategic managers, not just financial risk (Bromiley, 1990).

The finance issues inherent in using Jensen's alpha are generally beyond the interests of management researchers. Consequently, using a measure that requires significant effort to calculate based on financial information typically not reported by companies makes the use of this measure unusual. In fact, only four studies in our survey of empirical studies used this measure to represent overall organizational performance.

Tobin's Q

Tobin's Q is defined as the ratio of the market value of an organization to the replacement cost of its assets. The formula for this measure is as follows:

$$\text{Tobin's } Q = \frac{\text{Enterprise value}}{\text{Replacement cost of assets}}.$$

Chung and Pruitt (1994) suggest that this enterprise value calculation actually uses the book value of short- and long-term debt since market values of debt are often not available. They argue that the difference is not significant for most companies and, accordingly, not worth the effort of exact determination. The value of a firm's short-term debt is defined as the difference between a firm's short-term assets and its short-term liabilities.

Barney (2002) states that this measure has advantages over economic profit measures since its calculation does not rely on accounting profits or an accurate calculation of the weighted average cost of capital (WACC) for each company in the sample. A value of greater than 1.0 indicates that a firm is expected to create above-normal performance while a value of less than 1.0 suggests that a firm is producing below-normal returns.

The use of Tobin's Q is difficult for researchers because there is limited information about the replacement cost of assets. Accordingly, our survey of empirical articles summarized in Chapter 2 indicated that very few researchers used this measure as a dependent variable to represent overall organizational performance.

ECONOMIC VALUE MEASURES

The following is a discussion of the most frequently used economic value measures used in practice. In the recent empirical studies identified in Chapter 2, economic value measures are almost never used in academic research in the fields of entrepreneurship and strategic management. While there is no clear explanation for this observation, it is most likely a result of

the significant adjustments required to be made to reported financial statements for each of the measures. Much of the data necessary to make these
adjustments is not publicly available, making the use of these measures
infeasible. Each measure will be defined and examined for its strengths and
limitations as a measure of overall organizational performance.

Residual Income (RI)

RI is a measure that adjusts accounting net income (NI) by subtracting a
charge for the cost of equity capital utilized in the organization. The cost
of equity capital is equal to the beginning book value of equity capital (BV)
times the cost of equity capital (k). Therefore, RI is defined by the formula:

$$\text{Residual income} = \text{NI}_t - (k_t \times \text{BV}_{t-1}).$$

This calculation yields the economic profit generated by the organization.
Another way to define residual income or economic profit is the spread
between the organization's return on invested capital and its WACC times
the amount of capital invested by the organization.

$$\text{Economic profit} = \text{Invested capital} \times (\text{ROIC} - \text{WACC}).$$

As discussed in Chapter 4, empirical tests of association between
stock returns, EVA® and RI suggest that RI provides as much information
with less calculation effort (Chen and Dodd, 2001). Occam's razor would
suggest that RI is a superior measure for researchers since it provides equal
information with less effort.

Based upon the review of recent empirical articles, RI was not used as a
dependent measure in any research. While there is no apparent reason why
this is the case, it seems reasonable to suppose that it was due to the fact
that there is no readily available source of information on the WACC for
companies. It generally is not reported in financial statements or included
in popular databases. It can only be assumed that this added complexity in
calculation makes RI a less attractive measure for researchers.

Economic Value Added (EVA®)

Economic value added, or EVA®, is a proprietary evolution of the residual
income concept by Stern Stewart & Company ('Stern Stewart'). It began to
be included in journals as early as 1989 (Finegan, 1989). The measure
became popular in 1993 with the publication of an article in *Fortune
Magazine* by Tully (1993) that provided a detailed description of the

concept, the Stern Stewart approach to using EVA®, and examples of its successful implementations. EVA® is defined as adjusted operating income less a charge for the use of capital (Stewart, 1991). The cost of equity capital is based upon the CAPM, wherein the charge for equity is the opportunity cost which shareholders forgo by making the specific invest-ment. Specifically, the cost proposed by Stern Stewart is the company's stock beta (the covariance of the price of the specific company's stock with the market) multiplied by 6 percent plus the then current return on long-term government bonds (considered as the risk-free rate in the market).

Beyond simply adjusting accounting earnings for the cost of equity, EVA® calculations include adjustments to reported earnings for alleged distortions caused by GAAP. Stern Stewart recommend up to 160 different adjustments to reported earnings to approximate 'economic' profits. Table 5.3 summarizes some of the adjustments for what are referred to as 'equity equivalents'.

EVA® advocates argue that the cost of equity must be considered, since investors will withdraw their capital and invest it elsewhere if they cannot earn an equivalent risk-adjusted return by investing in the firm. Since

Table 5.3   Equity adjustments required when calculating EVA®

Add equity equivalents to capital for:	Add increase in equity equivalents to NOPLAT for:
Deferred tax reserve	Increase in deferred tax reserve
LIFO reserve	Increase in LIFO reserve
Cumulative goodwill amortization	Goodwill amortization
Unrecorded goodwill	
(Net) capitalized intangibles*	Increase in (net) capitalized intangibles
Full-cost reserve**	Increase in full-cost reserve
Cumulative unusual loss (gain) after tax	Unusual loss (gain) after tax
Other reserves such as:	Increase in other reserves
Bad debt	
Inventory obsolescence	
Warranty	
Deferred income	

Notes:
* Stewart recommends capitalizing cumulative R&D expenditures.
** Changes to full-cost accounting for natural resource companies that use successful-efforts accounting.

Source: Stewart (1991: 112).

reported accounting earnings do not include a charge for equity capital, they are incomplete measures of performance. The advantage of EVA® is to focus management attention on committing resources to projects that have expected returns in excess of the weighted average cost of capital for the project. This makes good financial sense, but does not recommend the measure for researchers who are simply seeking to measure organizational economic performance. The advantage of EVA® seems to be more of a driver of stock returns (value creation) rather than a measure of it. What researchers need is the simplest measure or set of measures that better reflects value creation. Not surprisingly, the survey of recent empirical articles summarized in Chapter 2 found that EVA® was not used as a dependent measure to represent performance.

Cash Flow Return on Investment (CFROI)

CFROI is an inflation-adjusted measure similar to internal rate of return that compares cash flows with total assets employed to generate those cash flows. It is defined by the formula:

$$\text{Cash flow return on investment} = \frac{\text{Cash operating profit}}{\text{Gross investment}}.$$

Clinton and Chen (1998) in a study of 325 firms over the years 1991 to 1995 found that operating cash flow per share and adjusted operating income after tax per share had a higher association with stock price and stock price return than both CFROI and EVA®. CFROI is a more complicated calculation than EVA® since it requires inflation-adjusted calculations of cash flows and investments. The added complications of calculation make the measure generally unacceptable to researchers and accordingly, no article included in the survey of empirical research in Chapter 2 used CFROI.

CHAPTER SUMMARY

This chapter has reviewed the individual strengths and weaknesses of organizational financial performance measures. Based upon the review of individual measures of organizational financial performance, it seems clear that no measure is perfect. Each measure individually has strengths and weaknesses. For the purposes of academic research, beyond the concerns of the individual information content of each measure, some measures can be eliminated from consideration because of the lack of sufficient information to calculate them, such as economic value added.

The most critical flaw with accounting-based, economic value and survival measures of organizational financial performance is that they primarily capture information about the past. Only market-based measures capture, albeit imperfectly, information about the future implications of current decisions. However, market-based measures are impractical for companies that are not publicly traded, since there is generally no information on the enterprise value of the organization.

Most individual measures of organizational financial performance capture different dimensions, or characteristics, of the overall organizational performance construct. Consequently, multidimensional measures will probably be required to capture more fully the concept of organizational financial performance. The identification of these dimensions, of this overall construct, is the aim of this research.

NOTES

1. Assumed taxes are calculated as the product of an organization's average tax rate times its net operating income.
2. Net operating profits equal operating earnings before interest and taxes (EBIT).
3. Interest-bearing debt includes both short- and long-term interest-bearing liabilities.

6. Measurement concepts and implications

This chapter addresses the measurement attributes and specifications appropriate for the variables that scholars use for dependent variables when undertaking a research study. These include decisions such as constructs and construct validation, timeframes, and samples, all of which affect the types of conclusions that can be made about the study's results, including (i) the generalizability to the population sampled with respect to external validity, (ii) the precision and accuracy in measuring the observed effects that are the subject of the study with respect to internal and construct validity, and (iii) the realism of context (Sackett and Larson, 1990; Scandura and Williams, 2000).

A review of the concepts underlying the development of effective measurement models for dependent measures, and the implications for the types of conclusions that can be drawn from research based upon the choices made by the researcher is included in this chapter. In particular, the implications for construct and statistical conclusion validity based upon the choice of variables are examined. The chapter concludes by applying the general concepts of measurement to the specific task of measuring overall organizational performance.

MEASUREMENT: A CONCEPTUAL OVERVIEW

Measurement is the process of making observations of real world phenomena for the purpose of describing the attributes of objects and actions in the form of a variable. Values are assigned to aspects of objects, not the objects themselves, or in other words, they are used to describe characteristics of the objects. For example, an observer does not assign a measurement to a box, rather he/she 'measures' its length, width and height. All other aspects of the object being observed, which are not assigned values, and on which similar objects could differ, are ignored. Therefore, when specific aspects of an object are chosen to be measured as representing the entire object, some features of the object (or information about it) are lost, and different people may choose to measure different aspects of the same object.

Observations can be categorized as direct, indirect and constructs (Babbie, 1998). *Direct observables* are attributes of an object that can be observed both simply and directly, such as color. Examples of direct observables in business research include behaviors of managers, inventory quantities and number of patents obtained. *Indirect observables* rely upon examining attributes that are related to the attribute of interest, but are not that attribute specifically. For instance, the volume of a box may not be directly observed but can be determined indirectly by measuring its length, width and height. In business, indirect observations include most financial measures that are calculated based upon financial statements. Net income is a function of revenues and expenses reported. It cannot be directly observed in nature, but it can be indirectly observed and a value assigned.

Finally, *constructs* are theoretical creations of phenomena that cannot be directly or indirectly observed. Overall organizational performance is a construct that cannot be directly observed and must be measured using theoretically derived indicators. As discussed in Chapter 2, these indicators can include growth, profitability, efficiency and so on. However, before using any of these indicators, they must be demonstrated to actually represent some aspect of the theoretical construct of interest. This is the essence of the problem with studies that purport to measure overall organizational performance, since the indicators that have been used to represent that construct have never been rigorously tested to determine their effectiveness as potential 'measures' of such performance.

Characteristics of Constructs

A construct may have multiple facets or dimensions. These dimensions can be characterized as groupings of similar attributes that are theoretically related to the phenomenon of interest, but are distinct from other groupings of similar attributes that also are related to the phenomenon of interest. Venkatraman and Ramanujam (1987) demonstrated that overall organizational performance was a construct that had at least two distinct dimensions, growth and profitability. Each of these dimensions can be 'described' using one or more attributes. For example, profitability can be described by measures of the returns to all resource providers such as return on invested capital, return on equity and return to shareholders. Likewise, growth can be described by increases in sales dollars and/or units, increase in total assets and increase in total employees. Each variable measures a different attribute of the same construct, growth. Through the specification of the different dimensions of a construct, researchers can often attain a more sophisticated understanding of the phenomenon of interest (Babbie, 1998).

Continuing with the example of a box, if a box is defined by the observer as its height, length and width, then its weight, color, shape and so on are ignored because they are deemed irrelevant to the task at hand. Since this is the judgment made by the observer, and different observers may deem other aspects of the object as equally or more relevant, it is essential that the characteristics of the different attributes be fully described so that the description of the object can be better understood from the perspective of what was being measured. Of course, what is relevant to measure can be determined only within the context of the theory about the phenomenon that the researcher is studying. Accordingly, measurement implies some of the relations among a set of variables appropriate to the phenomenon being investigated.

THE ROLE OF MEASUREMENT IN THEORY BUILDING AND TESTING

Theory building refers to making and testing a set of assertions that explain or predict a particular phenomenon that holds true across a prescribed range of specific instances (Weick, 1989). In entrepreneurship and strategic management research, most theories are developed to predict or explain the impact of management actions on performance. In some theories, the performance construct of interest is overall organizational performance. In other theories, the performance construct may be more narrowly defined to outcomes such as new venture formation or customer satisfaction.

Theories can be presented as relationships between independent and dependent variables. If the variables are well specified, the relationship may be able to be represented mathematically in equation form. The purpose of empirical research is to test propositions about the hypothesized relationships represented in the theoretical model (Bourgeois, 1979; Van de Ven, 1989). To accomplish this task, researchers must be able to make observations of all independent and dependent measures specified in the model or conceptual framework. Based upon the relationships that are found to exist among the variables observed, conclusions are drawn about the ability of the model or conceptual framework to adequately represent the phenomenon of interest. In other words, the theory becomes 'grounded' by the data.

There are three primary purposes for research: exploration, description and/or explanation (Babbie, 1998). Exploration is the attempt to develop an initial understanding of a phenomenon. Description is the precise measurement and reporting of the characteristics of a phenomenon. Explanation is the discovery and reporting of the relationships among aspects of a phenomenon.

Regardless of whether the purpose of the research being conducted is to explore, explain or describe, measurement is necessary for research to achieve these purposes. Since measurement involves the assignment of values to attributes of the phenomenon of interest, it is in the interests of the researcher to use measurement systems that capture the most accurate information possible about that phenomenon with the greatest reliability and utility. The utility of a measurement system can be judged by whether the form of the information it represents is useful in the testing the relationships portrayed in the theoretical model. The assignment of numbers to aspects of a phenomenon allows the use of mathematics in its explanation or description, and the use of mathematics allows for common interpretation of the results of tests of the relationships of interest.

The Components of Theories and Models

Most management researchers operate both as theorists and empiricists. As theorists, they operate at the theory–hypothesis–construct level while as empiricists they operate at the observation–evaluation level (Kerlinger, 1986). In transitioning from theory to empiricism, researchers must transform concepts into constructs that can be measured by variables.

A concept 'expresses an abstraction formed by generalization from particulars' (ibid.: 26). A concept cannot necessarily be measured directly. For instance, strategy is a concept. The concept of a strategy can be described as evolving from generalizations about the actions taken by managers relative to market scope, organizational resources and capabilities, and timing. Scope, resources and timing are deliberately and consciously created constructs that have been developed by scholars to describe certain measurable attributes of the concept of strategy. To measure such constructs of interest, various attributes of the construct are assigned numbers or values that can be directly observed.

Measurement involves the assignment of numbers or values to the attributes of an object based upon either direct or indirect observation. The point of measurement is to collect empirical evidence to 'test' the theories or hypotheses derived from them. The relationships of interest in a theoretical model are between the independent and dependent variables. Tests of these proposed relationships involve statistically determining how well the variation in the set of independent variables explains or predicts variation in the dependent variables. The unexplained variance in the dependent variable is assumed to result from other factors not included in the model or from random error. If there are specification or measurement errors in describing any of the independent or dependent measures, variance that could and should have been explained by the hypothesized relationships, remains unexplained. Therefore, it is critical to pay attention to the specification and the measurement of the variables of interest in empirical research.

EMPIRICAL CONSTRUCTS AND CLASSIFICATION SYSTEMS

Empirical research involves transforming concepts into constructs, then converting these constructs into measurable attributes, then making observations, and testing the hypothesized relationships among the variables of interest. The choices a researcher makes in operationalizing constructs into variables are many. They include the types of variables that will be employed and the information they will represent.

Single versus Multiple Attribute Measures

A variable can represent either a single attribute of the object or phenomenon of interest or multiple attributes. For instance, the length, width and height of a box can all be described by single-attribute measures. The volume of the box, by contrast, is a multi-attribute measure that can be described by a combination of single-attribute measures, namely length, width and height. If someone is interested in packaging a liquid, simply knowing the volume of the box may be sufficient information to make decisions. However, if the object to be packaged is a solid that will not conform to the shape of its package, it is critical to know all three dimensions of the object in order to know what size box to use. The greater the number of attributes a variable includes, the greater the information that must be collected about the object or phenomenon. The research question of interest determines whether this information is useful in aggregate or needs to be separated into multiple, individual measures. One of the key tasks facing the researcher is to properly specify the measures to be used in the study, so that they provide adequate information to confirm or reject the researcher's theoretical model.

For example, if a researcher is interested on the impact of research and development investments ('R&D') on net income over a three-year period, several choices have to be made. The researcher must be able to observe the amounts expended on R&D as well as the change in net income over the study. If all other sources of variation in net income have been controlled for during the same period, then the remaining change in net income would be assumed to result from the observed R&D expenditures. However, net income is a multi-attribute measure, including information about both sales and expenses. Just looking at that measure, it is impossible to tell whether the R&D investments resulted in higher sales or lower costs. Therefore, the only conclusions that can be drawn from the study would be that R&D does or does not impact future net income, but not necessarily how.

Types of Scales/Indices for Measuring Attributes

There are four principal types of measures: nominal, ordinal, interval and ratio (Babbie, 1998). The choice of the types of measures used in a study will impact the types of tests that can be employed and, consequently, the types of conclusions drawn.

- *Nominal measures* are variables whose attributes are only mutually exclusive and exhaustive. They have no other characteristics. Examples of nominal measures include gender, industry membership and strategy employed. The values are individually distinct but cannot be ordered or scaled. Nominal measures provide names or labels for the different 'categories' into which the object or phenomenon may fall, but provide no further information about it.
- *Ordinal measures* are variables that can be logically ranked along some dimension. An example would be level of education. A person may have an elementary school education, high school degree, college degree or post-graduate education. There is a clear rank order to the values for the variable 'education level', but there is not a clear spacing between the values.
- *Interval measures* are variables for which the distance between variables can be expressed in standard intervals. Interval measures do not have a true value for zero. An example would be IQ test scores. The meaning of the difference between a score of 100 and 110 is the same as the meaning of the difference between the scores of 120 and 130. However, an IQ test score of zero would mean that a person has absolutely no intelligence which would not be regarded as reasonable.
- *Ratio measures* are variables have all the characteristics of interval measures, and also have a true zero point. These measures can be mathematically manipulated in equation form. The advantage to ratio measures is that they can be interpreted over an infinite range of values and can be directly used in statistical analyses. Net income, sales, return on equity and market value added are all examples of a ratio measures.

One type of measure is not superior to another type. Each provides a unique kind of information. Ratio scales may allow for the greatest range of mathematical manipulation, but they cannot be used to represent every attribute of interest. The type of variables selected must conform to the nature of the attribute of interest. Consequently, it is the job of the researcher to weigh the information necessary for the study against the limitations inherent in the types of variables used.

ATTRIBUTES OF EFFECTIVE MEASUREMENT SYSTEMS

Measurement involves the mapping of some of the characteristics of a set of objects onto a set of numbers so that there is discrimination between the characteristics of the objects measured and the numbers assigned to them. There must be isomorphism, a one-to-one correspondence, between elements of two different classes (Babbie, 1998). However, measurement is indirect, and since it is up to the observer to select the attributes to represent a phenomenon, it is 'subjective'.

Specific criteria must be met in the development of measurement and classification systems: (i) for attribute selection, (ii) by all the 'taxa' in the measurement system, and (iii) by the measurement and classification system as a whole. Each of these three issues is discussed in greater detail in the following subsections.

Criteria for Attribute Selection

First, and perhaps most importantly, the attributes of an object or an event of interest that must be measured to accurately portray the phenomenon of interest should describe its basic properties. In addition, these attributes should be stable over time, so that current research can build upon prior research on the same phenomenon (Kuhn, 1970). Also, the selected attributes should be situationally generic or generalizable to other circumstances than those being currently observed. Otherwise, the model that is eventually developed on those attributes will not hold true across a prescribed range of specific instances, which is a necessary condition for a useful theory. Finally, the attributes selected for measurement should facilitate ease of identification and/or classification of real-world observations.

Criteria for Category Creation

All classification systems consist of two or more categories into which the object or phenomenon being observed can 'fall'. Those categories will comprise the domain that will be covered by any models built on the phenomenon's basic attributes. To be effective, there are four characteristics that the categories in the classification system must satisfy. First, they must be internally homogeneous, that is, all the phenomena grouped into that category must be the same. Second, the categories must be mutually exclusive. In other words, males and females cannot be put into the same category of gender. This means that a single phenomenon cannot be put into more that one category of the classification system. Third, the categories of the system must be collectively exhaustive, that is, there must be a category into which every real-world observation can be put. Finally, the categories should use relevant 'names' so that all observations of an object or phenomenon will be classified the same way by everyone in the field.

Criteria for the Entire Classification System

There are also four criteria that a classification system as a whole should satisfy. First, the system should be parsimonious with respect to both attributes used and the categories it contains. In general, the fewer the measures used to differentiate between all possible representations of the object or phenomenon, the better. Second, the attributes and categories should produce reasonable differentiation among different forms of the same object or phenomenon, that is, all of the observations should not, in general, fall into only one category. Third, if the classification system is to be used for more than basic description, it should be hierarchical. Finally, the classification system should be timeless. It should not be necessary to continue to add new categories in order to classify an object or phenomenon in future instances of using the system. In essence, this means that the system's basic categories should have various subcategories, and these subcategories should have various sub-subcategories, and so on.

ISSUES OF ATTRIBUTE MEASUREMENT: ACCURACY AND PRECISION

Researchers make myriad choices when they design a study, including the measures they choose to operationalize in their models. McGrath et al. (1981) discussed these choices as a 'three horned dilemma' that involves issues of: (i) generalizability and external validity, (ii) precision, internal and construct validity in measurement, and (iii) realism of context. In wrestling with this dilemma, researchers should be guided by the principle of parsimony, which is using the fewest measures possible to provide sufficient information to perform the study.

Measurements systems must be both accurate and precise to effectively represent the object or event being observed. A measurement is accurate when it adequately describes the real meaning of the phenomenon being studied. For a measurement system to be precise, it must yield the same description of the phenomenon when applied repeatedly. Using the example of a target, a clustering of hits around the bull's-eye would be accurate, while a tight clustering of hits anywhere on the target would imply precise shooting. A tight clustering of hits around the bull's-eye would be both accurate and precise.

Measurement errors can arise from problems with either accuracy or precision, or both. The impact of measurement errors in the dependent measures of a study does not cause bias in the estimation of the relationships with the independent measures, but does lead to an increase in the standard error of estimate, thereby weakening tests of statistical significance (Pedhazur, 1997). Issues pertaining to accuracy and precision will be discussed individually in the following sections.

THE REPLICABILITY OF MEASURES: PRECISION AND RELIABILITY

Precision is how closely distinctions between attributes composing a variable are made (Babbie, 1998). A measurement system is reliable if the values assigned to observations of the same phenomenon, when repeatedly applied, are the same. While reliability does not ensure accuracy, it is the function of consistency. Therefore, reliability of measurement depends upon the methods employed, the skill of the person taking the measures, and the instrumentation utilized (Ghiselli et al., 1981).

Since measurement consists of the rules for assigning values or numbers to attributes of a phenomenon, it is imperative that the rules be applied consistently. Generally accepted accounting principles (GAAP) exist in part to achieve reliability of financial statements. However, it is well known that different accountants applying the same GAAP can result in different values in the financial statements. The reliability of the measures employed must be sufficient to provide consistency of evaluation.

There are many tests for reliability of measurement systems. Two of the most frequently used are the split-half and the test–retest methods. The split-half method involves taking a sample from a population, dividing that sample in half, and performing the analysis on both half samples. Comparing the results of the two analyses should yield statistically similar results. The test–retest method involves taking two separate measurements of the same sample and comparing the results. Unless intervening forces have acted upon the members of the sample, the results should be statistically the same. If not, the measurement method is unreliable to the extent of the variation.

It is acceptable to rely upon measures that have been established in prior research as reliable. Unfortunately, in entrepreneurship and strategic management, the reliability of organizational performance measures used in previous studies has never been established. If the reliability of measures has not been established, then replication is not justifiable.

ASSESSING THE 'EFFECTIVENESS' OF MEASUREMENT SYSTEMS: ISSUES OF VALIDITY AND ACCURACY

For a measurement to be meaningful, it must be valid. Validity is the extent that a measure actually represents the true nature of the phenomenon of interest (Cook and Campbell, 1979). There are four validity criteria discussed by Babbie (1998) with respect to measurement: (i) face validity; (ii) content validity; (iii) criterion-related validity; and (iv) construct validity. Included in these criteria are the issues of internal validity and external validity as they relate to measurement, but not necessarily how they relate to overall research design.

Internal validity deals with issues of causality. Accordingly, internal validity issues include whether there is true covariation between the independent and dependent variables being studied, the methods used in the study demonstrate that cause preceded effect, and that alternative explanations of the phenomenon of interest have been addressed (Cook and Campbell, 1976; Scandura and Williams, 2000). While the issues of internal validity are critical to a proper experimental design, the critical aspect with respect to overall organizational performance measurement is whether the measures selected to represent the performance construct actually covary with the underlying definition of the construct. External validity deals with the ability to generalize the results of a study across times, settings and other members of the population sampled.

Face Validity

The first criterion for an empirical measure is that it must be valid at face value. Face validity deals with whether there is common agreement among experts in the discipline that the empirical measures being employed describe the phenomenon being studied. With respect to organizational performance, this cannot be true given the large number of different measures used to describe the same phenomenon in spite of prior research that indicates that the measures are not interchangeable (see Venkatraman and Ramanujam, 1987 as one example).

Content Validity

A second criterion for the validity of an empirical measure is content validity, or whether a measure covers the range of possible meanings within a concept. A system of measurement appropriate to an object or phenomenon of interest must be collectively exhaustive so that any form of the phenomenon of interest can be represented by a value that is unique and understandable. There are no specific tests for content validity. Nunnally summed up the issue as follows: 'inevitably content validity rests mainly on appeals to reason regarding the adequacy with which important content has been sampled and on the adequacy with which the content has been cast in the form of test items' (1978: 93). The qualitative assessment of the adequacy of the measures is made by both the researcher and the individual readers of a study (Ghiselli et al., 1981; Bollen, 1989).

Criterion-related or Predictive Validity

The third requirement for an empirical measure is criterion-related validity, also known as predictive validity. The criterion is the attribute of interest for a study (Ghiselli et al., 1981). As such, the criterion is the dependent measure in a study, since research is interested in predicting or explaining variation in the phenomenon of interest.

   Criterion-related validity is studied by comparing the values for the object or phenomenon of interest with one or more external variables, or criteria, which are believed to measure the attribute under study (Kerlinger, 1986). For instance, if organizational performance is defined as creating value for its participants, using return on sales as the measure of organizational performance is valid only if it corresponds to what is deemed to be valuable by the participants. If these 'participants' are shareholders, and if from the perspective of shareholders higher returns on sales do not translate into higher returns to them (the shareholders), it does not have criterion or predictive validity. When doing empirical research, this implies that the researcher must explicitly establish correspondence between the research perspective of overall organizational performance and the variables used to represent it.

   Another aspect of criterion-related validity is statistical conclusion validity, that is the ability to draw statistical conclusions or make predictions on the basis of covariation with the criterion of interest (Cook and

Campbell, 1976; Scandura and Williams, 2000). While covariation is necessary, it is not a sufficient precondition for causation (Cook et al., 1990). Therefore, it is incumbent upon researchers to select measures that are reasonably expected to covary based upon the hypothesized relationship being studied.

Another aspect of criterion-related validity is the correspondence of the level of analysis for the model being tested with the nature of the variables used. If the theory being tested purports to test a macro-level concept, then the dependent measures should also be at the macro level.

Criterion-related validity also deals with the stability of the measures over time. The criterion used to evaluate effectiveness at one point in time may not be appropriate at a future point in time. Different criteria may be necessary in the short, intermediate and long runs. Continuing with the example of creating value for shareholders as the criterion of interest, different variables may be better 'proxies' at different points in the life of the organization. For instance, profitability may be sacrificed in the short run in favor of accelerated product development schedules. The required increased spending on R&D in the short run which for accounting purposes is counted as an expense in the period in which it is incurred, results in reduced profitability. However, in the long run, being first to market with a new product may result in much higher cumulative profits. A researcher must select the appropriate variable, or set of variables, that covaries with the criterion of value creation for shareholders during the time period being observed.

Construct Validity

Cook and Campbell (1979) define construct validity as how well the operationalization of a construct by use of selected variables actually measures the concept of interest. In other words, the indicators used to measure a construct must actually capture the relevant concepts under investigation (Campbell and Fiske, 1959; Davies, 2000). Since measurement errors, both random and methodological, are potential threats to the validity of empirical research, measures should be validated before they are used in theory testing (Bagozzi et al., 1991). Tests of construct validity offer weight of evidence that the measure either does or does not adequately describe the aspect a researcher wishes to measure, but does not provide conclusive proof (Babbie, 1998). These tests examine constructs from two perspectives: convergent validity of multiple variables that purport to measure the same object or phenomenon, and discriminant validity where multiple constructs are demonstrated to represent different attributes.

Convergent validity

Construct validity requires that variables that are purported to measure the same phenomenon demonstrate convergent validity (consistently covary). For example, to measure the construct of growth, multiple measures might be employed including sales dollar or unit growth, growth in total assets and growth in number of employees. To test the validity of using all of these measures to represent the growth construct, each measure would first have to be demonstrated to be associated with growth, and then it must be determined whether the identified criteria are affected similarly when acted upon by external factors. Continuing with the example of growth, if demand for a company's product increases dramatically, as sales increase the company should also experience growth in total assets and employment.

Generalizability is questionable when different measures are used to represent the same phenomenon, particularly when it has not been shown that those measures have convergent validity. Further, measures that may be appropriate for one sample may not be appropriate to another sample. For instance, profitability in large, publicly held corporations may not be directly analogous to profitability in small, privately held corporations, because in privately held firms, the owners may take comparatively larger salaries or benefits to minimize overall tax exposure. Thus, the selection of measures must be internally consistent with the goals and purposes of the sample being studied and externally consistent with the goals and purposes of other organizations to which observed effects are being generalized.

Campbell and Fiske (1959) suggest that using multiple measures and multiple methods is the best way to understand what portion of variance is due to method and what portion is due to the trait of interest. Multiple indicators of the same trait are preferable to single indicators to minimize measurement bias, so long as there is convergent validity of the indicators of a construct. Convergent validity is the level of congruence across the multiple indicators. The indicators should be significantly correlated, indicating that they do measure the same aspect of a phenomenon. Another way to express this concept is that the indicators need to be internally homogeneous.

Discriminant validity

If different constructs purport to measure individually unique aspects of a phenomenon, it is incumbent upon a researcher to demonstrate that the constructs have discriminant validity. Accordingly, constructs should not be significantly correlated. For example, Venkatraman and Ramanujam (1987) demonstrated that growth and profitability were different constructs. Therefore, different indicators of growth should be more highly correlated with each other than with indicators of profitability. Likewise, different indicators of profitability should be more highly correlated with each other than with indicators of growth.

In multivariate models of performance (using several variables under a single unifying framework), the indirect measures used to represent overall organizational performance may be negatively correlated, which could result in findings for such multivariate models being contradictory. For example, if both profitability and sales growth are used independently as separate criteria for measuring the performance of a new venture, the results of an analysis may well be significantly contradictory. If both measures are hypothesized to represent organizational effectiveness, the organization may simultaneously be both effective and ineffective.

ISSUES IN MEASURING ORGANIZATIONAL FINANCIAL PERFORMANCE

In the review of empirical research summarized in Chapter 2, researchers claimed to establish validity for the criterion measures used in their studies primarily by citing prior use of the same measures in similar empirical research. Actual tests of validity were not conducted by the researchers, and the studies they cite generally did not test the validity of the measures used. Basically, these researchers relied on only face validity for their choice of dependent measures. However, face validity requires that there be common agreement among experts in the discipline that the empirical measures being employed describe the phenomenon being studied. Unfortunately, as established in the summary of performance measures in Chapter 2, the primary criterion for face validity is routinely violated. Clearly, among the authors of the studies summarized, there is no common agreement on the empirical measures that represent overall organizational performance. This is evidenced by the fact that there were more measures of supposedly the same construct than there were studies published.

Establishing the validity of measures of organizational financial performance should be considered fundamental for macro-level empirical research, and it is the aim of this research. To accomplish this aim, the principles of measurement discussed in this chapter must be applied.

First, the question of whether organizational financial performance is a single or a multiple attribute construct must be empirically established. If organizational financial performance construct is found to be a multiple attribute construct, as the prior literature has indicated, the set of separate performance dimensions should be examined to determine what are the appropriate attributes of the construct. The critical characteristics of this set of measures, as discussed in this chapter, are that they actually describe the phenomenon of organizational financial performance, allow for differentiation between separate levels of performance, be as few as possible without losing too much information (that is, parsimonious), easy to observe, stable over time and generalizable.

Any set of measures of the overall organizational performance construct must be demonstrated to be valid. In establishing face and content validity for the dimensions of the performance construct, the starting place for this investigation should be those dimensions previously identified in the literature. To establish construct validity, the dimensions of performance that are identified should be demonstrated to have discriminant validity. Empirically these measures must be demonstrated to be different. Further, convergent validity should be demonstrated between variables that represent the same dimension of performance. Empirically, these variables must be demonstrated to be statistically significantly correlated. Finally, the measurement model for organizational financial performance must be shown to have criterion-related validity by covariance with an external criterion.

CHAPTER SUMMARY

This chapter addressed the measurement attributes and specifications appropriate for the variables that scholars use for dependent variables when undertaking a research study. In this context, the chapter first reviewed the role of measurement in theory building and testing. Next, the chapter reviewed the nature of empirical constructs and classification systems, and the criteria for them to be effective. These include issues that affect (i) the accuracy and precision in measuring the observed effects that are the subject of the study with respect to internal and construct validity, and (ii) the generalizability to the population sampled with respect to external validity. The chapter concluded by applying the general concepts of measurement to the specific task of measuring overall organizational performance.

In the following chapters, this research examines individual measures that are demonstrated to discriminate between high- and low-performing organizations with respect to financial performance. These measures will be examined for their relative and incremental information content as well as their reliability and validity. The primary dimensions of the construct of organizational financial performance will be examined and tested. Based upon these findings, a multidimensional model of organizational financial performance will be developed and tested.

7. Developing a generalizable model for measuring organizational financial performance

This chapter outlines the methodology used to answer the research questions detailed in Chapter 1. It contains three main sections. The first section discusses the research approach that guides this research. The second section discusses the research design and methods including operationalization of the variables that will comprise the empirical data for this research and the sample, including the data-gathering procedures and measurement issues. The third section discusses the methodology for developing and testing a model of organizational financial performance including data analysis techniques.

AN EMPIRICAL APPROACH TO ESTABLISHING THE BOUNDARIES OF A MODEL OF ORGANIZATIONAL FINANCIAL PERFORMANCE

Cameron and Whetten (1983) proposed seven critical questions for bounding and assessing overall organizational effectiveness. These seven questions were used as the basis for developing and bounding the model of organizational financial performance developed in this research:

1. Why is effectiveness being assessed?
2. What level of analysis is being used?
3. What timeframe is being used for the assessment?
4. From whose perspective is effectiveness being judged?
5. What is the referent against which effectiveness is being judged?
6. What is the domain for assessment?
7. What data are being used for the assessment?

Cameron and Whetten argued that the answers to these questions lead to a unique combination of effectiveness criteria for each set of existing circumstances. In other words, organizational effectiveness is unique to the circumstances of each individual organization. However, if effectiveness criteria are not generalizable across organizations, then it becomes impossible to generalize research results across different studies, since without a common framework for comparison, incremental advances in knowledge that build upon prior studies is impossible.

This research deals with the measurement of organizational financial performance. While different levels of financial performance may be acceptable for different firms, if one accepts that resource providers have a minimum expectation of risk-adjusted return for the use of their assets, then there is a common basis for financial comparisons across companies. This research adopts this point of view and uses the seven questions posed by Cameron and Whetten as a guide to developing a model of organizational financial performance. This approach does not accept or deny Cameron and Whetten's assertions about organizational uniqueness. Rather it seeks to examine one dimension of organizational effectiveness that is generalizable across different organizations, which is financial performance.

Measurement models consist of both constructs and indicators of the constructs. Since one objective of this research was to develop a generalizable model of organizational performance, the relative and incremental information content of performance measures were examined to determine the most parsimonious set of constructs and variables that adequately represent organizational performance. Accordingly, this section includes a discussion of the nature of the information content of measures.

Answering Cameron and Whetten's Seven Questions for Bounding Organizational Effectiveness

The framework proposed by Cameron and Whetten is applicable to bounding any model of organizational effectiveness or performance. The first four questions establish some boundaries for such a model. The final three questions deal with the operationalization of the model. Specific operationalization decisions for this research are discussed in the 'research design and methods' section of this chapter.

Why is organizational financial performance being assessed?

There is little dispute that one of the core purposes of both entrepreneurship and strategic management theory and research is the improvement of organizational financial performance (Venkatraman and Ramanujam, 1986; Eisenhardt and Zbaracki, 1992). However, there seems to be no consensus regarding the best, or even sufficient, measures of organizational financial performance. This is in no small part due to the many varied views of what are desirable outcomes of organizational effectiveness and because performance has often been characterized by the theory and purposes of the research being performed.

In general, organizational financial performance is being addressed to provide researchers and managers with an understanding of the implications of selecting variables for use in empirical studies and practice where organizational financial performance is the criterion of interest. The paradox of management research, as expressed by Cameron (1986), is that empirical studies tend to explain average performance, while the focus should be on understanding what makes firms either successful or unsuccessful. By better understanding the construct of organizational financial performance, researchers and managers should be able to identify firms that are performing well, from those that are poorly performing.

Specifically for management practice, providing a greater understanding of which dimensions of performance covary with shareholder returns permits better strategic focus in for-profit companies. This information may allow management to track critical financial performance metrics that anticipate market reactions during interim periods between public disclosures of performance information. Further, a better understanding of the relative and incremental information content of financial performance metrics can assist managers in selecting non-financial metrics to fill information gaps about overall organizational performance.

The validity of the operationalizations of concepts and constructs, in the form of both independent and dependent measures, is fundamental to the interpretation of theoretical relationships being tested in substantive research and is the essence of the measurement stream of research. The summary of empirical research presented in Chapter 2 found that measures of financial performance are the most commonly used dependent measures to represent the overall organizational performance construct. However, if the validity of these measures has not been established, then the conclusions of the studies are suspect.

What level of analysis is being used?
The focus of this research is the financial performance dimension of the overall organizational performance construct. Accordingly, the level of analysis for this study is the entire organization.

What timeframe is being used?
Strategic management deals with the long-term, not day-to-day management. The appropriate timeframe for any research must account for the lag between cause and effect proposed in the model being tested. Unfortunately, the longer the time lag between cause and effect, the more

intervening events occur that can obscure the phenomenon of interest. Our summary of empirical research studies dealing with organizational performance found that the most commonly used timeframes were one and three years. However, it is incumbent upon the researcher to select a time-frame appropriate to the question being tested.

One- and three-year timeframes were selected for this research because they are the most commonly used in entrepreneurship and strategic management research. One question of interest being addressed is whether the same model of organizational performance is appropriate over the two different timeframes. This is an important question if researchers wish to rely upon findings from prior studies that used a different timeframe.

From whose perspective is organizational financial performance being judged?

As noted in Chapter 3, there are three primary dimensions of overall organizational performance: financial, operational and stakeholder. The overriding consideration in financial operations of for-profit organizations is satisfying providers of critical resources to the organization. Since shareholders are residual claimants, all other resource providers must be satisfied before they receive a return. Consequently, maximizing returns to shareholders requires balancing the satisfactions to all other stakeholders. Shareholders maximize the value of other claims in an attempt to maximize their own value (Freeman, 1984; Stewart, 1991; Copeland et al., 2000). Gifford summed up the matter from a finance perspective as follows: 'While academics have been busily proving that capital structure can affect shareholder value, few have questioned that shareholder value creation itself is the goal of the corporation' (1998: 76).

Strategic management is concerned with managing an organization for the long term. Therefore, it is important to select a perspective for measuring organizational performance that is compatible. Since common stockholders commit resources to the organization for the longest time period (they get their capital back only after all other claimants against organizational assets are first satisfied), their perspective is closest to the focus of strategic management issues. Common stockholders have long-term interests and must balance short-term satisfactions against long-term benefits. In other words, modern corporations give control over decision making to shareholders (or their agents) because they are the only claimants that require complete information to make decisions in their self-interest.

One final argument in favor of using the common stockholders' perspective is that they are considered to have a relatively homogeneous perspective of performance. Common stock investors can invest in any number of organizations. As a consequence, shareholders require, at a minimum, a risk-adjusted return on their capital that is comparable to similar equity investment opportunities. Shareholder returns for an investment in a specific organization over a given period of time reflect the changes in actual and expected payouts to shareholders as a result of management and market actions (Miller and Modigliani, 1961). Those firms that investors perceive as having created greater opportunity for present and future payouts will have higher returns to common stockholders over the measured timeframe. Therefore, the common referent for shareholder value, across all for-profit organizations, is present and risk-adjusted expectations of future cash flows. Consequently, this research addresses the financial dimension of organizational performance.

What is the referent against which organizational financial performance is being judged?
Having argued that organizational financial performance should be viewed from the perspective of common stockholders, it is appropriate that shareholder value creation be used as the referent for evaluating various potential measures of financial performance. For public companies, return to shareholders is the appropriate measure of shareholder value creation (Copeland et al., 2000). Return to shareholders includes the appreciation in the value of shareholders' ownership stake in the organization plus dividends they received. This position is supported by Robinson's 1995 study of new venture performance measures for publicly traded entrepreneurial companies in which he found that return to shareholders provided the most empirical power compared with nine other new venture performance measures.

It is generally preferable to use multiple methods of measuring a phenomenon of interest to minimize the effects of method bias (Campbell and Fiske, 1959; Venkatraman and Ramanujam, 1987). In this research, return to shareholders is measured using objective, secondary data. The change in stock analyst ratings was considered as a second measure of the criterion. However, only current stock analyst ratings were found to be generally available. The Compustat® database includes only the current ratings, not historical. Further, Thompson One Analytics publishes a composite of all analyst recommendations, but historical data are not available in hardcopy or in publicly accessible databases. A search of library resources and the internet in conjunction with the business research librarian at the University of Georgia found no source for historical analyst recommendations. Additionally, an interview with a vice president at Merrill Lynch revealed that while they have access to current analyst recommendations, they do not have access to historical data. Consequently, this research used only a single measure of the referent return to shareholders.

What is the domain for assessment?

For the purposes of this study, the domain for assessment is public companies that are widely traded on US stock exchanges. There are four primary reasons for this choice. First, shareholders of public companies have a homogeneous concept of performance. Rational investors will seek out investments that provide a minimally satisfactory return and will continually adjust their portfolios to achieve this level of satisfaction. Investors can and do, easily and readily change investments from one company to another as they seek to meet their investment goals. The choice to limit the population to US stock exchange-traded companies is appropriate because the values of shares listed are expressed in a common currency, further allowing for ease of value comparison.

The second criterion for using widely traded public companies as the domain of assessment is that the population must have financial information that is readily observable. Public companies must issue financial statements that are available for public review at least quarterly. This information is readily available through the Securities and Exchange Commission (SEC) either in hardcopy or over the internet. Further, many companies such as Standard and Poor's and Dun and Bradstreet publish annual summaries of public company financial information that can be accessed in research libraries or for a fee from the data provider. In addition to annual financial information, return to shareholders is readily observable in public companies. Appreciation in the value of equity securities as well as dividends paid to shareholders are reported daily and summarized in multiple publications annually.

The third criterion is that the financial information reported must be internally consistent and reliable. While accounting irregularities receive great notoriety in the press, the actual instances of fraudulent financial reporting in public companies are very few. One of the most critical elements in attracting capital from outside investors is the integrity of management. To ensure that management reports accurate financial information, public companies are required to have an annual audit by independent certified public accountants qualified to perform audits of SEC reporting companies. The work of the auditors and the quality of financial reporting are subject to review by an audit committee of the board of directors, typically comprising outside directors. The information filed with the SEC is reviewed by Commission staff and subject to revision if found to be non-compliant or inconsistent with prior years' reporting. Further, managers deemed to be the most knowledgeable about and responsible for financial reporting are required to certify that the financial information reported is materially correct and are personally subject to civil and criminal penalties for fraud. While all of these controls are not always effective, there are relatively few instances of documented fraudulent reporting by public companies.

The fourth criterion is that the financial information reported by public companies must be prepared and presented in a consistent fashion. Consistency in the meaning of the content of financial statements across organizations is critical for the results of statistical tests to be generalizable to the entire population. Public companies meet this criterion in two respects. First, companies that trade on US stock exchanges are required to use generally accepted accounting principles (GAAP), consistently applied. While GAAP allow for judgment in preparing financial statements, they do provide a common framework within which management judgment is exercised. A second source of consistency in reporting for public companies is the disclosure requirements of the SEC for financial disclosures by public companies. The SEC has enforcement powers to ensure that companies do provide accurate, sufficient and timely financial disclosures. The consistent application of a common set of rules for reporting financial information across companies allows for the generalization of the findings from a sample of the population of public companies to the entire population.

The Standard and Poor's 1500 (a combination of the Standard and Poor's 500, Standard and Poor's Mid Cap 400 and the Standard and Poor's Small Cap 600 indices) was the population of public companies used for this research. These companies include the biggest large cap, mid cap and small cap public companies in the United States. Accordingly, there is a considerable amount of secondary data available on these companies that have been well vetted by independent auditors, the SEC and independent stock analysts.

As the companies that comprise the indices that make up the S&P 1500 regularly change, it is important to note that the sample was based on those companies identified as being in the indices at December 31, 2002. The sample was selected based upon the firms included in the indices at the end of the measurement period rather than at the beginning in order to ensure that as many companies as possible had four full years of data. The purpose of this research is to measure the effects of management actions, and no management actions are taken for companies that are out of business. Using the companies in the indices at the beginning of the measurement period would have required eliminating companies from at least the three-year sample that ceased to exist as separate entities because of acquisition, merger, delisting or failure. Those firms in the indices at the end of the measurement period clearly had not suffered any of those fates. It is clear that this approach has a bias in favor of companies that survived, but does include the full range of financial performance that ongoing ventures can achieve (good and bad).

What data are being used for assessment?
A model of performance should include constructs that represent the primary dimensions of performance. For each construct, individual variables must be identified that capture the essence of the construct. This research uses secondary data collected from publicly available databases, such as the Standard and Poor's Compustat® database, for the public companies included in the sample. The reason for using secondary data in this study is that publicly reported financial information receives the most scrutiny from independent observers such as public accountants and the SEC. Another and more pragmatic reason is that secondary data is most commonly used in entrepreneurship and strategic management research because it is readily available. This research requires a large sample to have sufficient data to analyse all the different financial performance variables and constructs. To obtain such a large sample from primary sources is generally impractical.

The Information Content of Measures

Since this research examines the measurement of organizational financial performance, it inherently must address the question of the information content of individual variables. When selecting variables, researchers must consider both the relative and the incremental information content of each measure. This research considers both issues in developing an effective and a parsimonious model.

As stated earlier, constructs are theoretical characterizations of phenomena that cannot be directly or indirectly observed. Accordingly, observable indicators of the construct that conceptually represent the meaning of the construct, must be used to measure the construct (Babbie, 1998). The indicators or variables used to represent a construct must be selected based upon the amount of information they provide about its nature at the time of observation (Chen and Dodd, 2001). A researcher must decide whether a single indicator or multiple indicators are necessary to adequately measure the construct. Further, the researcher must decide whether the construct represents the condition of a phenomenon at a static point in time or a change in condition over an appropriate period of time.

Relative versus incremental information content of measures
Researchers have employed two approaches to compare information usefulness of different measures, namely relative and incremental (ibid., 2001). The relative information content of measures represents the degree of association with a measure of interest, such as stock returns, relative to the degree of association with the same referent by other measures. The greater

the correlation of a measure with a criterion, the greater the relative information content of the measure.

The incremental information content of measures addresses whether a measure adds information about a referent that is not already provided by another measure. When attempting to measure a specific construct with a single variable, knowledge of the relative information content of different measures allows the researcher to select the single 'best' variable. With knowledge of the incremental information content of different measures, a researcher can select multiple measures that in combination will most effectively represent the construct of interest.

The first question that a researcher must ask is whether a single measure can adequately represent the construct of interest. For the purposes of the study being conducted, if the single measure selected does not adequately explain variation in the construct of interest, then the researcher must either select another measure that explains more variance in the construct or select multiple measures that in combination will more effectively represent the construct of interest.

Prior research has demonstrated that performance is multidimensional. Although multiple measures are frequently used, no prior research has identified which single measure, or combination of measures, is the most effective in representing the construct of organizational financial performance. That is the primary objective of this research.

Static measures versus change scores
Change scores measure a change in the value of an indicator of interest over a period of time, while static measures represent the value of an indicator at a given point in time. In the context of this research, performance is viewed as the creation of value for the unit of analysis, be it an individual, an organization, or even society. Creating value implies a change in condition. Therefore, measuring organizational performance at any level involves measuring a change in condition.

Although change scores seem to be the most appropriate type of measure to represent performance, they are subject to two potential problems (Cronbach and Furby, 1970; Cohen and Cohen, 1983; Allison, 1990). First is the problem of 'floor/ceiling' effects, which relate to the magnitude of the change. A startup or early-stage company can exhibit significant sales growth simply because the starting sales level is either zero or very small. For example, when Planet Java was a new soft drink company in the United States, it exhibited exceptional percentage increases in sales in its early years, while an established company such as the Coca-Cola Company was able to grow only slightly faster than the population growth rate in such a saturated market. The second problem with change scores is that the pre-change value is generally correlated with the post-change value. Accordingly, it is often appropriate to use the pre-change value as the control variable as suggested by Cohen and Cohen (1983).

Static measures represent values of an indicator at a given point in time. They do not represent a change in condition. Accordingly, the value of a static measure is influenced by many factors, primarily the starting value of the measure at the beginning of the period of interest. Further, static measures may not represent the true condition of the phenomenon of interest at different points in time. For instance, a jewelry company may have a very low debt-to-equity ratio right after the Christmas holiday season, while at the start of the holiday buying season, it may have a very high debt-to-equity ratio to pay for the increased inventory levels. Consequently, a researcher must take care to account for cyclical effects when using static measures.

This research includes both static and change scores in the initial evaluation of variables. Answering the question of whether change scores provide greater relative information or incremental information about value creation than static measures is one intended finding of this research.

RESEARCH DESIGN AND METHODS

The preceding section discussed the general conceptual approach to developing a generalizable model of organizational financial performance. The level of analysis, timeframes, referents, the domain for assessment and the nature of the data utilized were presented. This section describes how the conceptual approach to this research was operationalized including the variables, sample and methods.

Operationalization of Variables

There were two timeframes of interest for this research, annual and three-year periods. Further, both static and change scores were used for variables for both timeframes. As change scores require both a beginning and an ending value to be calculated, it required four years of data to calculate the change in a three-year period measure. Accordingly, 6,000 annual firm years of data (four years of data for 1,500 companies) were extracted from the Compustat® database for the fiscal years ending between January 1, 1999 and December 31, 2002. These data included balance sheets, income statements and statements of cash flows. Additionally, company information such as SIC code, fiscal year end during each of the calendar years, number of employees and Altman's Z-scores were extracted. Return to shareholders was extracted for both annual and three-year periods and company betas were extracted for each month of each year.

Calculation of Measures

Twenty-six measures of financial performance and the market-adjusted return to shareholders were calculated for each annual and three-year period for each company in the sample. Variables were selected to represent each of the primary categories of performance discussed in Chapter 4. Individual measures for each category were selected based upon their historical frequency of use in prior empirical studies, as summarized in the survey in Chapter 2, as well as measures that are frequently used in practice, as discussed in Chapter 5, but which may not have been used frequently in strategic management or entrepreneurship research. Since many alternative calculations of some variables are commonly accepted, the following is a brief description of the operationalization of each variable used.

Profitability measures

- *Return on assets* was calculated as net income divided by total assets. This ratio was calculated by using both ending total assets as well as average total assets as the denominator.
- *Return on equity* was calculated as net income divided by total stockholders' equity. This ratio was calculated by using both ending stockholders' equity as well as average stockholders' equity as the denominator.
- *Return on investment* was calculated as net income divided by the sum of stockholders' equity plus interest-bearing liabilities. This ratio was calculated by using both ending stockholders' equity plus ending interest-bearing liabilities as well as average stockholders' equity plus average interest-bearing liabilities as the denominator.
- *Return on invested capital* was calculated as net operating profit less assumed taxes divided by stockholders' equity plus interest-bearing liabilities.
- *EBITDA return on investment* was calculated as earnings before interest, taxes depreciation and amortization divided by the sum of stockholders' equity plus interest-bearing liabilities. This ratio was calculated by using both ending stockholders' equity plus ending interest-bearing liabilities as well as average stockholders' equity plus average interest-bearing liabilities as the denominator.

- *Return on sales* was calculated as net income divided by sales.
- *Operating margin* was calculated as earnings before interest and taxes divided by sales.

Growth measures

All growth measures were calculated as the value for the period of interest (either annual or three-year) minus the value for the immediately preceding equivalent period, divided by the value of the immediately preceding equivalent period. Growth measures were calculated for sales, operating expenses, total assets and total employees.

Leverage, liquidity and cash flow measures

- *Debt-to-equity ratio* was calculated as long-term debt divided by stockholders' equity.
- *Liabilities-to-total assets ratio* was calculated as total liabilities divided by total assets.
- *Operating cash flow-to-equity ratio* was calculated as operating cash flow (as reported on the statement of cash flows) divided by stockholders' equity.
- *Free cash flow-to-equity ratio* was calculated as the sum of net cash flow from operations plus net cash flows from investing activities divided by stockholders' equity.
- *Growth rate of operating cash flow* was calculated as operating cash flow for the period of interest minus the value for the immediately preceding equivalent period, divided by the value of the immediately preceding equivalent period.

Market-based measures

- *Cost of equity capital* was calculated using the capital asset pricing model. The formula for this calculation is the risk-free rate plus the product of beta multiplied by the market risk premium. For the purposes of this calculation, the ten-year US Treasury bill rate (as suggested by Copeland et al., 2000) was used as the risk-free rate. The historical US Treasury bill rates were obtained from the Federal Statistical Release prepared by the Federal Reserve. Company betas were extracted from the Compustat® database. Compustat® betas were calculated based on a trailing 60-month covariance with the S&P 500 index. If less data were available, at least 24 months was used. A market risk premium of 4.9 percent was used as recommended by Copeland et al. (2000).

- *Price-to-book ratio* was extracted from the Compustat® database and was calculated as the ending market value of the company divided by the net book value of the company.

Economic value measures

- *Residual income* was calculated as net income less a charge for equity calculated as the product of the cost of equity capital multiplied by common stockholders' equity.
- *Residual income return on investment* was calculated as residual income divided by the sum of the average interest-bearing debt plus stockholders' equity.

Survival measure

- *Altman's Z-score* was extracted from the Compustat® database and was calculated using the public company formula discussed in Chapter 5.

Efficiency measure

- *Asset turnover* was calculated as sales divided by average total assets.

Market-adjusted return to shareholders

Both annual and three-year returns to shareholder values were extracted from the Compustat® database. These measures were calculated by Standard and Poor's as ending closing price of the stock divided by the closing price 12 months earlier for annual returns, or 36 months earlier for three-year returns, adjusted for dividends paid. It is assumed that dividends are reinvested at the time they are paid.

Since companies in the sample had different fiscal year ends, the return to shareholders reported in the Compustat® database was adjusted by subtracting the overall market return during the equivalent fiscal period. The change in the New York Stock Exchange Composite Index was used to represent the market rate of return. The NYSE Composite measures all common stocks listed on the New York Stock Exchange. The index tracks the change in aggregate market value of NYSE common stocks, adjusted to eliminate the effects of capitalization changes, new listings and delistings. The market value of each stock included in the index is calculated by multiplying its closing price per share times the number of shares listed. This index was considered to best represent the entire equities market, since over 80 percent of the market value of stock transactions in the United States is traded on the NYSE (www.nyse.com/marketinfo).

Using the Absolute Value of the Denominator in Certain Cases

Although none of the calculations of the variables used in this research specifies the use of the absolute value of the denominator, in certain instances it is necessary to preserve the underlying meaning of the measure being utilized. This is particularly true in the case of any measure that utilizes equity as the denominator, and in evaluating change scores.

Consider the measure return on equity. In the Compustat® database, the ratio is calculated as net income divided by ending stockholders' equity. A company that loses money during the year and ends the year with negative stockholder equity will report positive return on equity. As positive return on equity implies that the company is creating shareholder value, it is inconsistent with the actual facts. Conversely, a company that makes money during the year but still has negative stockholder equity at the end of the year would report negative return on equity. Again, this is inconsistent with the actual facts. Unfortunately, Standard and Poor's does not compensate for this problem in their calculation of ratios in the Compustat® database, making it questionable to use their statistics without careful scrutiny. In our sample of 1,500 companies, for fiscal years ending in 2002, the Compustat® database reported that 16 companies, just over 1 percent, had positive returns on equity when in actuality they had losses during the year.

Although it is not common that companies have negative equity, there are several instances where these circumstances occur. The first example involves companies that have large amounts of intangible value that are not reflected on their balance sheets. If these companies engage in large share repurchase programs as treasury stock, the repurchased shares are recorded at their purchase price as a reduction of shareholder equity. The result can be a negative amount of total shareholder equity. A second example involves companies that have substantially appreciated real estate holdings. These companies can refinance the properties with new mortgages and use the proceeds for distributions to shareholders, as would be the case with many publicly traded real estate investment trusts. Since GAAP require that real property, other than land, be carried at the lower of depreciated book value or market, and since most real estate has actually appreciated over time, the amount refinanced on real estate is often many times the book value of the properties recorded on the books. The result is that many real estate ventures normally have negative equity balances. One final example is early-stage ventures that use convertible subordinated debt in lieu of equity. These ventures often have losses in the early years, leaving them with negative equity balances on their books. To entice investors, the companies use debt with equity-like returns (that is, convertible debt), which gives these investors preferred positions for claims on company assets over the founders. As a consequence, the companies reflect negative equity on their balance sheets.

In the case of change scores, if both the beginning and ending balances of the measurement period are negative, and the ending balance is a larger negative number than the beginning balance, the ratio will reflect a positive change score. For instance, if return on assets was minus 5 percent at time zero and minus 10 percent at time one, then calculating the change score results in a positive 100 percent change. Typically, a positive change of 100 percent in return on assets would be interpreted as favorable. However, under the circumstances just described, the actual effects are negative for the company. In our sample of 1,500 companies, such circumstances occurred in 191 instances, or just under 13 percent of the sampled companies.

To adjust for the circumstances described above, the absolute value of the denominator was used to preserve the direction of the numerator. In all other respects, the calculated ratio was equal to those normally calculated. The numerator will reflect the correct direction of the change and the absolute value of the denominator will provide the proper effect size of the change. Accordingly, the calculations in this research used the absolute value of the denominator for all change scores and for all ratios that used stockholder equity as the denominator.

Operationalization of Three-year Data

The three-year measures used in this research were generally calculated as the annually compounded rates. In other words, the ratios were calculated as $[(1 + R_1) * (1 + R_2) * (1 + R_3)] - 1$. However, there were several exceptions to this approach as follows.

Residual income and asset turnover were calculated as the sum of the three annual values. These measures, by their nature, accumulate over time rather than compound. Debt-to-equity, liabilities-to-assets, Altman's Z-score and price-to-book ratios were calculated as the average of the three annual values, since they are point-in-time measures and do not either accumulate or compound. Return on sales and operating margin were calculated as the sum of net income and operating profits divided by the sum of sales for the three-year period, respectively. All change scores were calculated as the change in the measure from the beginning of the three-year period through the end of the three-year period.

Developing a Sample

Three fiscal years of data and one three-year period were calculated for each of the 1,500 companies in the sample. This resulted in 4,500 annual firm years and 1,500 three-year periods of data. The sample included companies in 329 different industries as represented by the four-digit SIC code. Annual sales for the companies in the sample ranged from a high of $217.8 billion to a low of $2 million. The median sales level was $1.2 billion and the average sales level was $4.8 billion. Total assets for the companies in the sample ranged from a high of $1,097.2 billion to a low of $21.0 million. The median total assets for the sample was $1.6 billion and the average was $13.4 billion. Total employees for companies in the sample ranged from a high of 1.4 million to a low of just 3 employees. The median employment was 5,200 and the average was 19,400. A total of 216 companies had fewer than 1,000 employees. The companies were all listed on US stock exchanges in the following proportions: 1,029 on the NYSE, 460 on the NASDAQ and 11 on the AMEX.

For a firm year of data to be included in the final sample, it had to be complete in all respects. Further, the firm years of data had to be for a complete 12-month period. Accordingly, firm years of data were eliminated from the sample for a variety of reasons detailed in the following discussion.

In a year that a firm changed its fiscal year end, the amounts reported in the Compustat® database were for a 'stub period', or in other words, for the period between the end of the old fiscal year end and the end of the new fiscal year end, which is always less than 12 months. Since these stub periods were not comparable with full firm years, they were eliminated from the sample.

Firms that were not public companies for a period of at least 24 months were eliminated from the sample because beta could not be calculated, making the calculation of residual income, residual income return on investment and the cost of equity variables impossible. Additionally, firm years that did not have complete data for any of the other variables included in this research were eliminated.

There were several reasons why firm years of data were incomplete. Financial institutions such as banks and insurance companies often report their balance sheet information without classification as current or long term. Accordingly, regular Altman's Z-scores and debt-to-equity ratios could not be calculated for these companies and they were eliminated from the sample.

Two variables were eliminated from the dataset because of the number of companies with insufficient data to calculate them. Return on invested capital could not be calculated for any company that did not separately disclose deferred taxes on its balance sheet, since it is not a GAAP requirement. About 15 percent of the companies in the sample did not have separately disclosed deferred taxes. Consequently, return on invested capital was eliminated from the dataset. The debt-to-equity ratio was also eliminated because of the number of companies that did not have any debt or did not report the amount of debt separately on their balance sheet. Since the liabilities-to-assets ratio captures substantially the same data, and since the number of records that would have to be eliminated from the dataset because of this one measure was high, the ratio was eliminated from the data rather than further reducing the sample.

In total, 1,236 firm years of data (27.5 percent) and two variables were eliminated from the sample due to incomplete information. Of the firm years of data eliminated, approximately half related to financial service companies such as commercial banks, investment banks, finance companies and insurance companies. These types of firms generally do not report classified balance sheets, making the calculation of certain ratios impossible.

Next, the remaining 3,264 firm years of data were examined for the presence of outliers in individual variables. To accomplish this, all variables were standardized and any firm year that had a variable that was ten or more standard deviations from the mean was eliminated. Some of the outliers in the sample were so extreme that they severely skewed the distribution of the variables to the point that when they were eliminated, the remaining standardized values for the variables in the sample still had outliers greater than ten standard deviations from the mean. To account for the effects of these extreme outliers on the distributions of the variables, three iterations of removing outliers that were ten or more standard deviations from the mean were performed. A total of 370 firm years of data were removed because one or more of the variables in a firm year for a specific company was an outlier. It should be noted that the majority of the outliers were caused by floor/ceiling effects on change scores.

The same procedures for identifying outliers were applied to the dataset of three-year periods. A total of 442 records was eliminated as a result of incomplete information and an additional 133 records were eliminated because the value of an individual measure was deemed an outlier.

In summary, a total of 2,894 individual firm years of data and 925 three-year periods of data were retained. A total of 24 static variables and 24 change scores were retained for evaluation for both the annual and the three-year datasets.

METHODOLOGY FOR DEVELOPING AND TESTING A MODEL OF ORGANIZATIONAL FINANCIAL PERFORMANCE

Since no prior research empirically established the domain of organizational financial performance, this research was by necessity exploratory in nature. The first step was to test the relative and incremental information content of individual financial performance measures with respect to the referent market-adjusted return to shareholders. Next, an initial model of financial performance was inferred from empirical data that included the primary constructs of organizational financial performance and empirical measures of those constructs. Next, the validity of the constructs was tested. Finally, the overall model was statistically evaluated using return to shareholders as the referent.

The results from this research attempt to answer three of the research questions posed in Chapter 1:

RQ2: What are the primary constructs underlying organizational financial performance?
RQ3: What are the best measures of the primary constructs underlying organizational financial performance?
RQ4: Can the model of organizational financial performance developed in this research distinguish between high- and low-performing companies?

Empirically Inferring a Model of Organizational Financial Performance

The first two research questions involved the exploratory research necessary to empirically infer a model of organizational financial performance. The process employed for inferring this model included six phases. First, the sample of public companies was segregated into high, medium and low performers based upon both annual and three-year financial performance, as indicated by their return to shareholders over the period of time. Second, the high- and low-performing groups were compared using the most commonly used financial measures from past research and from the literature review, for the purpose of identifying specific measures that differentiate the two groups. Third, the variables identified that differentiated between high- and low-performing companies were grouped into constructs. Fourth, the measures of each construct were tested for relative and incremental information content to select the 'best' measures of each construct. Fifth, the validity of the constructs was tested. Finally, both the annual and three-year models of financial performance were tested using return to shareholders as a referent.

Developing a sample of high and low financial-performing companies
The individual annual firm year and three-year periods in the sample were classified as high, medium or low financial performance based upon return to shareholders. A firm was classified as high performing if its standardized value of return to shareholders was one or greater. A firm was

classified as low performing if its standardized value of return to share-holders was minus one or greater. All other firms were classified as medium performing.

A total of 309 firm years were classified as 'high', 321 firm years were classified as 'low', and the remaining 2,264 firm years were classified as 'medium'. In the case of three-year period data, a total of 124 three-year periods were classified as 'high', 143 three-year periods were classified as 'low' and the remaining 658 three-year periods were classified as 'medium'.

Comparing the high and low financial-performing companies
The two samples of high- and low-performing companies were compared with respect to the most commonly used financial measures from past research and from the literature. The measures were compared using *t*-tests to determine whether there is a statistically significant difference between the two groups with respect to each measure.

Those measures that indicated a statistically significant difference between the groups were retained for further evaluation. Variables that did not discriminate between high and low financial-performing companies were not utilized further. Each variable that was included in this research was evaluated both as a static value and for the change in the value over the period of interest to examine the relative information content of static versus change scores.

Robinson (1995) found that many of the variables used to measure per-formance violate the assumptions underlying parametric tests. Given the size of the samples being utilized, the *t*-test is robust with respect to viola-tions of the two underlying assumptions for *t*-tests of normal distributions and homogeneity of variance of the parent populations (Weinberg and Goldberg, 1990). As a consequence, the results of the *t*-tests should be valid even if the underlying samples are not normally distributed or if there is not equality of variance between the samples.

Grouping the variables that discriminate into constructs
Once variables that discriminate between the high- and low-performing groups were identified, they were grouped into constructs. The groupings were based upon the literature review in Chapter 4. In prior research, Murphy et al. (1996) used exploratory factor analysis to group perform-ance measures into constructs. As indicated in Chapter 2, our evaluation of the proposed constructs from that study found that the constructs had no theoretical basis; nor were they valid when tested using confirmatory factor analysis. Accordingly, the categories of measures in Chapter 4 were used as the basis for proposing constructs used in this study, and the validity of the constructs were subsequently tested.

Selecting the 'best' measures for each construct

As stated earlier, the information content of measures can be evaluated on both a relative and an incremental basis. The relative information content of a measure examines how much variance in a criterion is explained by the single measure. The greater the variation explained, the greater the relative information provided by the measure. In contrast, the incremental information provided by a variable is measured by the change in variation in the criterion explained by the addition of another variable. If the change in the variation explained by the addition of another measure is statistically significant, the conclusion is that the variable adds significant additional information about the criterion.

The approach employed to determine the relative information content of the measures was to use a regression of each variable of interest against the criterion return to shareholders (see Cheng and Cheung, 1993; Chen and Dodd, 1997 as examples). Variables were ranked by R^2 value. The higher the R^2 value, the greater the relative information content of the variable. In addition to the simple ranking of variables by relative information content, the information content of return on assets, return on equity, return on investment and EBITDA return on investment calculated using ending balances in the denominators was compared to the same measures calculated using average balances in the denominators. Further, the relative and incremental information content of static measures versus the corresponding change score measures was tested.

The incremental information content of a measure was determined using a combination of structural equation modeling and forward stepwise regression. For each combination of variables, the first variable selected was the one with the most relative information content. Subsequently, the addition of variables was tested to identify the variable that in combination with the first variable provides the most additional explanation of variance in the criterion as indicated by the largest increment in R^2 for the regression. If the addition of a variable increases R^2 by a statistically significant amount, the variable adds significant incremental information (Keppel and Zedeck, 1989). The final result was to develop parsimonious regression models for annual and three-year timeframes that maximized the explanation of variance in the criterion, market-adjusted return to shareholders. These regression equations were then used to calculate a composite measure of financial performance and the classification rate for companies for either high, medium or low financial performance was tested against the entire sample of annual and three-year data.

Based upon the comparison of variables for both relative and incremental information content, a set of variables was selected to measure each construct. The combination of theoretical constructs and the variables used to represent the constructs became the model of organizational financial performance tested in the next stage of this research.

Testing the validity of the constructs
The validity of the constructs was tested using confirmatory factor analysis (CFA) through the use of AMOS 5.0 structural equation modeling software (Venkatraman and Ramanujam, 1987; Bollen, 1989). The CFA framework uses a maximum likelihood approach to providing a statistical analysis of the entire validity of a construct and a decomposition of the measurement variance into its constituent components (Bagozzi et al., 1991).

Convergent validity refers to whether different measures of the same construct are in agreement and is tested using a model that 'hypothesizes that all the variation and covariation in the measurement be accounted for by the [constructs] that the measurements are intended to capture plus random error' (Venkatraman and Ramanujam, 1987: 114). Figure 7.1 depicts an example of a model of convergent validity that would be tested. If the data 'fit' the model, the implication is that the variations in the unobservable construct of profitability are caused by the underlying traits (the variables being tested) and random error. If the data do not fit the model, the implication is that there is not convergent validity among the variables utilized.

Discriminant validity refers to whether the constructs represent different attributes of the higher-order construct of organizational financial performance. Using a CFA framework, discriminant validity is achieved when the correlations between the separate constructs are statistically significantly

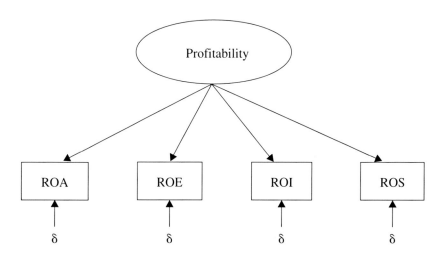

Figure 7.1   A model of convergent validity

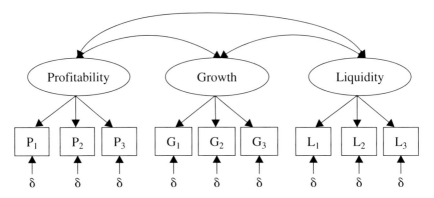

Figure 7.2   A model of discriminant validity

lower than unity (Bollen, 1989). The process of testing for discriminant validity involves testing a model similar to Figure 7.2, first with the correlations unconstrained, and then retesting the same model with the correlations constrained to unity. If the chi square value (χ^2) of the unconstrained model is significantly different from the constrained model, then there is support for discriminant validity.

TESTING AN OVERALL MODEL OF ORGANIZATIONAL FINANCIAL PERFORMANCE

Having determined constructs and tested them for validity, the next step in this research was to test the overall model of organizational financial performance. This was accomplished by testing a model similar to Figure 7.3.

Using structural equation modeling, the model of organizational financial performance was tested using a random sample consisting of 300 annual periods and 120 three-year periods from the high/low sample. Confirmatory factor analysis, using maximum likelihood estimation, was utilized to test the null hypothesis that the data fit the model. Three fit indices, as recommended by Bollen (1989), were chosen to determine whether the data fit the model. The three indices included: (i) comparative fit index (CFI; Bentler, 1990), (ii) the Tucker–Lewis coefficient (TLI; Bentler and Bonnet, 1980) which is also known as the Bentler and Bonnet non-normed fit index (NNFI), and (iii) the root mean square error of approximation (RMSEA; Brown and Cudeck, 1993). A value of 0.90 or greater for the CFI and the TLI indicates a reasonable fit of the data with the model (Bollen, 1989; Arbuckle and Wothke, 1999). Arbuckle and Wothke suggest that an RMSEA value of less than 0.08, but certainly no

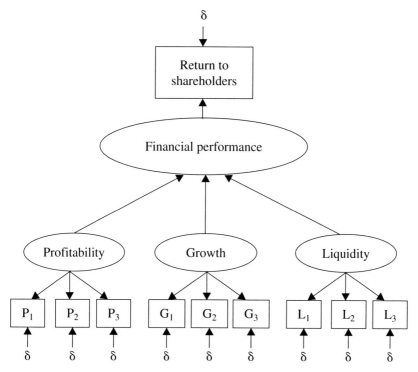

Figure 7.3   A model of financial performance

greater than 0.10 indicates an acceptable error rate for a model. If the model satisfies the rules of thumb for the three fit indices, the alternative hypothesis that the data do not fit the model cannot be accepted. A good fit indicates that the data fit the model of organizational financial performance inferred from empirical data in the first part of this research.

Once an acceptable model was developed that fit the data, the model was retested using separate random samples of 300 annual periods and 120 three-year periods. After determining whether the retest of the model continued to indicate an acceptable fit with the data, the model was tested against all annual and all three-year periods of data. Again, revisions were made to the annual and three-year models to achieve an acceptable fit with the data.

CHAPTER SUMMARY

Chapter 7 detailed the research design for this study. It included a discussion of the philosophy underlying the research design and the critical assumptions for the operationalization of the study. Using Cameron and Whetten's seven questions for bounding and evaluating organizational effectiveness, the research design, the population of interest, data-gathering issues and measurement issues for this research were detailed. An exploratory approach to inferring a model of organizational financial performance from empirical data was presented. Finally, a discussion of the data analysis techniques utilized to test the model concluded the chapter.

Because this research is exploratory in nature, it was not possible to develop a priori hypotheses. However, it was possible to develop working hypotheses as to what might or might not be found as each part of the exploratory work was performed. These working hypotheses are put forth in Chapters 8 and 9 where the exploratory research is presented. Chapter 8 presents the tests of the relative and incremental information content of individual financial performance measures. This information is used in Chapter 9 to develop and test annual and three-year models of financial performance.

8. Tests of the information content of individual measures of organizational financial performance

This chapter presents the exploratory work performed to examine individual measures of organizational financial performance as a first step in developing a measurement model of the construct. The first section addresses the relationship among ratios calculated with ending balances and average balances with return to shareholders to determine if they are statistically significantly different. The second section presents the results of statistical comparisons between high- and low-performing companies to identify measures that discriminate between the two groups. The third section examines the relative information content of various individual measures of financial performance. The fourth section examines the incremental and relative information content of static measures versus change scores.

THE RELATIONSHIP BETWEEN RATIOS CALCULATED USING AVERAGE AND ENDING BALANCES WITH RETURN TO SHAREHOLDERS

Certain ratios in this research can be calculated with either average or ending balances for the variables in the denominator. In the Compustat® database, all ratios are calculated using ending balances. However, this can present potentially misleading results in several instances. In the case of a ratio calculated with period information in the numerator (such as net income) and point-in-time information in the denominator (such as stockholders' equity), significant changes in the denominator, over the period measured in the numerator, may be lost. For instance, if a company completes a substantial equity offering in the last month of its fiscal year, its return on equity calculation at the end of the fiscal year will be significantly lower than its return on equity calculated using its average equity outstanding during the year. In other words, since these resources were not available for management to deploy for the majority of the year, the end-of-year calculation will give the impression that management was less effective in their use of assets than they actually were. Consequently, it was hypothesized that:

H1: The ratios return on assets, return on equity, return on investment and EBITDA return on investment, calculated using average balances for the denominators, will have a stronger statistical relationship with market-adjusted returns to shareholders than the same ratios calculated with ending balances for the denominators.

To test this hypothesis, simple regressions, with market-adjusted return to shareholders as the dependent variable, were performed using all annual firm years and all three-year periods in the sample. The adjusted R-square values for each variable were compared between the two formulations of the ratio to determine whether there was a significant difference. Table 8.1 presents the results of these tests. All of the correlations between the paired variables were at least 0.95 and all were statistically significant. The adjusted R-square values for the individual regressions also indicated almost no difference between the two formulations of the variables, although the F-statistic in almost every case was higher for the formulation using average balances. In short, the hypothesis was not supported. There was no statistically significant difference between the two formulations of the ratios. Consequently, only the ratios calculated with average balances will be used in the remainder of this research.

Return on equity had the most significant differences between the two formulations of the variables. A total 12.9 percent of the companies had a 20 percent or greater difference between the two calculations. A review of a sample of these companies revealed that the cause was typically due to a significant equity offering or stock repurchase during the year, again supporting the use of formulations using average balances.

DETERMINING VARIABLES THAT DISCRIMINATE BETWEEN HIGH- AND LOW-PERFORMING FIRMS

As noted earlier, the first step in developing a model of organizational financial performance was to determine which financial measures discriminate between high- and low-performing firms. This analysis required three steps. First, a random sample of approximately half of the high- and low-performing firms was selected from the annual and three-year period datasets (reserving the other half to retest the final models). Second,

Table 8.1   *Results of correlation and regression analyses comparing ending and average balances*

	Mean	SD	Adj. R^2	F	Coefficient[c]	Correlation
All annual firm years[a]						
Return on assets						0.99**
Ending balance	5.05	7.88	0.04	111.63	0.19**	
Average balance	5.55	8.15	0.04	122.45	0.20**	
Return on equity						0.96**
Ending balance	10.64	18.00	0.03	87.81	0.17**	
Average balance	11.95	17.15	0.03	103.20	0.19**	
Return on investment						0.99**
Ending balance	7.30	11.29	0.04	108.30	0.19**	
Average balance	8.03	11.60	0.04	113.96	0.20**	
EBITDA return on investment						0.98**
Ending balance	21.68	13.68	0.02	63.28	0.15**	
Average balance	22.94	14.75	0.02	72.72	0.16**	
All three-year periods[b]						
Return on assets						0.99**
Ending balance	16.58	21.08	0.12	130.00	0.35**	
Average balance	18.53	21.73	0.12	129.07	0.35**	
Return on equity						0.95**
Ending balance	37.90	57.05	0.08	86.00	0.29**	
Average balance	43.41	55.94	0.10	98.00	0.31**	
Return on investment						0.98**
Ending balance	24.93	33.96	0.11	116.92	0.33**	
Average balance	28.09	35.05	0.10	106.48	0.32**	
EBITDA return on investment						0.99**
Ending balance	84.09	58.44	0.08	83.33	0.29**	
Average balance	90.76	65.83	0.08	86.07	0.29**	

Notes:
[a] $n = 2894$.
[b] $n = 925$.
[c] Values are standardized regression coefficients.
** $p < 0.001$.

independent *t*-tests were performed for each variable comparing the high and low groups. Finally, those variables that were demonstrated to discriminate between the two groups were retained for further testing. The exploratory null hypothesis tested was:

H2: The individual static and change score variables will discriminate between high- and low-performing companies.

There were 300 annual firm years selected for the first sample and 120 three-year periods selected for the second sample. Variable means and standard deviations for all the annual and three-year periods are presented in Tables 8.2 and 8.3, respectively, and the correlations between variables for all the annual and three-year periods are presented in Tables 8.4 and 8.5, respectively. Variable means and standard deviations for the annual and three-year period high/low samples are presented in Tables 8.6 and 8.7, respectively, and the correlations between variables for the annual and three-year period high/low samples are presented in Tables 8.8 and 8.9, respectively.

Table 8.10 presents the results of the independent *t*-tests. The null hypothesis was not supported at the $p < 0.10$ level in the annual data for the static measures liabilities to total assets, and free cash flow to equity, or for the change scores liabilities to total assets, operating cash flow to equity and free cash flow to equity. Consequently, these variables were not retained, but 30 annual variables and 29 three-year variables were retained for further analysis.

This research identified only the variables that discriminated between high- and low-performing companies. It did not examine why they did or did not discriminate. However, there are several possible explanations for these findings.

First, liabilities to total assets, and its corresponding change score, probably did not discriminate because firms have some control over their capital structures. In periods of significant losses, firms can raise new equity capital. In periods of significant profits, firms can engage in share re-purchase programs and reinvestment in the business. In other words, management may attempt to maintain leverage within a specific range in both good times and bad, and as a result this variable does not discriminate between high- and low-performing companies.

Free cash flow to equity, and its corresponding change score, probably did not discriminate because of the control that management can exercise over free cash flow through the investing activities of the firm. During times of significant profits, firms may reinvest free cash flow in the business, while in times of significant losses, firms may significantly reduce capital expenditures. The result is that free cash flow does not discriminate between high- and low-performing firms over an annual period.

One possible explanation why asset turnover did not discriminate is that assets may increase in successful companies and decrease in unsuccessful companies in proportion to changes in sales, leaving the ratio substantially unchanged. However, if there is a change in the ratio of assets to sales, either for the good or bad, then performance is impacted. Accordingly, the

Table 8.2   Means and standard deviations of all annual firm years[a]

Variable	Description	Mean	SD
ROA	Return on assets	5.55	8.15
ROE	Return on equity	11.95	17.15
ROS	Return on sales	4.77	12.73
ROI	Return on investment	8.03	11.60
EBITDA ROI	EBITDA return on investment	22.94	14.75
Op. Margin	Operating margin	10.77	12.03
GR Sales	Growth rate of sales	11.12	29.25
GR Op Exp	Growth rate of operating expenses	112.12	28.58
GR OCF	Growth rate of operating cash flow	19.88	230.23
GR Assets	Growth rate of total assets	14.10	31.30
GR Employ	Growth rate of employees	7.10	24.18
Resid Income	Residual income	48.36	596.37
Resid Inc ROI	Residual income return on investment	1.19	11.95
Asset Turn	Asset turnover	1.19	0.78
Liab/Assets	Total liabilities to total assets	50.22	20.45
OCF/Eqty	Operating cash flow to equity	26.54	23.28
FCF/Eqty	Free cash flow to equity	3.71	30.37
Alt Z Score	Altman's Z-score	5.49	6.15
Price/Book	Price-to-book ratio	3.12	3.19
CAPM Rate	Cost of equity capital	9.77	3.06
ΔROA	Change in return on assets	17.33	299.29
ΔROE	Change in return on equity	13.95	293.45
ΔROS	Change in return on sales	10.73	310.90
ΔROI	Change in return on investment	18.24	305.16
ΔEBITDA ROI	Change in EBITDA return on investment	1.90	108.53
ΔOp. Margin	Change in operating margin	3.56	153.53
ΔGR Sales	Change in growth rate of sales	29.44	528.13
ΔGR Op Exp	Change in growth rate of operating expenses	−1.10	28.24
ΔGR OCF	Change in growth rate of operating cash flow	85.05	946.70
ΔGR Assets	Change in growth rate of total assets	106.12	799.51
ΔGR Employ	Change in growth rate of employees	45.52	589.09
ΔResid Income	Change in residual income	−19.06	562.59
ΔResid Inc ROI	Change in residual income return on investment	−25.03	506.77
ΔAsset Turn	Change in asset turnover	−2.92	19.32
ΔLiab/Assets	Change in total liabilities to total assets	0.51	20.60
ΔOCF/Eqty	Change in operating cash flow to equity	27.84	203.66
ΔFCF/Eqty	Change in free cash flow to equity	17.45	817.85
ΔAlt Z Score	Change in Altman's Z-score	−1.29	40.64
ΔPrice/Book	Change in price-to-book ratio	−3.64	50.90
ΔCAPM Rate	Change in cost of equity capital	−2.97	14.22
1yr Rtn MA	1-year market-adjusted return	17.24	52.07

Note: [a] $n = 2,894$.

Table 8.3   Means and standard deviations of three-year periods[a]

Variable	Description	Mean	SD
ROA	Return on assets	18.53	21.73
ROE	Return on equity	43.41	55.94
ROS	Return on sales	5.29	9.38
ROI	Return on investment	28.09	35.05
EBITDA ROI	EBITDA return on investment	90.76	65.83
Op. Margin	Operating margin	11.18	10.05
GR Sales	Growth rate of sales	34.73	61.43
GR Op Exp	Growth rate of operating expenses	37.25	59.55
GR OCF	Growth rate of operating cash flow	55.22	307.41
GR Assets	Growth rate of total assets	51.84	78.96
GR Employ	Growth rate of employees	23.36	52.13
Resid Income	Residual income	153.15	1,427.14
Resid Inc ROI	Residual income return on investment	5.65	29.64
Asset Turn	Asset turnover	3.54	2.22
Liab/Assets	Total liabilities to total assets	0.50	0.20
OCF/Eqty	Operating cash flow to equity	112.49	107.44
FCF/Eqty	Free cash flow to equity	14.68	78.86
Alt Z Score	Altman's Z-score	5.62	6.23
Price/Book	Price-to-book ratio	3.22	2.69
CAPM Rate	Cost of equity capital	9.29	3.21
ΔROA	Change in return on assets	−17.47	87.68
ΔROE	Change in return on equity	−19.59	91.69
ΔROS	Change in return on sales	−17.68	127.79
ΔROI	Change in return on investment	−17.18	83.29
ΔEBITDA ROI	Change in EBITDA return on investment	−8.23	24.42
ΔOp. Margin	Change in operating margin	−6.50	62.48
ΔGR Sales	Change in growth rate of sales	−33.74	256.02
ΔGR Op Exp	Change in growth rate of operating expenses	6.43	424.19
ΔGR OCF	Change in growth rate of operating cash flow	63.16	892.50
ΔGR Assets	Change in growth rate of total assets	13.17	338.31
ΔGR Employ	Change in growth rate of employees	−2.35	397.22
ΔResid Income	Change in residual income	−49.03	301.80
ΔResid Inc ROI	Change in residual income return on investment	−37.87	273.64
ΔAsset Turn	Change in asset turnover	−4.19	9.66
ΔLiab/Assets	Change in total liabilities to total assets	−0.71	11.02
ΔOCF/Eqty	Change in operating cash flow to equity	5.03	56.61
ΔFCF/Eqty	Change in free cash flow to equity	36.99	355.43
ΔAlt Z Score	Change in Altman's Z-score	−4.47	17.56
ΔPrice/Book	Change in price-to-book ratio	−8.53	23.76
ΔCAPM Rate	Change in cost of equity capital	−2.53	11.62
3yr Rtn MA	3-year market-adjusted return	26.46	24.11

Note: [a] $n = 925$.

change in asset turnover was found to be significant while the static ratio was not.

Liabilities to assets and free cash flow to equity, and the associated change score for free cash flow to equity probably did not discriminate in three-year periods for the same reasons that they not discriminate in the annual periods. The ability to manage investment levels in line with profitability could be the root cause.

Altman's Z-score probably did not adequately discriminate over the three-year timeframe because it is a point in time measure that is being compared to a period measure, return to shareholders. However, Altman's Z-score may actually be capturing information over a shorter period of time, such as a single year, about a firm's ability to succeed over future periods. For example, the higher Altman's Z-score, the greater amount of available slack resources a firm possesses, which has been demonstrated to be associated with higher firm performance (Chakravarthy, 1986). Further, Altman's Z-score has a significant market component that is more likely to yield a significant statistical effect over a single year than over a three-year period. Accordingly, the change in Altman's Z-score over the period was the most significantly correlated variable with return to shareholders. In fact, Altman (1993) recommended that the proper use of the measure was to examine its change over time, rather than simply use the point-in-time value.

Price-to-book value most likely did not adequately discriminate for the same reasons as Altman's Z-score. It is a point-in-time measure being compared to a period measure. However, just as with Altman's Z-score, the change in the price-to-book value was highly correlated with return to shareholders.

The change in the growth rate of employees did not discriminate, probably because significant productivity gains can allow companies to succeed without a corresponding increase in the workforce. Also, companies are slow to increase staff during times of expansion and slow to reduce staff during periods of contraction, such as using attrition rather than layoffs.

The null hypothesis was not supported at $p < 0.10$ for either the static or change scores for liabilities to total assets and free cash flow to equity, or the change in operating cash flow for the annual data. The null hypothesis was not supported at $p < 0.10$ in the three-year period data for the static measures asset turnover, liabilities to assets, free cash flow to equity, Altman's Z-score and price-to-book value, or for the change scores growth rate of operating cash flow, growth rate of employees or free cash flow to equity. Consequently, these variables were not retained for further analysis in this research.

Table 8.4   Correlations for all annual firm years[a]

	Variable	1	2	3	4	5	6	7	8	9
1	ROA									
2	ROE	0.84								
3	ROS	0.79	0.65							
4	ROI	0.97	0.88	0.73						
5	EBITDA ROI	0.77	0.76	0.46	0.83					
6	Op. Margin	0.63	0.55	0.77	0.58	0.53				
7	GR Sales	0.27	0.22	0.19	0.25	0.24	0.22			
8	GR Op Exp	0.14	0.11	0.06	0.13	0.14	0.07	0.09		
9	GR OCF	0.09	0.06	0.06	0.07	0.08	0.08	0.09	0.05	
10	GR Assets	0.23	0.17	0.17	0.21	0.17	0.17	0.52	0.53	0.05
11	GR Employ	0.19	0.14	0.13	0.17	0.15	0.14	0.54	0.56	0.05
12	Resid Income	0.32	0.38	0.30	0.34	0.27	0.23	0.07	0.02	0.01
13	Resid Inc ROI	0.92	0.89	0.72	0.95	0.80	0.59	0.23	0.11	0.07
14	Asset Turn	0.25	0.24	−0.01	0.30	0.37	−0.18	0.11	0.08	0.05
15	Liab/Assets	−0.21	0.07	−0.10	−0.13	0.00	−0.06	−0.02	−0.02	−0.02
16	OCF/Eqty	0.37	0.57	0.27	0.43	0.58	0.34	0.06	0.01	0.14
17	FCF/Eqty	0.20	0.28	0.12	0.23	0.27	0.12	−0.22	−0.28	0.07
18	Alt Z Score	0.40	0.18	0.24	0.34	0.26	0.23	0.13	0.11	0.05
19	Price/Book	0.38	0.43	0.24	0.40	0.43	0.28	0.15	0.12	0.04
20	CAPM Rate	−0.08	−0.17	−0.15	−0.09	−0.08	−0.14	0.03	0.05	−0.01
21	ΔROA	0.26	0.26	0.24	0.25	0.14	0.15	0.15	0.03	0.04
22	ΔROE	0.26	0.27	0.25	0.25	0.14	0.15	0.15	0.03	0.04
23	ΔROS	0.29	0.28	0.29	0.28	0.15	0.18	0.12	0.01	0.04
24	ΔROI	0.25	0.25	0.24	0.25	0.14	0.15	0.15	0.03	0.04
25	ΔEBITDA ROI	0.15	0.14	0.16	0.14	0.13	0.15	0.21	0.06	0.01
26	ΔOp. Margin	0.23	0.19	0.28	0.21	0.16	0.27	0.18	−0.01	0.07
27	ΔGR Sales	0.09	0.11	0.06	0.09	0.09	0.06	0.38	0.33	0.00
28	ΔGR Op Exp	0.11	0.12	0.08	0.11	0.11	0.08	0.61	0.63	0.00
29	ΔGR OCF	0.13	0.11	0.10	0.12	0.12	0.12	0.13	0.07	0.36
30	ΔGR Assets	0.07	0.09	0.05	0.07	0.06	0.05	0.14	0.12	0.01
31	ΔGR Employ	0.07	0.06	0.04	0.06	0.04	0.05	0.19	0.18	0.01
32	ΔResid Income	0.30	0.29	0.25	0.30	0.19	0.18	0.18	0.07	0.05
33	ΔResid Inc ROI	0.28	0.28	0.22	0.28	0.18	0.16	0.17	0.07	0.04
34	ΔAsset Turn	0.14	0.15	0.12	0.14	0.17	0.11	0.65	0.50	0.05
35	ΔLiab/Assets	−0.19	−0.16	−0.15	−0.17	−0.13	−0.10	0.03	0.06	−0.03
36	ΔOCF/Eqty	0.03	0.02	0.06	0.03	0.01	0.03	0.04	−0.01	0.28
37	ΔFCF/Eqty	0.03	0.02	0.02	0.03	0.04	0.03	−0.06	−0.09	0.04
38	ΔAlt Z Score	0.22	0.21	0.21	0.20	0.16	0.16	0.19	0.07	0.04
39	ΔPrice/Book	−0.01	−0.01	0.00	−0.02	−0.01	−0.02	0.01	−0.04	0.04
40	ΔCAPM Rate	−0.04	−0.08	−0.07	−0.04	−0.03	−0.06	0.00	0.01	−0.01
41	1yr Rtn MA	0.20	0.19	0.16	0.19	0.16	0.12	0.14	0.06	0.06

Note: [a] $n = 2,894$

10	11	12	13	14	15	16	17	18	19	20	21
0.60											
0.01	0.04										
0.17	0.14	0.36									
0.00	0.05	0.06	0.28								
−0.11	−0.08	0.07	0.10	0.02							
0.01	−0.02	0.18	0.49	0.13	0.29						
−0.40	−0.34	0.07	0.24	0.12	0.01	0.47					
0.19	0.14	0.06	0.18	0.10	−0.63	0.00	0.06				
0.21	0.15	0.24	0.35	0.04	−0.10	0.28	0.13	0.43			
0.07	0.07	−0.15	−0.34	−0.04	−0.32	−0.16	−0.06	0.23	0.06		
0.05	0.04	0.10	0.26	0.05	0.01	0.08	0.06	0.00	0.04	−0.08	
0.05	0.04	0.10	0.27	0.06	0.02	0.09	0.06	0.00	0.04	−0.09	0.99
0.05	0.04	0.12	0.29	0.05	0.02	0.09	0.06	0.01	0.05	−0.11	0.96
0.05	0.04	0.10	0.26	0.05	0.01	0.08	0.07	0.00	0.04	−0.09	0.00
0.02	0.01	0.05	0.15	0.06	0.03	0.10	0.09	−0.01	0.01	−0.01	0.25
0.08	0.04	0.07	0.23	0.05	0.03	0.09	0.05	0.01	0.03	−0.08	0.41
0.22	0.22	0.01	0.11	0.04	0.04	0.02	−0.09	0.00	0.01	−0.03	0.12
0.33	0.35	0.05	0.12	0.04	0.04	0.03	−0.13	−0.02	0.04	−0.06	0.10
0.08	0.05	0.06	0.13	0.04	0.01	0.19	0.09	0.03	0.06	−0.04	0.09
0.36	0.18	0.02	0.08	0.00	0.04	0.01	−0.18	−0.02	0.04	−0.04	0.04
0.23	0.41	−0.01	0.06	0.02	−0.01	−0.03	−0.16	0.02	0.01	−0.02	0.02
0.07	0.07	0.15	0.31	0.06	0.01	0.11	0.06	0.03	0.07	−0.13	0.22
0.06	0.07	0.13	0.29	0.05	0.00	0.10	0.06	0.03	0.06	−0.12	0.22
−0.08	0.14	0.09	0.18	0.15	0.12	0.10	0.09	−0.07	0.01	−0.13	0.22
0.13	0.12	−0.03	−0.17	−0.07	0.15	−0.07	−0.21	−0.18	−0.04	0.02	−0.10
−0.04	−0.02	−0.02	0.04	0.06	0.02	0.21	0.16	−0.01	−0.04	−0.03	0.07
−0.18	−0.16	0.03	0.03	0.02	−0.01	0.10	0.31	0.00	−0.03	−0.02	0.03
−0.13	−0.05	0.08	0.23	0.10	−0.08	0.10	0.22	0.20	0.13	−0.14	0.21
−0.10	−0.05	0.01	0.03	0.09	0.08	0.01	0.09	−0.03	0.20	−0.16	0.11
0.00	0.02	−0.08	−0.13	−0.02	−0.10	−0.09	−0.04	0.04	−0.06	0.40	−0.06
0.15	0.12	0.06	0.23	0.11	−0.02	0.12	0.05	0.15	0.19	−0.20	0.16

Table 8.4 (continued)

	Variable	22	23	24	25	26	27	28	29	30
1	ROA									
2	ROE									
3	ROS									
4	ROI									
5	EBITDA ROI									
6	Op. Margin									
7	GR Sales									
8	GR Op Exp									
9	GR OCF									
10	GR Assets									
11	GR Employ									
12	Resid Income									
13	Resid Inc ROI									
14	Asset Turn									
15	Liab/Assets									
16	OCF/Eqty									
17	FCF/Eqty									
18	Alt Z Score									
19	Price/Book									
20	CAPM Rate									
21	ΔROA									
22	ΔROE									
23	ΔROS	0.96								
24	ΔROI	0.99	0.96							
25	ΔEBITDA ROI	0.25	0.23	0.25						
26	ΔOp. Margin	0.40	0.40	0.41	0.38					
27	ΔGR Sales	0.12	0.09	0.12	0.14	0.12				
28	ΔGR Op Exp	0.09	0.06	0.10	0.11	0.07	0.40			
29	ΔGR OCF	0.09	0.09	0.09	0.05	0.10	0.05	0.02		
30	ΔGR Assets	0.04	0.04	0.04	0.05	0.06	0.15	0.17	0.01	
31	ΔGR Employ	0.02	0.02	0.02	0.02	−0.01	0.20	0.20	−0.01	0.21
32	ΔResid Income	0.22	0.22	0.21	0.14	0.15	0.10	0.09	0.06	0.04
33	ΔResid Inc ROI	0.22	0.22	0.22	0.13	0.15	0.10	0.09	0.05	0.04
34	ΔAsset Turn	0.22	0.18	0.22	0.34	0.24	0.34	0.58	0.07	0.03
35	ΔLiab/Assets	−0.08	−0.10	−0.10	−0.02	−0.08	0.04	0.06	0.01	0.04
36	ΔOCF/Eqty	0.08	0.07	0.07	0.11	0.13	0.00	−0.02	0.21	−0.03
37	ΔFCF/Eqty	0.03	0.03	0.03	0.03	0.02	−0.04	−0.06	0.06	−0.10
38	ΔAlt Z Score	0.20	0.19	0.21	0.20	0.21	0.12	0.11	0.08	−0.04
39	ΔPrice/Book	0.11	0.11	0.11	0.06	0.09	0.05	0.07	0.06	−0.02
40	ΔCAPM Rate	−0.06	−0.07	−0.06	−0.03	−0.06	−0.02	−0.04	−0.02	−0.07
41	1yr Rtn MA	0.16	0.16	0.17	0.09	0.14	0.10	0.14	0.07	0.09

31	32	33	34	35	36	37	38	39	40
0.05									
0.06	0.98								
0.11	0.20	0.20							
0.05	−0.05	−0.06	−0.02						
−0.02	0.04	0.04	0.09	−0.03					
−0.10	0.02	0.03	0.03	−0.11	0.08				
0.01	0.17	0.16	0.34	−0.46	0.09	0.09			
0.01	0.09	0.09	0.20	0.03	0.08	0.04	0.39		
−0.01	−0.12	−0.12	−0.10	0.02	−0.03	−0.02	−0.19	−0.20	
0.09	0.20	0.19	0.16	−0.06	0.07	0.02	0.60	0.56	−0.34

Table 8.5   Correlations for all three-year periods[a]

	Variable	1	2	3	4	5	6	7	8	9
1	ROA									
2	ROE	0.74								
3	ROS	0.71	0.50							
4	ROI	0.94	0.80	0.61						
5	EBITDA ROI	0.77	0.71	0.37	0.86					
6	Op Margin	0.58	0.42	0.75	0.49	0.41				
7	GR Sales	0.14	0.09	0.01	0.13	0.13	0.12			
8	GR Op Exp	0.09	0.04	−0.04	0.08	0.09	0.08	0.93		
9	GR OCF	0.10	0.07	0.07	0.09	0.11	0.13	0.23	0.19	
10	GR Assets	0.21	0.12	0.11	0.18	0.14	0.17	0.60	0.60	0.19
11	GR Employ	0.14	0.07	0.01	0.11	0.09	0.11	0.61	0.62	0.21
12	Resid Income	0.30	0.37	0.28	0.33	0.25	0.20	−0.02	−0.04	−0.03
13	Resid Inc ROI	0.88	0.84	0.59	0.94	0.83	0.49	0.10	0.04	0.09
14	Asset Turn	0.23	0.20	−0.11	0.27	0.34	−0.29	0.01	−0.02	0.02
15	Liab/Assets	−0.28	0.09	−0.16	−0.17	−0.04	−0.12	−0.09	−0.11	−0.02
16	OCF/Eqty	0.35	0.67	0.21	0.43	0.60	0.27	0.06	0.02	0.06
17	FCF/Eqty	0.23	0.25	0.09	0.31	0.33	0.06	−0.17	−0.20	0.04
18	Alt Z Score	0.38	0.12	0.22	0.30	0.22	0.25	0.18	0.20	0.04
19	Price/Book	0.47	0.57	0.24	0.54	0.52	0.29	0.22	0.16	0.07
20	CAPM Rate	−0.10	−0.21	−0.15	−0.10	−0.09	−0.12	0.05	0.11	−0.03
21	ΔROA	0.25	0.22	0.22	0.23	0.16	0.13	0.08	−0.02	0.06
22	ΔROE	0.23	0.22	0.20	0.21	0.16	0.13	0.07	−0.03	0.06
23	ΔROS	0.24	0.20	0.25	0.22	0.15	0.13	0.02	−0.05	0.07
24	ΔROI	0.24	0.22	0.21	0.22	0.17	0.13	0.08	−0.02	0.07
25	ΔEBITDA ROI	0.18	0.16	0.13	0.17	0.18	0.09	0.32	0.12	0.16
26	ΔOp Margin	0.18	0.15	0.16	0.17	0.14	0.16	0.15	0.02	0.11
27	ΔGR Sales	0.08	0.09	0.03	0.08	0.07	0.02	0.17	0.15	0.05
28	ΔGR Op Exp	0.06	0.11	0.03	0.06	0.08	0.03	0.07	0.07	0.04
29	ΔGR OCF	0.03	0.02	0.03	0.02	0.01	0.03	0.09	0.08	0.36
30	ΔGR Assets	0.16	0.21	0.11	0.18	0.16	0.08	0.08	0.04	0.04
31	ΔGR Employ	0.03	0.05	0.05	0.01	−0.02	0.06	0.08	0.06	0.04
32	ΔResid Income	0.13	0.14	0.07	0.13	0.12	0.05	0.08	0.01	0.08
33	ΔResid Inc ROI	0.14	0.14	0.08	0.13	0.13	0.09	0.14	0.06	0.07
34	ΔAsset Turn	0.01	0.05	−0.02	0.01	0.07	−0.02	0.32	0.21	0.07
35	ΔLiab/Assets	−0.25	−0.16	−0.22	−0.21	−0.15	−0.16	0.06	0.09	−0.01
36	ΔOCF/Eqty	−0.03	−0.03	0.01	−0.02	−0.02	−0.04	0.12	0.05	0.13
37	ΔFCF/Eqty	−0.05	−0.06	−0.05	−0.05	−0.04	−0.03	−0.05	−0.05	0.03
38	ΔAlt Z Score	0.30	0.22	0.31	0.26	0.24	0.21	0.08	−0.04	0.08
39	ΔPrice/Book	0.06	0.09	0.04	0.07	0.13	0.01	0.02	−0.09	0.08
40	ΔCAPM Rate	−0.10	−0.13	−0.11	−0.09	−0.09	−0.07	0.03	0.07	−0.02
41	1yr Rtn MA	0.35	0.31	0.29	0.32	0.29	0.24	0.26	0.15	0.13

Note: [a] $n = 925$.

10	11	12	13	14	15	16	17	18	19	20	21
0.59											
−0.05	−0.02										
0.10	0.07	0.37									
−0.07	−0.01	0.05	0.25								
−0.21	−0.14	0.10	0.08	0.02							
0.00	0.01	0.22	0.52	0.12	0.32						
−0.33	−0.23	0.10	0.32	0.14	0.05	0.35					
0.32	0.20	0.03	0.12	0.05	−0.65	−0.05	0.01				
0.29	0.18	0.27	0.49	0.02	−0.09	0.44	0.21	0.43			
0.18	0.10	−0.19	−0.37	−0.07	−0.37	−0.20	−0.08	0.32	0.12		
0.04	0.00	0.09	0.28	0.09	0.04	0.13	0.12	−0.01	0.10	−0.27	
0.02	−0.01	0.11	0.26	0.10	0.05	0.15	0.09	−0.01	0.10	−0.26	0.88
0.05	−0.06	0.04	0.26	0.09	0.04	0.11	0.07	0.00	0.08	−0.25	0.81
0.02	−0.02	0.10	0.27	0.09	0.04	0.14	0.12	−0.02	0.10	−0.26	0.94
−0.01	0.09	0.07	0.25	0.08	0.13	0.18	0.18	−0.09	0.10	−0.33	0.48
0.08	0.08	0.04	0.22	0.06	0.05	0.13	0.12	0.01	0.12	−0.20	0.40
0.08	0.14	−0.07	0.10	0.06	0.06	0.06	0.00	−0.02	0.02	−0.09	0.16
0.06	0.07	−0.04	0.08	0.02	0.04	0.19	0.02	−0.02	0.04	−0.06	0.05
0.02	0.05	−0.02	0.05	−0.01	0.07	0.01	0.00	−0.03	0.00	−0.08	0.09
0.17	0.13	0.02	0.19	0.02	−0.04	0.12	−0.02	0.04	0.12	−0.10	0.16
0.15	0.20	0.02	0.03	−0.05	0.00	0.01	−0.08	−0.01	0.01	−0.06	0.07
−0.08	−0.02	0.11	0.20	0.11	0.12	0.12	0.09	−0.05	0.05	−0.30	0.24
−0.05	0.02	0.10	0.19	0.05	0.09	0.12	0.10	−0.04	0.04	−0.26	0.27
−0.35	−0.02	0.05	0.11	0.17	0.20.	0.12	0.22	−0.21	−0.07	−0.35	0.24
0.04	0.03	0.02	−0.17	−0.06	0.22	−0.04	−0.14	−0.21	−0.01	−0.04	−0.19
−0.06	0.05	−0.02	0.01	0.04	0.12	0.05	0.09	−0.08	−0.03	−0.13	0.11
−0.16	−0.06	−0.04	−0.04	0.01	0.0.4	0.00	0.19	−0.05	−0.06	−0.01	−0.01
−0.15	−0.02	0.08	0.33	0.18	0.0.2	0.18	0.22	−0.01	−0.05	−0.39	0.40
−0.20	−0.05	0.06	0.21	0.18	0.28	0.28	0.25	−0.22	−0.02	−0.53	0.26
0.12	0.08	−0.11	−0.14	−0.14	−0.14	−0.14	−0.11	0.11	0.03	0.40	−0.19
0.18	0.18	0.10	0.40	0.11	0.02	0.25	0.08	0.01	0.10	−0.45	0.36

Table 8.5   (continued)

	Variable	22	23	24	25	26	27	28	29	30
1	ROA									
2	ROE									
3	ROS									
4	ROI									
5	EBITDA ROI									
6	Op Margin									
7	GR Sales									
8	GR Op Exp									
9	GR OCF									
10	GR Assets									
11	GR Employ									
12	Resid Income									
13	Resid Inc ROI									
14	Asset Turn									
15	Liab/Assets									
16	OCF/Eqty									
17	FCF/Eqty									
18	Alt Z Score									
19	Price/Book									
20	CAPM Rate									
21	ΔROA									
22	ΔROE									
23	ΔROS	0.80								
24	ΔROI	0.96	0.83							
25	ΔEBITDA ROI	0.46	0.39	0.50						
26	ΔOp Margin	0.40	0.38	0.42	0.63					
27	ΔGR Sales	0.14	0.11	0.16	0.20	0.09				
28	ΔGR Op Exp	0.03	0.04	0.04	0.06	0.03	0.39			
29	ΔGR OCF	0.07	0.08	0.09	0.14	0.14	0.08	0.05		
30	ΔGR Assets	0.13	0.16	0.15	0.20	0.14	0.18	0.30	0.00	
31	ΔGR Employ	0.06	0.03	0.06	0.11	0.10	0.22	0.11	0.04	0.21
32	ΔResid Income	0.24	0.18	0.25	0.30	0.10	0.10	0.02	0.05	0.04
33	ΔResid Inc ROI	0.28	0.19	0.29	0.37	0.09	0.10	0.02	0.04	0.05
34	ΔAsset Turn	0.24	0.15	0.26	0.57	0.20	0.24	0.11	0.12	0.08
35	ΔLiab/Assets	−0.12	−0.18	−0.17	−0.06	−0.12	0.03	0.00	0.05	−0.04
36	ΔOCF/Eqty	0.14	0.12	0.15	0.30	0.10	0.07	−0.02	0.03	−0.04
37	ΔFCF/Eqty	−0.01	−0.02	0.00	0.04	0.01	−0.05	−0.06	0.07	−0.17
38	ΔAlt Z Score	0.34	0.32	0.40	0.55	0.31	0.12	0.04	0.04	0.12
39	ΔPrice/Book	0.26	0.20	0.27	0.45	0.25	0.13	0.19	0.08	0.07
40	ΔCAPM Rate	−0.19	−0.18	−0.20	−0.20	−0.12	−0.08	−0.03	0.01	0.00
41	1yr Rtn MA	0.34	0.30	0.38	0.53	0.29	0.15	0.07	0.06	0.21

31	32	33	34	35	36	37	38	39	40

0.04									
0.05	0.73								
0.06	0.27	0.29							
0.02	0.00	0.00	0.05						
0.01	0.13	0.12	0.20	0.07					
−0.12	0.03	0.02	0.03	−0.10	0.14				
0.04	0.25	0.27	0.45	−0.52	0.16	0.09			
0.04	0.28	0.30	0.42	0.03	0.27	0.04	0.50		
0.01	−0.24	−0.18	−0.21	−0.04	−0.10	−0.06	−0.24	−0.27	
0.11	0.28	0.32	0.31	−0.14	0.16	−0.02	0.67	0.55	−0.24

Table 8.6   Means and standard deviations of annual data high/low sample[a]

Variable	Description	Mean	SD
ROA	Return on assets	5.293	11.004
ROE	Return on equity	9.611	19.140
ROS	Return on sales	3.415	18.455
ROI	Return on investment	7.451	15.149
EBITDA ROI	EBITDA return on investment	22.290	16.944
Op Margin	Operating margin	9.148	15.374
GR Sales	Growth rate of sales	17.251	34.736
GR Op Exp	Growth rate of operating expenses	117.633	31.702
GR OCF	Growth rate of operating cash flow	19.433	251.582
GR Assets	Growth rate of total assets	20.709	42.770
GR Employ	Growth rate of employees	12.894	33.907
Resid Income	Residual income	−87.969	573.760
Resid Inc ROI	Residual income return on investment	−1.203	15.602
Asset Turn	Asset turnover	1.264	0.860
Liab/Assets	Total liabilities to total assets	43.376	21.246
OCF/Eqty	Operating cash flow to equity	22.450	20.629
FCF/Eqty	Free cash flow to equity	2.702	28.855
Alt Z Score	Altman's Z-score	7.352	7.917
Price/Book	Price-to-book ratio	3.437	3.681
CAPM Rate	Cost of equity capital	11.310	3.529
ΔROA	Change in return on assets	19.864	321.843
ΔROE	Change in return on equity	10.103	295.944
ΔROS	Change in return on sales	7.284	311.419
ΔROI	Change in return on investment	20.875	337.329
ΔEBITDA ROI	Change in EBITDA return on investment	−8.154	129.990
ΔOp Margin	Change in operating margin	−9.480	206.095
ΔGR Sales	Change in growth rate of sales	54.565	494.313
ΔGR Op Exp	Change in growth rate of operating expenses	1.814	35.821
ΔGR OCF	Change in growth rate of operating cash flow	20.602	1,065.021
ΔGR Assets	Change in growth rate of total assets	79.422	740.487
ΔGR Employ	Change in growth rate of employees	95.371	765.746
ΔResid Income	Change in residual income	−36.636	805.630
ΔResid Inc ROI	Change in residual income return on investment	−39.776	740.924

Table 8.6   (continued)

Variable	Description	Mean	SD
ΔAsset Turn	Change in asset turnover	−2.968	22.992
ΔLiab/Assets	Change in total liabilities to total assets	−0.144	25.793
ΔOCF/Eqty	Change in operating cash flow to equity	32.986	213.781
ΔFCF/Eqty	Change in free cash flow to equity	19.232	545.462
ΔAlt Z Score	Change in Altman's Z-score	8.401	74.611
ΔPrice/Book	Change in price-to-book ratio	4.821	81.395
ΔCAPM Rate	Change in cost of equity capital	1.062	19.083
1yr Rtn MA	1-year market-adjusted return	34.454	103.402

Note: [a] $n = 300$.

THE RELATIVE INFORMATION CONTENT OF INDIVIDUAL MEASURES OF ORGANIZATIONAL FINANCIAL PERFORMANCE

To determine the relative information content of measures, an examination was made of how much of the variance in the criterion (market-adjusted return to shareholders) was explained by a single variable. The greater amount of variance explained, the greater the relative information provided by the variable. The measure that explains the greatest amount of variance in the criterion is said to be the 'best' single measure for the construct (Chen and Dodd, 1997).

Using similar methodology to Chen and Dodd, a regression of each individual measure of financial performance against the criterion (market-adjusted return to shareholders) was performed for the annual and three-year high/low samples. Additionally, regressions were also performed using the entire database of annual and three-year data to contrast the relative information content between the two populations. The results of these regression analyses for annual periods are presented in Table 8.11.

An observation about the comparison of the results of the regressions for the high/low sample and for the entire database is that the ranking of the relative information content of the measures is generally the same. In addition, all of the regression coefficients were significant for the entire database primarily because of the large sample size. However, the relative amount of information provided for the high/low sample was considerably more than the relative information for the entire database.

Table 8.7　Means and standard deviations of three-year data high/low sample[a]

Variable	Description	Mean	SD
ROA	Return on assets	15.491	25.345
ROE	Return on equity	35.669	64.984
ROS	Return on sales	4.390	12.515
ROI	Return on investment	23.279	38.507
EBITDA ROI	EBITDA return on investment	88.021	63.365
Op Margin	Operating margin	10.801	11.743
GR Sales	Growth rate of sales	44.809	73.324
GR Op Exp	Growth rate of operating expenses	43.302	57.940
GR OCF	Growth rate of operating cash flow	53.373	304.448
GR Assets	Growth rate of total assets	57.050	67.039
GR Employ	Growth rate of employees	32.432	57.309
Resid Income	Residual income	−63.009	1,426.284
Resid Inc ROI	Residual income return on investment	−0.611	34.744
Asset Turn	Asset turnover	3.546	2.221
Liab/Assets	Total liabilities to total assets	0.476	0.199
OCF/Eqty	Operating cash flow to equity	109.233	101.338
FCF/Eqty	Free cash flow to equity	15.462	97.245
Alt Z Score	Altman's Z-score	5.818	5.118
Price/Book	Price-to-book ratio	3.618	2.755
CAPM Rate	Cost of equity capital	10.442	3.911
ΔROA	Change in return on assets	−27.412	95.955
ΔROE	Change in return on equity	−33.507	102.557
ΔROS	Change in return on sales	−55.695	198.028
ΔROI	Change in return on investment	−28.632	98.661
ΔEBITDA ROI	Change in EBITDA return on investment	−7.464	35.717
ΔOp Margin	Change in operating margin	−19.465	107.048
ΔGR Sales	Change in growth rate of sales	−41.156	276.226
ΔGR Op Exp	Change in growth rate of operating expenses	−36.838	233.916
ΔGR OCF	Change in growth rate of operating cash flow	−161.993	1,092.970
ΔGR Assets	Change in growth rate of total assets	−20.007	315.006
ΔGR Employ	Change in growth rate of employees	−48.899	279.923
ΔResid Income	Change in residual income	−66.653	294.490

Table 8.7   (continued)

Variable	Description	Mean	SD
ΔResid Inc ROI	Change in residual income return on investment	−64.393	370.116
ΔAsset Turn	Change in asset turnover	−4.319	11.182
ΔLiab/Assets	Change in total liabilities to total assets	−0.657	13.212
ΔOCF/Eqty	Change in operating cash flow to equity	3.331	56.167
ΔFCF/Eqty	Change in free cash flow to equity	15.957	361.224
ΔAlt Z Score	Change in Altman's Z-score	−5.155	27.426
ΔPrice/Book	Change in price-to-book ratio	−10.581	34.621
ΔCAPM Rate	Change in cost of equity capital	0.376	14.691
3yr Rtn MA	3-year market-adjusted return	26.646	40.403

Note: [a] $n = 120$.

The Results of Regression Analyses Testing the Relative Information Content of Annual Financial Performance Measures

Overall, six categories of measures were tested for their relative information content: (i) profitability measures; (ii) growth measures; (iii) efficiency measures; (iv) cash flow measures; (v) survival measures; and (vi) market-based measures. In general, the measures that provided the greatest amount of relative information about return to shareholders were those that included a market component in the measure such as Altman's Z-score (a survival measure), price-to-book value (a market-based measure), and the cost of equity capital (a market-based measure). Although cost of equity capital is not intuitively a market-based measure, it does have a significant correlation with market-adjusted returns since beta (the covariation of firm-specific returns with the market) is a key component in calculating the cost of capital.

The information content of profitability measures

The profitability measures that provided the most information about return to shareholders were those that in some way represented the residual income available to common stockholders. These included return on equity, residual income and residual income return on investment. The economic value measures were included in this category because they include profitability as their primary component. Residual income and residual

Table 8.8   Correlations for annual high/low sample[a]

	Variable	1	2	3	4	5	6	7	8
1	ROA								
2	ROE	0.92**							
3	ROS	0.82**	0.74**						
4	ROI	0.98**	0.95**	0.75**					
5	EBITDA ROI	0.77**	0.77**	0.48**	0.81**				
6	Op Margin	0.68**	0.62**	0.81**	0.62**	0.59**			
7	GR Sales	0.42**	0.40**	0.38**	0.39**	0.32**	0.37**		
8	GR Op Exp	0.26**	0.24**	0.18**	0.24**	0.18**	0.13*	0.89**	
9	GR OCF	0.20**	0.20**	0.16**	0.19**	0.15**	0.18**	0.11*	0.02
10	GR Assets	0.28**	0.27**	0.19**	0.27**	0.16**	0.06	0.59**	0.61**
11	GR Employ	0.27**	0.26**	0.20**	0.26**	0.21**	0.18**	0.64**	0.67**
12	Resid Income	0.35**	0.41**	0.29**	0.37**	0.30**	0.24**	0.21**	0.10+
13	Resid Inc ROI	0.94**	0.93**	0.73**	0.96**	0.78**	0.61**	0.37**	0.21**
14	Asset Turn	0.24**	0.25**	0.06	0.26**	0.39**	−0.05	0.06	0.05
15	OCF/Eqty	0.43**	0.53**	0.33**	0.47**	0.60**	0.41**	0.15**	0.02
16	Alt Z Score	0.38**	0.25**	0.25**	0.33**	0.25**	0.23**	0.23**	0.21**
17	Price/Book	0.34**	0.37**	0.21**	0.37**	0.38**	0.21**	0.21**	0.21**
18	CAPM Rate	−0.10+	−0.16**	−0.10+	−0.11+	−0.10+	−0.05	−0.01	0.05
19	ΔROA	0.19**	0.18**	0.15*	0.18**	0.15**	0.17**	0.15**	−0.01
20	ΔROE	0.19**	0.17**	0.15*	0.17**	0.15**	0.17**	0.17**	0.01
21	ΔROS	0.19**	0.18**	0.13*	0.18**	0.15**	0.16**	0.08	−0.06
22	ΔROI	0.18**	0.17**	0.14*	0.16**	0.15*	0.16**	0.15**	0.00
23	ΔEBITDA ROI	0.36**	0.33**	0.35**	0.34**	0.29**	0.39**	0.25**	0.06
24	ΔOp Margin	0.37**	0.37**	0.48**	0.35**	0.28**	0.49**	0.29**	0.04
25	ΔGR Sales	0.17**	0.19**	0.15**	0.18**	0.10+	0.15*	0.40**	0.33**
26	ΔGR Op Exp	0.22**	0.26**	0.22**	0.22**	0.19**	0.21**	0.56**	0.52**
27	ΔGR OCF	0.20**	0.21**	0.22**	0.20**	0.12*	0.19**	0.17**	0.11*
28	ΔGR Assets	0.07	0.10+	0.07	0.08	0.03	−0.01	0.23**	0.19**
29	ΔGR Employ	0.11+	0.11+	0.07	0.10+	0.07	0.05	0.23**	0.22**
30	ΔResid Income	0.33**	0.32**	0.22**	0.32**	0.25**	0.22**	0.22**	0.08
31	ΔResid Inc ROI	0.31**	0.31**	0.20**	0.30**	0.22**	0.21**	0.20**	0.08
32	ΔAsset Turn	0.22	0.24**	0.22**	0.21**	0.23**	0.27**	0.55**	0.36**
33	ΔOCF/Eqty	0.04	0.06	0.04	0.05	0.02	0.04	0.03	−0.03
34	ΔAlt Z Score	0.32**	0.33**	0.27**	0.30**	0.26**	0.27**	0.23**	0.03
35	ΔPrice/Book	0.12*	0.18*	0.13*	0.13*	0.12*	0.13*	0.06	−0.04
36	ΔCAPM Rate	−0.12*	−0.14**	−0.09	−0.11+	−0.08	−0.03	−0.07	−0.01
37	1yr Rtn MA	0.32**	0.35**	0.22**	0.31**	0.27**	0.20**	0.29**	0.14*

Note: [a] $n = 300$; $+p<0.10$; $*p<0.05$; $**p<0.01$.

income return on investment both include a charge for the use of common shareholder investments, not included in other measures. Return on equity excludes a direct charge for the use of equity capital, but represents the total amount available for distribution to common shareholders. Intuitively, these measures should covary significantly with the returns to shareholders

9	10	11	12	13	14	15	16	17	18
0.01									
0.04	0.65**								
0.07	0.07	0.06							
0.19**	0.25**	0.23**	0.37**						
−0.04	−0.02	0.07	0.19**	0.27**					
0.20**	−0.02	0.00	0.17**	0.50**	0.22**				
0.09	0.31**	0.16**	0.10+	0.22**	0.00	0.04			
0.07	0.38**	0.16**	0.16**	0.33**	−0.01	0.28**	0.54**		
−0.06	−0.02	0.03	−0.15**	−0.32**	−0.09	−0.11*	0.10+	−0.02	
0.09	0.02	0.04	0.09	0.20**	0.02	0.15**	0.01	0.03	−0.10+
0.09	0.03	0.04	0.08	0.19**	0.02	0.15**	0.00	0.03	−0.09
0.10+	0.00	0.02	0.09	0.19**	0.01	0.13*	0.03	0.04	−0.08
0.09	0.02	0.04	0.08	0.18**	0.02	0.14*	0.01	0.03	−0.09
0.10	0.03	0.08	0.14*	0.37**	0.09	0.21**	0.03	0.01	−0.12*
0.15**	0.01	0.08	0.24**	0.37**	0.10+	0.23**	0.03	0.06	−0.11+
0.00	0.34**	0.28**	0.10+	0.19**	−0.04	0.01	0.10+	0.06	−0.10+
−0.01	0.33**	0.36**	0.15**	0.25**	−0.03	0.16**	0.02	0.13*	−0.16**
0.40**	0.08	0.09	0.19**	0.20**	0.05	0.20**	0.14*	0.08	−0.13*
0.01	0.50**	0.25**	0.07	0.10+	−0.04	−0.04	0.10+	0.09	−0.15*
0.05	0.21**	0.33**	0.06	0.09	0.00	0.03	0.06	0.05	−0.02
0.08	0.14*	0.13*	0.28**	0.34**	0.04	0.06	0.08	0.10+	−0.14*
0.05	0.12*	0.12*	0.23**	0.32**	0.02	0.04	0.06	0.09	−0.13*
0.05	−0.08	0.13*	0.26**	0.25**	0.09	0.26**	−0.05	−0.01	−0.17**
0.19**	−0.08	−0.07	0.06	0.07	0.15**	0.25**	0.00	−0.01	−0.03
0.14*	0.03	0.02	0.22**	0.35**	0.05	0.18**	0.31**	0.29**	−0.30**
0.12*	−0.03	−0.03	0.14*	0.20**	0.12*	0.15**	0.04	0.27**	−0.34**
−0.10	−0.12*	−0.01	−0.16**	−0.19**	−0.04	−0.04	−0.14*	−0.20**	0.48**
0.14*	0.26**	0.21**	0.22**	0.37**	0.11*	0.19**	0.28**	0.36**	−0.34**

actually realized. This relationship was replicated in the test of the entire database, although the inclusion of the moderate-performing companies reduced the amount of relative information captured by the profitability measures. Return on assets and return on investment also had significant relative information content, but to a lesser degree than measures directly associated with the return to common shareholders.

Table 8.8   (continued)

	Variable	19	20	21	22	23	24	25	26
1	ROA								
2	ROE								
3	ROS								
4	ROI								
5	EBITDA ROI								
6	Op Margin								
7	GR Sales								
8	GR Op Exp								
9	GR OCF								
10	GR Assets								
11	GR Employ								
12	Resid Income								
13	Resid Inc ROI								
14	Asset Turn								
15	OCF/Eqty								
16	Alt Z Score								
17	Price/Book								
18	CAPM Rate								
19	ΔROA								
20	ΔROE	0.98**							
21	ΔROS	0.95**	0.94**						
22	ΔROI	0.99**	0.98**	0.95**					
23	ΔEBITDA ROI	0.25**	0.26**	0.21**	0.24**				
24	ΔOp Margin	0.33**	0.35**	0.32**	0.32**	0.38**			
25	ΔGR Sales	0.08	0.06	0.02	0.07	0.13*	0.18**		
26	ΔGR Op Exp	0.21**	0.21**	0.13*	0.21**	0.15**	0.10+	0.39**	
27	ΔGR OCF	−0.05	−0.08	−0.07	−0.06	0.09	0.15**	0.26**	0.09
28	ΔGR Assets	0.00	−0.01	−0.05	0.00	0.10+	0.05	0.36**	0.24**
29	ΔGR Employ	0.07	0.08	0.04	0.07	0.03	0.10+	0.16**	0.17**
30	ΔResid Income	0.19**	0.20**	0.20**	0.19**	0.15**	0.15**	0.13*	0.19**
31	ΔResid Inc ROI	0.19**	0.20**	0.19**	0.18**	0.15*	0.15*	0.13*	0.18**
32	ΔAsset Turn	0.30**	0.32**	0.20**	0.30**	0.33**	0.34**	0.29**	0.58**
33	ΔOCF/Eqty	0.09	0.09	0.08	0.09	0.14*	0.10	−0.04	0.01
34	ΔAlt Z Score	0.25**	0.23**	0.21**	0.24**	0.31**	0.32**	0.29**	0.22**
35	ΔPrice/Book	0.22**	0.20**	0.19**	0.21**	0.07	0.17**	0.13*	0.16**
36	ΔCAPM Rate	−0.09	−0.09	−0.09	−0.08	−0.14*	−0.08	−0.15**	−0.14*
37	1yr Rtn MA	0.23**	0.22**	0.20**	0.23**	0.21**	0.20**	0.29**	0.30*

The information content of growth measures

The growth measures that provided the greatest relative information about return to shareholders were the growth rate of sales, the change in the growth rate of sales and the change in the growth rate of operating expenses. The growth rate of total assets also provided significant relative information. The growth in sales has traditionally been used as an indicator of

27	28	29	30	31	32	33	34	35	36
0.05									
0.10^+	0.21^{**}								
0.02	-0.02	0.09							
0.01	-0.06	0.08	0.98^{**}						
0.10^+	0.05	0.15^*	0.24^{**}	0.23^{**}					
0.25^{**}	-0.09	-0.08	-0.11^+	-0.11^+	0.11^+				
0.18^{**}	0.09	0.10^+	0.21^{**}	0.20^{**}	0.42^{**}	0.07			
0.15^*	-0.02	0.00	0.23^{**}	0.24^{**}	0.26^{**}	0.15^{**}	0.52^{**}		
-0.07	-0.17^{**}	-0.02	-0.21^{**}	-0.20^{**}	-0.17^{**}	-0.04	-0.35^{**}	-0.35^{**}	
0.12^*	0.21^{**}	0.15^{**}	0.33^{**}	0.31^{**}	0.33^{**}	0.06	0.71^{**}	0.63^{**}	-0.48^{**}

organizational performance. However, few researchers have used the growth in total assets as an indicator of organizational performance, even though acquiring slack resources has been shown to be associated with higher levels of firm performance (Chakravarthy, 1986). It is, therefore, understandable why the growth rate of assets provided relatively high information about return to shareholders as well as the growth rate of sales.

Table 8.9   Correlations for three-year high/low sample[a]

	Variable	1	2	3	4	5	6	7	8
1	ROA								
2	ROE	0.77**							
3	ROS	0.77**	0.59**						
4	ROI	0.97**	0.79**	0.70**					
5	EBITDA ROI	0.80**	0.64**	0.48**	0.85**				
6	Op Margin	0.69**	0.53**	0.66**	0.65**	0.60**			
7	GR Sales	0.16+	0.20*	0.02	0.15	0.19*	0.14		
8	GR Op Exp	0.15+	0.21*	0.01	0.14	0.18+	0.12	0.93**	
9	GR OCF	0.08	0.00	0.09	0.05	0.05	0.05	0.18+	0.07
10	GR Assets	0.27**	0.18*	0.30**	0.25**	0.25**	0.24**	0.46**	0.52**
11	GR Employ	0.17+	0.15	0.05	0.15	0.13	0.08	0.56**	0.60**
12	Resid Income	0.42**	0.39**	0.50**	0.41**	0.31**	0.39**	0.06	0.08
13	Resid Inc ROI	0.93**	0.82**	0.68**	0.95**	0.82**	0.67**	0.16+	0.12
14	Asset Turn	0.14	0.17+	−0.07	0.17+	0.18*	−0.27**	0.05	0.09
15	OCF/Eqty	0.49**	0.64**	0.37**	0.51**	0.67**	0.48**	0.28**	0.24**
16	Alt Z Score	0.33**	0.12	0.09	0.28**	0.22*	0.14	0.26**	0.28**
17	Price/Book	0.24**	0.42**	0.01	0.29**	0.31**	0.21*	0.22*	0.21*
18	CAPM Rate	−0.47**	−0.45**	−0.49**	−0.44**	−0.35**	−0.39**	−0.05	0.04
19	ΔROA	0.48**	0.38**	0.34**	0.45**	0.35**	0.31**	0.22*	0.10
20	ΔROE	0.46**	0.39**	0.28**	0.43**	0.36**	0.29**	0.16+	0.07
21	ΔROS	0.45**	0.33**	0.39**	0.41**	0.33**	0.27**	−0.03	−0.08
22	ΔROI	0.46**	0.37**	0.31**	0.43**	0.35**	0.29**	0.17+	0.06
23	ΔEBITDA ROI	0.31**	0.24**	0.32**	0.28**	0.17+	0.17+	0.49**	0.31**
24	ΔOp Margin	0.30**	0.19*	0.24**	0.30**	0.25**	0.28**	0.28**	0.15
25	ΔGR Sales	0.00	−0.01	−0.02	−0.03	−0.12	−0.09	0.15+	0.14
26	ΔGR Op Exp	0.19*	0.23**	0.19*	0.22*	0.24**	0.15+	0.21*	0.22*
27	ΔGR OCF	0.06	0.03	0.05	0.03	0.05	0.07	0.14	0.14
28	ΔGR Assets	0.27**	0.28**	0.22*	0.30**	0.24**	0.22*	0.13	0.11
29	ΔGR Employ	−0.04	0.08	0.01	−0.05	−0.16+	−0.08	0.13	0.17+
30	ΔResid Income	0.22*	0.22*	0.10	0.23*	0.25**	0.15	0.26**	0.20*
31	ΔResid Inc ROI	0.22*	0.20*	0.08	0.21*	0.24**	0.13	0.18+	0.11
32	ΔAsset Turn	0.21*	0.25**	0.07	0.20*	0.19*	0.09	0.54**	0.41**
33	ΔOCF/Eqty	0.19*	0.12	0.16+	0.18+	0.14	0.07	0.35**	0.23**
34	ΔAlt Z Score	0.48**	0.39**	0.50**	0.44**	0.36**	0.27**	0.21*	0.10
35	ΔPrice/Book	0.23*	0.13	0.20*	0.22*	0.21*	0.18+	0.20*	0.06
36	ΔCAPM Rate	−0.27**	−0.20*	−0.26**	−0.23**	−0.17+	−0.14	−0.06	−0.03
37	3yr Rtn MA	0.50**	0.47**	0.49**	0.46**	0.40**	0.35**	0.30**	0.21*

Note: [a] $n = 120$; $+p < 0.10$; $*p < 0.05$; $**p < 0.01$.

The information content of efficiency measures

The change in asset turnover provided a significant amount of information about return to shareholders. This is consistent with the amount of information provided by the growth rate of sales and assets. Since the

9	10	11	12	13	14	15	16	17	18
0.29**									
0.30**	0.53**								
0.02	0.03	0.02							
0.05	0.20*	0.13	0.40**						
−0.07	−0.08	0.01	0.07	0.19*					
0.10	−0.09	0.03	0.20*	0.58**	0.08				
0.04	0.20*	0.26**	0.16+	0.12	0.03	−0.04			
0.07	0.11	0.17+	0.11	0.28**	−0.12	0.34**	0.34**		
−0.03	−0.04	0.01	−0.35**	−0.64**	−0.18*	−0.33**	0.18+	0.04	
0.19*	0.17+	0.09	0.11	0.53**	0.18*	0.32**	0.07	0.17+	−0.53**
0.17+	0.09	0.04	0.09	0.51**	0.22*	0.34**	0.06	0.14	−0.51**
0.14	0.14	−0.04	0.11	0.48**	0.17+	0.25**	−0.01	0.12	−0.49**
0.17+	0.11	0.05	0.09	0.51**	0.20*	0.32**	0.05	0.17+	−0.52**
0.31**	0.27**	0.23*	0.13	0.37**	0.08	0.24**	0.01	0.14	−0.48**
0.28**	0.20*	0.06	0.06	0.35**	0.09	0.25**	0.07	0.23*	−0.29**
0.05	0.06	0.17+	−0.27**	−0.01	0.14	−0.02	−0.05	−0.20*	−0.11
0.16+	0.21*	0.17+	0.11	0.28**	0.16+	0.26**	0.02	0.03	−0.31**
0.30**	0.09	0.16+	0.00	0.05	0.05	0.05	0.02	0.02	0.00
0.10	0.22*	0.14	0.15+	0.35**	0.08	0.16+	0.05	0.16+	−0.32**
0.07	0.01	0.23*	0.06	−0.01	0.03	0.04	−0.06	0.07	−0.07
0.17+	0.17+	0.23*	0.15+	0.31**	0.20*	0.23*	−0.06	0.09	−0.36**
0.22*	0.13	0.17+	0.14	0.25**	0.17+	0.22*	−0.04	0.00	−0.27**
0.06	−0.23*	0.17+	0.13	0.29**	0.21*	0.38**	−0.02	0.16+	−0.41**
0.03	0.01	0.15+	0.07	0.26**	0.06	0.22*	−0.07	0.10	−0.34**
0.03	0.16+	0.09	0.20*	0.52**	0.19*	0.34**	0.01	−0.01	−0.64**
0.21*	−0.04	0.04	0.09	0.35**	0.18*	0.36**	−0.14	0.13	−0.54**
0.02	0.06	0.05	−0.25**	−0.28**	−0.23**	−0.10	0.00	−0.03	0.48**
0.16+	0.28**	0.22*	0.23*	0.54**	0.06	0.45**	0.02	0.09	−0.63**

ratio is calculated by the change in sales divided by the change in assets, this result is logical. Interestingly, the combination of the change in the two variables provides more information than does the change in either of the individual variables, suggesting that there is unique information provided by both the change in sales and the change in total assets.

Table 8.9 (continued)

	Variable	19	20	21	22	23	24	25	26
1	ROA								
2	ROE								
3	ROS								
4	ROI								
5	EBITDA ROI								
6	Op Margin								
7	GR Sales								
8	GR Op Exp								
9	GR OCF								
10	GR Assets								
11	GR Employ								
12	Resid Income								
13	Resid Inc ROI								
14	Asset Turn								
15	OCF/Eqty								
16	Alt Z Score								
17	Price/Book								
18	CAPM Rate								
19	ΔROA								
20	ΔROE	0.93**							
21	ΔROS	0.85**	0.78**						
22	ΔROI	0.96**	0.98**	0.80**					
23	ΔEBITDA ROI	0.68**	0.54**	0.42**	0.62**				
24	ΔOp Margin	0.53**	0.44**	0.37**	0.50**	0.61**			
25	ΔGR Sales	0.17+	0.15+	0.10	0.16+	0.19*	-0.07		
26	ΔGR Op Exp	0.16+	0.14	0.09	0.15	0.22*	0.12	0.22*	
27	ΔGR OCF	0.06	0.03	0.03	0.04	0.14	0.29**	0.00	0.05
28	ΔGR Assets	0.40**	0.30**	0.39**	0.31**	0.29**	0.16+	0.18*	0.33**
29	ΔGR Employ	0.04	0.02	0.01	0.03	0.14	0.01	0.09	0.18+
30	ΔResid Income	0.41**	0.38**	0.22*	0.39**	0.44**	0.19*	0.17+	0.27**
31	ΔResid Inc ROI	0.38**	0.37**	0.21*	0.37**	0.39**	0.14	0.16+	0.19*
32	ΔAsset Turn	0.38**	0.37**	0.14	0.39**	0.57**	0.25**	0.28**	0.22*
33	ΔOCF/Eqty	0.44**	0.35**	0.31**	0.43**	0.68**	0.30**	0.19*	0.15+
34	ΔAlt Z Score	0.68**	0.62**	0.55**	0.67**	0.69**	0.31**	0.21*	0.18*
35	ΔPrice/Book	0.47**	0.44**	0.40**	0.47**	0.55**	0.40**	0.18*	0.22*
36	ΔCAPM Rate	-0.29**	-0.26**	-0.26**	-0.27**	-0.25**	-0.15	-0.13	-0.19*
37	3yr Rtn MA	0.57**	0.52**	0.43**	0.55**	0.62**	0.32**	0.19*	0.28**

The information content of cash flow measures

The only significant cash flow measure for the high/low sample was operating cash flow to equity. The relative information provided by this measure was considerably less than that provided by the profit, growth and efficiency measures. Accordingly, using any of these cash flow measures in isolation is questionable. Further, the relatively high correlation between operating

27	28	29	30	31	32	33	34	35	36
−0.06									
−0.03	0.11								
0.02	0.15⁺	0.10							
0.02	0.13	0.09	0.76**						
0.04	0.14	0.20*	0.36**	0.29**					
−0.05	0.17⁺	0.09	0.28**	0.23*	0.53**				
0.00	0.31**	−0.01	0.42**	0.35**	0.49**	0.58**			
0.07	0.28**	0.11	0.40**	0.36**	0.58**	0.51**	0.56**		
0.00	−0.03	0.04	−0.26**	−0.24**	−0.31**	−0.30**	−0.33**	−0.31**	
0.06	0.34**	0.12	0.42**	0.42**	0.43**	0.46**	0.77**	0.59**	−0.29**

cash flow to equity and return on equity (0.53 for the high/low sample) suggests that there might be little incremental information provided by this variable.

The information content of survival measures
Altman's Z-score and the change in Altman's Z-score both provided significant relative information about return to shareholders. In particular,

Measuring organizational performance

Table 8.10 Independent t-*test results comparing high- and low-performing firms*

Variable	Annual firm years[a]		Three-year periods[b]	
	Static score	Change score	Static score	Change score
Return on assets	-5.18^{**}	-4.83^{**}	-5.53^{**}	-7.54^{**}
Return on equity	-6.07^{**}	-4.96^{**}	-5.24^{**}	-6.81^{**}
Return on sales	-3.49^{**}	-4.27^{**}	-5.39^{**}	-4.83^{**}
Return on investment	-5.14^{**}	-4.76^{**}	-4.94^{**}	-7.22^{**}
EBITDA return on investment	-4.54^{**}	-3.14^{**}	-4.01^{**}	-8.16^{**}
Operating margin	-3.27^{**}	-3.19^{**}	-3.85^{**}	-3.75^{**}
Growth rate of sales	-5.29^{**}	-4.92^{**}	-3.35^{**}	-2.08^{*}
Growth rate of operating expenses	-2.84^{**}	-5.91^{**}	-2.33^{*}	-3.08^{**}
Growth rate of operating cash flow	-2.11^{*}	-2.43^{*}	-2.07^{*}	-0.99
Growth rate of total assets	-4.33^{**}	-3.36^{**}	-2.90^{**}	-3.68^{**}
Growth rate of employees	-3.30^{**}	-3.08^{**}	-2.27^{*}	-0.99
Residual income	-4.13^{**}	-5.68^{**}	-1.92^{+}	-5.08^{**}
Residual income return on investment	-6.53^{**}	-5.46^{**}	-6.24^{**}	-4.76^{**}
Asset turnover	-1.97^{+}	-6.85^{**}	-0.34	-4.88^{**}
Liabilities to total assets	0.19	1.55	0.28	3.02^{**}
Operating cash flow to equity	-3.62^{**}	-1.10	-4.50^{**}	-4.93^{**}
Free cash flow to equity	-1.08	-0.52	-1.16	0.07
Altman's Z-score	-4.17^{**}	-15.35^{**}	-0.22	-11.42^{**}
Price-to-book ratio	-6.58^{**}	-13.18^{**}	-0.66	-6.95^{**}
Cost of equity capital	7.60^{**}	10.34^{**}	8.01^{**}	3.26^{**}

Notes:
[a] $n = 300$.
[b] $n = 120$.
** $p < 0.01$.
* $p < 0.05$.
+ $p < 0.10$.

Table 8.11   *Results of regression analyses testing annual data relationship with market-adjusted returns*

Variable	Annual high/low sample[a]			All firm years[b]		
	Adj. R^2	F	Coefficient	Adj. R^2	F	Coefficient
Profitability measures						
Return on assets	0.10	34.45	0.32**	0.04	122.45	0.20**
Return on equity	0.12	41.39	0.35**	0.03	103.20	0.19**
Return on sales	0.05	15.46	0.22**	0.02	71.69	0.16**
Return on investment	0.10	32.69	0.31**	0.04	113.96	0.20**
EBITDA return on investment	0.07	23.81	0.27**	0.02	72.72	0.16**
Operating margin	0.04	12.38	0.20**	0.01	42.32	0.12**
Residual income	0.04	14.50	0.22**	0.00	11.13	0.06**
Residual income return on investment	0.13	47.02	0.37**	0.05	154.70	0.23**
Δreturn on assets	0.08	27.33	0.29**	0.03	80.05	0.16**
Δreturn on equity	0.08	27.34	0.29**	0.03	76.93	0.16**
Δreturn on sales	0.07	22.66	0.27**	0.03	76.64	0.16**
Δreturn on investment	0.08	26.41	0.29**	0.03	81.09	0.17**
ΔEBITDA return on investment	0.04	13.09	0.21**	0.01	21.92	0.09**
Δoperating margin	0.04	12.90	0.20**	0.02	61.97	0.15**
Δresidual income	0.11	36.32	0.33**	0.04	118.57	0.20**
Δresidual income return on investment	0.09	30.95	0.31**	0.04	108.48	0.19**
Growth measures						
Growth rate of sales	0.08	27.35	0.29**	0.02	58.31	0.14**
Growth rate of operating expenses	0.02	6.31	0.14*	0.00	10.44	0.06**
Growth rate of total assets	0.07	22.30	0.26**	0.02	62.82	0.15**
Growth rate of employees	0.04	13.36	0.21**	0.02	44.38	0.12**
Δgrowth rate of sales	0.08	27.67	0.29**	0.01	27.15	0.10**
Δgrowth rate of operating expenses	0.09	30.27	0.30**	0.02	60.27	0.14**
Δgrowth rate of total assets	0.04	13.76	0.21**	0.01	24.19	0.09**
Δgrowth rate of employees	0.02	6.74	0.15**	0.01	22.40	0.09**
Efficiency measures						
Asset turnover	0.01	3.96	0.11*	0.01	38.08	0.11**
Δasset turnover	0.11	36.71	0.33**	0.03	78.70	0.16**

Table 8.11   (continued)

Variable	Annual high/low sample[a]			All firm years[b]		
	Adj. R^2	F	Coefficient	Adj. R^2	F	Coefficient
Cash flow measures						
Operating cash flow to equity	0.03	10.65	0.19**	0.01	39.68	0.12**
Growth rate of operating cash flow	0.02	6.15	0.14*	0.00	10.57	0.06**
ΔGrowth rate of operating cash flow	0.01	4.47	0.12*	0.01	14.81	0.07**
Survival measures						
Altman's Z-score	0.08	25.81	0.28**	0.02	64.91	0.15**
ΔAltman's Z-score	0.50	299.90	0.71**	0.36	1,637.18	0.60**
Market-based measures						
Price-to-book ratio	0.13	43.72	0.36**	0.03	104.36	0.19**
Cost of equity capital	0.11	38.38	−0.34**	0.04	123.09	−0.20**
Δprice-to-book ratio	0.39	194.30	0.63**	0.32	1,344.30	0.56**
Δcost of equity capital	0.23	88.61	−0.48**	0.11	372.86	−0.34**

Notes:
[a] $n = 300$.
[b] $n = 2,894$.
**$p < 0.01$; *$p < 0.05$.

the change in Altman's Z-score provided the greatest amount of relative information about the return to shareholders. Because this measure has five components, including asset turnover, a profit measure (EBIT return on assets), a leverage measure, a working capital measure, and most importantly, a market-value measure, and since it has already been shown that profitability and asset turnover provide significant relative information about return to shareholders, a composite measure such as Altman's Z-score should logically provide even more relative information. The more interesting observation is that the change in Altman's Z-score provides over five times the relative information as does the static measure. This is consistent with the premise that value creation involves a change in organizational state. Four of the five components of the static Altman's Z-score are based upon single point-in-time observations such as working capital to assets. Consequently, the static measure provides information primarily about the organization on a single date, while the change in the measure represents the change in the organization over a period of time.

The information content of market-based measures

Cost of equity capital provided significant relative information about return to shareholders both as a static measure and as a change score. As with Altman's Z-score, the change score provided significantly more relative information because it represents a change in the condition of the organization. Cost of equity capital contains a market component, since it uses the covariation with the market over the prior 24 to 60 months in its calculation. So long as this covariation remains relatively consistent, the return to shareholders will have a strong association with the cost of equity capital. Further, the change in the cost of equity capital implicitly includes the change in the covariation with the market, strengthening the association with return to shareholders. For non-public companies, a proxy for the covariation with the market return must be estimated to calculate the cost of equity capital. This may be accomplished by using betas from comparable public companies or by using expert opinions. However, the answer to this question is beyond the scope of this research and will remain an open question for future investigation.

The ratio of price-to-book value provided significant relative information about return to shareholders both as a static measure and as a change score. The price-to-book ratio is an approximation of the unrealized value of organizational assets and opportunities (options) at a point in time. Therefore, the static measure represents unrealized economic value based upon prior organizational actions, while the change in the price-to-book ratio represents the creation of new unrealized asset appreciation and opportunities, as valued by the market. In other words, the change in the price-to-book value represents organizational performance other than financial, such as operational and stakeholder performance as proposed by Venkatraman and Ramanujam (1986). Accordingly, it is not surprising that the change in the price-to-book ratio provides three times greater relative information about the return to shareholders than the static measure.

The Results of Regression Analyses Testing the Relative Information Content of Three-year Performance Measures

The same six categories of measures were also tested for their relative information content using three-year performance measures, that is: (i) profitability measures; (ii) growth measures; (iii) efficiency measures; (iv) cash flow measures; (v) survival measures; and (vi) market-based measures. In general, the relative information content of three-year period financial performance measures was considerably higher than the equivalent annual period measures. This suggests that there were significant short-term fluctuations in financial performance that were smoothed by the longer timeframe. As with the annual data, the relative information for the high/low sample was considerably greater than for the database as a whole. Another general observation is that profitability and cash flow measures were much more significant over the longer period than for the shorter annual periods. This suggests that markets tolerate short-term fluctuations in these dimensions, but they value execution over the longer term. In other words, the conversion of opportunity into economic value creation appears to be more important over longer periods. Table 8.12 presents the results of the regression analyses for three-year periods.

The information content of profitability measures
The change in EBITDA return on investment provided the most information about return to shareholders among the profitability measures. This is quite different from the findings for the annual periods. EBITDA is often used as a proxy for operating cash flow and the increased explanatory power of this measure parallels the increase in the explanatory power of operating cash flow return on equity. This suggests that over longer periods, cash flow takes on increased significance to investors.

Return on sales and operating margin also provided significantly more information about return to shareholders over the longer term, suggesting that spending discipline becomes more important over the longer term. The change in return on assets, return on equity and return on investment provided greater relative information than the corresponding static profitability measures. This suggests that the change in organizational execution on opportunities becomes more important in generating return to shareholders.

The information content of growth measures
Growth rates and the change in these rates do not seem to provide greater information over the longer term than in the short term. The notable exception was that the growth rate of sales provided much more information about return to shareholders for the entire database.

The information content of efficiency measures
The change in asset turnover provided a significant amount of information about return to shareholders. As with the annual periods, this is consistent with the amount of information provided by the growth rate of sales and assets, the numerator and the denominator in calculating asset turnover.

The information content of leverage measures
The change in the leverage measure liabilities to total assets provided significant information about the return to shareholders. Further, as

Table 8.12   Results of regression analyses testing three-year data relationship with market-adjusted returns

Variable	Three-year high/low sample[a]			All three-year periods[b]		
	Adj. R^2	F	Coefficient	Adj. R^2	F	Coefficient
Profitability measures						
Return on assets	0.24	38.59	0.50**	0.12	129.07	0.35**
Return on equity	0.22	33.51	0.47**	0.10	98.00	0.31**
Return on sales	0.24	37.88	0.49**	0.08	86.09	0.29**
Return on investment	0.21	31.66	0.46**	0.10	106.48	0.32**
EBITDA return on investment	0.15	22.69	0.40**	0.08	86.07	0.29**
Operating margin	0.12	16.62	0.35**	0.06	54.38	0.24**
Residual income	0.05	6.55	0.23*	0.01	9.81	0.10**
Residual income return on investment	0.29	49.16	0.54**	0.16	178.11	0.40**
Δreturn on assets	0.32	56.80	0.57**	0.13	140.45	0.36**
Δreturn on equity	0.27	44.36	0.52**	0.12	124.70	0.35**
Δreturn on sales	0.18	26.87	0.43**	0.09	89.21	0.30**
Δreturn on investment	0.29	50.59	0.55**	0.14	152.39	0.38**
ΔEBITDA return on investment	0.38	72.54	0.62**	0.28	352.06	0.53**
Δoperating margin	0.09	13.39	0.32**	0.09	87.36	0.29**
Δresidual income	0.17	25.56	0.42**	0.08	75.95	0.28**
Δresidual income return on investment	0.17	24.68	0.42**	0.10	107.77	0.32**
Growth measures						
Growth rate of sales	0.08	11.34	0.30**	0.07	68.97	0.26**
Growth rate of operating expenses	0.04	5.43	0.21*	0.02	22.70	0.16**
Growth rate of total assets	0.07	9.82	0.28*	0.03	31.55	0.18**
Growth rate of employees	0.04	6.15	0.22**	0.03	32.01	0.18**
Δgrowth rate of sales	0.03	4.58	0.19*	0.02	21.86	0.15**
Δgrowth rate of operating expenses	0.07	10.18	0.28**	0.00	4.87	0.07*
Δgrowth rate of total assets	0.11	15.94	0.35**	0.04	40.80	0.21**
Efficiency measures						
Δasset turnover	0.18	27.08	0.43**	0.09	95.56	0.31**
Leverage measure						
Δliabilities to total assets	0.08	11.88	−0.30**	0.02	18.20	−0.14**

Table 8.12   (continued)

Variable	Three-year high/low sample[a]			All three-year periods[b]		
	Adj. R^2	F	Coefficient	Adj. R^2	F	Coefficient
Cash flow measures						
Operating cash flow to equity	0.20	30.71	0.45**	0.06	59.07	0.25**
Growth rate of operating cash flow	0.02	2.95	0.16+	0.02	15.35	0.13**
Δoperating cash flow to equity	0.20	31.12	0.46**	0.02	24.09	0.16**
Survival measures						
ΔAltman's Z-score	0.59	172.73	0.77**	0.45	767.59	0.67**
Market-based measures						
Cost of equity capital	0.39	77.76	−0.63**	0.20	231.00	−0.45**
Δprice-to-book ratio	0.35	63.97	0.59**	0.30	395.16	0.55**
Δcost of equity capital	0.08	11.12	−0.29**	0.06	55.43	−0.24**

Notes:
[a] $n = 120$.
[b] $n = 925$.
**$p < 0.01$; *$p < 0.05$; +$p < 0.10$.

leverage increased, return to shareholders decreased, as evidenced by the sign of the standardized regression coefficient. This is consistent with the information provided by Altman's Z-score since higher leverage levels can suggest that the organization has assumed greater risk (Penman, 2001).

The information content of cash flow measures
The static and change score measures of operating cash flow to equity, as well as the growth rate of operating cash flow, provided significant information about return to shareholders. As with the annual periods, the relatively high correlation between operating cash flow to equity and return on equity and EBITDA return on investment (both as a static and a change score measure) suggests that there might be little incremental information provided by this variable.

The information content of survival measures
As was the case with the annual periods (and for the same reasons), the composite measure change in Altman's Z-score individually provided the greatest relative information about the market-adjusted return to shareholders.

The information content of market-based measures

The relative information provided by the change in price-to-book value was very similar to the annual data findings. However, the relative information provided by the static measure price-to-book value was not significant for the three-year data. This suggests that the creation of new opportunities is more important to creating shareholder value than simply maintaining a static level of opportunities.

For the three-year periods, the cost of equity capital provided more relative information than the change in the cost of equity capital. This is the opposite of the findings for the annual periods. This may be a result of using an average cost of capital over the three-year period that incorporates the average beta for the period. This appears to have a greater association with return to shareholders than the change in the cost of capital, which would capture information only about the change in beta over the three-year period, but not include information about the actual covariation with the market over the entire performance period.

THE INCREMENTAL AND RELATIVE INFORMATION CONTENT OF STATIC MEASURES VERSUS CHANGE SCORES

Static measures represent values of an indicator at a given point in time or over a specific period of time. Conversely, change scores represent the change in static measures. In the context of this research, performance is viewed as the creation of shareholder value, and creating this value implies a change in condition. Therefore, measuring organizational financial performance involves measuring a change in condition. However, to date organizational financial performance has been measured almost exclusively by static measures in entrepreneurship and strategic management research, as the summary of past empirical research in Chapter 2 indicated.

There are two questions yet to be investigated in the context of static measures and change scores. First, does the change in the underlying static measure of organizational financial performance provide additional information beyond that provided by the static measure alone? Second, does the change in the underlying static measure provide more relative information about organizational financial performance than the static measure?

The Incremental Information Content of Change Scores

The following exploratory null hypothesis was tested to examine the first question:

H3:   The change score associated with the change in a static measure of
organizational financial performance will provide statistically significant
incremental information with respect to market-adjusted return to shareholders.

To test whether the change scores associated with the static measures provided statistically significant incremental information, the difference between
a simple regression of the static variable with market-adjusted return to shareholders, and a regression that included both the static measure and the associated change score, was tested for statistical significance for both the annual
and three-year period high/low samples. Only those measures found to be
significant in the last section were tested. The static variable was tested first
and then the change score added to the regression equation, because static
measures have been typically used in previous research. Thus, this hypothesis
explores the *added* information of change scores in addition to the information from the static measures. Table 8.13 presents the regression results.

Results of the Tests for Annual Periods

Regressions were run both for the static measures and for the combination
of the static measures and the corresponding change scores for the 18
financial performance measures previously found to be statistically
significant in this research. The change scores for each static variable provided statistically significant incremental information for 14 out of 18
measures in the annual high/low sample at the $p < 0.05$ level. The four variables that change scores did not add incremental information for were the
growth rate of cash flow, the growth rate of total assets, the growth rate of
employees and operating cash flow to equity. Three of these four variables
were growth measures. This indicates that the growth rates provided more
information about the change in the condition of the organization than the
change in the rate of growth.

   In the case of measures that are not growth measures, 12 of the 13 change
scores provided statistically significant incremental information. Given that
only one change score was correlated with the corresponding underlying
variable at greater than 0.50, it is reasonable to surmise that the change
scores not only provide incremental information, but are part of a separate
organizational performance construct.

   The question of collinearity must be addressed in any instance where the
change of a variable is included in a regression with the underlying
measure. Tests for collinearity, as suggested by Pedhazur (1997), were performed by examining plots of residuals, tolerances and variance inflation
factors for each multiple regression equation. All of these procedures

Table 8.13   *Results of regression analyses to determine the incremental information content of change scores*

Variable	Model 1			Model 2			
	Static coeff.	F	R^2	Static coeff.	Change coeff.	ΔF	ΔR^2
Annual high/low sample[a]							
Return on assets	0.32**	34.45	0.10	0.26**	0.21**	14.55	0.04**
Return on equity	0.35**	41.39	0.12	0.28**	0.19**	10.85	0.03**
Return on sales	0.22**	15.48	0.05	0.16**	0.22**	15.13	0.05**
Return on investment	0.31**	32.69	0.10	0.25**	0.21**	14.08	0.04**
EBITDA return on investment	0.27**	23.81	0.07	0.23**	0.14*	5.78	0.02*
Operating margin	0.20**	12.38	0.04	0.13*	0.14*	4.65	0.02*
Residual income	0.22**	14.50	0.04	0.13*	0.29**	26.78	0.08**
Residual income return on investment	0.37**	47.02	0.14	0.30**	0.21**	14.31	0.04**
Growth rate of sales	0.29**	27.35	0.08	0.21**	0.21**	12.28	0.04**
Growth rate of operating expenses	0.14*	6.31	0.02	−0.19	0.31**	23.47	0.07**
Growth rate of operating cash flow	0.14*	6.15	0.02	0.11+	0.08	1.54	0.01
Growth rate of total assets	0.26**	22.30	0.07	0.21**	0.10	2.63	0.01
Growth rate of employees	0.21**	13.36	0.04	0.18**	0.09	2.24	0.01
Asset turnover	0.11*	3.96	0.01	0.08	0.32**	34.81	0.10**
Operating cash flow to equity	0.19**	10.65	0.04	0.18**	0.02	0.10	0.00
Altman's Z-score	0.28**	25.81	0.08	0.07	0.68**	256.31	0.43**
Price-to-book ratio	0.39**	43.72	0.13	0.20**	0.57**	158.85	0.30**
Cost of equity capital	−0.34**	38.38	0.11	−0.14*	−0.41**	51.44	0.13**
Three-year period high/low sample[b]							
Return on assets	0.50**	38.59	0.25	0.29**	0.43**	27.21	0.14**
Return on equity	0.47**	33.51	0.22	0.31**	0.40**	24.62	0.14**
Return on sales	0.49**	37.88	0.24	0.38**	0.28**	11.59	0.07**
Return on investment	0.46**	31.66	0.21	0.28**	0.43**	27.60	0.15**
EBITDA return on investment	0.40**	22.69	0.16	0.31**	0.57**	68.39	0.31**
Operating margin	0.35**	16.62	0.12	0.29**	0.24**	7.55	0.05**
Residual income	0.23*	6.55	0.05	0.17*	0.40**	22.54	0.15**
Residual income return on investment	0.54**	49.16	0.29	0.48**	0.30**	15.59	0.08**
Growth rate of sales	0.30**	11.34	0.08	0.27**	0.15+	2.95	0.02+

Table 8.13   (continued)

Variable	Model 1			Model 2			
	Static coeff.	F	R^2	Static coeff.	Change coeff.	ΔF	ΔR^2
Growth rate of operating expenses	0.21^*	5.43	0.04	0.16^+	0.25^{**}	7.66	0.06^{**}
Growth rate of operating cash flow	0.16^+	2.95	0.02	0.15	0.01	0.02	0.00
Growth rate of total assets	0.28^{**}	9.82	0.08	0.21^*	0.30^{**}	11.81	0.09^{**}
Growth rate of employees	0.22^*	6.15	0.05	0.21^*	0.07	0.63	0.01
Asset turnover	0.06	0.45	0.00	-0.031	0.44^{**}	26.47	0.18^{**}
Liabilities to total assets	-0.03	0.11	0.00	0.01	-0.30^{**}	11.66	0.09^{**}
Operating cash flow to equity	0.45^{**}	30.71	0.21	0.37^{**}	0.38^{**}	23.73	0.13^{**}
Altman's Z-score	0.02	0.04	0.00	0.01	0.77^{**}	171.31	0.59^{**}
Price-to-book ratio	0.09	0.99	0.01	0.02	0.59^{**}	62.00	0.34^{**}
Cost of equity capital	-0.63^{**}	77.76	0.40	-0.63^{**}	0.01	0.01	0.00

Notes:
[a] $n = 300$.
[b] $n = 120$.
$** \ p < 0.01; * \ p < 0.05; \ ^+ p < 0.10$.

clearly indicated that there were no problems with collinearity. However, in the case of the growth rate of operating expenses, the signs of the static variable and the change score were inverse, which is an indication that there could be a problem with collinearity. Further investigation revealed that the static variable was not significant in the equation, indicating that the change score by itself included substantially all of the explanation of variance in the dependent variable provided by the two independent variables. Accordingly, the static variable growth rate of operating expenses should be excluded in a model of organizational financial performance that includes the change in the growth of operating expenses. The signs of all of the other combinations of static and change scores were the same in the annual high/low sample and in the direction anticipated.

Results of the Tests for Three-year Periods

As indicated in Table 8.13, regressions were run on each of the 19 three-year financial performance measures previously found to be statistically significant in this research. Once again, the change scores provided statistically significant incremental information for 15 out of 19 variables at $p <$ 0.05. The four variables for which change scores did not add significant incremental information were the growth rate of sales, the growth rate of operating cash flow, the growth rate of employees and the cost of equity capital. Once again, three of these four variables were growth measures. This again suggests that growth rates provide more information about the change in condition of the organization than the change in the rate of growth. For non-growth rate measures, the change scores provided statistically significant incremental information in 12 of 13 cases. In the three-year period high/low sample, no change score was correlated with its corresponding underlying variable at greater than 0.50. Again, it is reasonable to surmise that the change scores not only provide incremental information, but are part of a separate organizational performance construct.

Once again, tests for collinearity were performed by examining plots of residuals, tolerances and variance inflation factors for each multiple regression equation. No collinearity problems were detected. Thus, while both asset turnover and liabilities to assets had conflicting directions of the signs on the standardized coefficients, in both cases the static measure coefficient was not significant in the equation, indicating that the change score by itself included all of the significant explanation provided by the two independent measures of variance in the dependent variable. Accordingly, the static variables asset turnover and liabilities to assets should be excluded in a model of organizational financial performance that includes the change scores for these variables. The sign of the change in cost of equity capital was also opposite of what would logically be expected. Again, the coefficient of the change score measure in model 2 was not significant. All of the signs of the other combinations of static and change scores were the same, and in the anticipated direction, for the annual high/low sample.

In summary, it is reasonable to conclude that change scores represent one or more distinct dimensions of organizational financial performance. Further, in cases where either the static measure or the change score do not provide statistically significant incremental explanation of variance in the dependent variable, the measure that has greater relative information should be retained and the other measure excluded in a model of organizational financial performance.

The Relative Information Content of Static Measures versus Change Scores

The following exploratory null hypothesis was tested to examine the second question:

H4:   The relative information content of change scores will be statistically significantly greater than the relative information content of the corresponding static measures, with respect to market-adjusted return to
shareholders.

To test the relative information content of static measures versus change
scores, the R-square of the simple regression of each measure and the
market-adjusted return to shareholders were compared. The measure with
the higher R-square provides greater relative information about variation in
the dependent measure (Chen and Dodd, 2001). Table 8.14 presents the
results of the simple regressions for the annual high/low sample and the
three-year period high/low samples, respectively. The results of these regressions were consistent with the results of the independent t-tests. The same
variables that did not discriminate between the high- and low-performing
groups did not have significant R-square values in the simple regressions.

   With respect to the relative information content of static measures versus
change scores, the only clear pattern that emerges from the data is that for
point-in-time measures, such as Altman's Z-score, price-to-book value and
residual income, the change scores consistently provided more information
about variation in the dependent variable than the static measures.

   In the case of different profitability and growth measures, the evidence
was mixed. In the annual high/low sample, the static profitability measures
generally provided more information than the change scores, while in the
three-year period high/low sample, just the opposite occurred. No clear
pattern emerged with the growth measures. Consequently, the null hypothesis that change scores would provide relatively more information than the
static measures can only be supported with respect to the point-in-time
measures. Otherwise, the data support the previous conclusion that
the change scores represent distinct dimensions of organizational financial
performance.

CHAPTER SUMMARY AND CONCLUSIONS

Chapter 8 presented the results of statistical tests of the relative and incremental information content of various measures of financial performance
relative to the criterion market-adjusted return to shareholders. First, a
comparison of the use of average versus ending balances for the measures
return on assets, return on equity, return on investment and EBITDA return
on investment was performed. It was found that there was no significant
difference in the relative information provided by these measures calculated
using ending balances as compared with the same measures calculated using

Table 8.14   Results of regression analyses to determine the relative information content of change scores

Variable	Static measures			Change score measures		
	R^2	F	Coefficient	R^2	F	Coefficient
Annual high/low sample[a]						
Return on assets	0.10	34.45	0.32**	0.08	27.33	0.29**
Return on equity	0.12	41.39	0.35**	0.08	27.34	0.29**
Return on sales	0.05	15.46	0.22**	0.07	22.66	0.27**
Return on investment	0.10	32.69	0.31**	0.08	26.41	0.29**
EBITDA return on investment	0.07	23.81	0.27**	0.04	13.09	0.21**
Operating margin	0.04	12.38	0.20**	0.04	12.90	0.20**
Growth rate of sales	0.08	27.35	0.29**	0.09	27.67	0.29**
Growth rate of operating expenses	0.02	6.31	0.14*	0.09	30.27	0.30**
Growth rate of operating cash flow	0.02	6.15	0.14*	0.02	4.47	0.12*
Growth rate of total assets	0.07	22.30	0.26**	0.04	13.76	0.21**
Growth rate of employees	0.04	13.36	0.21**	0.02	6.74	0.15*
Residual income	0.04	14.50	0.22**	0.11	36.32	0.33**
Residual income return on investment	0.14	47.02	0.37**	0.09	30.95	0.31**
Asset turnover	0.01	3.96	0.11*	0.11	36.71	0.33**
Operating cash flow to equity	0.04	10.65	0.19**	0.00	1.18	0.06
Altman's Z-score	0.08	25.81	0.28**	0.50	299.90	0.71**
Price-to-book ratio	0.13	43.72	0.36**	0.40	194.30	0.63**
Cost of equity capital	0.11	38.38	−0.34**	0.23	88.61	−0.48**
Three-year period high/low sample[b]						
Return on assets	0.25	38.59	0.50**	0.33	56.80	0.57**
Return on equity	0.22	33.51	0.47**	0.27	44.36	0.52**
Return on sales	0.24	37.88	0.49**	0.19	26.87	0.43**
Return on investment	0.21	31.66	0.46**	0.30	50.59	0.55**
EBITDA return on investment	0.16	22.69	0.40**	0.38	72.54	0.62**
Operating margin	0.12	16.62	0.35**	0.10	13.39	0.32**
Growth rate of sales	0.08	11.34	0.30**	0.04	4.58	0.19*
Growth rate of operating expenses	0.04	5.43	0.21*	0.08	10.18	0.28**

Table 8.14   (continued)

Variable	Static measures			Change score measures		
	R^2	F	Coefficient	R^2	F	Coefficient
Growth rate of operating cash flow	0.02	2.95	0.16^+	0.00	0.42	0.06
Growth rate of total assets	0.08	9.82	0.28^{**}	0.12	15.94	0.35^{**}
Growth rate of employees	0.05	6.15	0.22^*	0.02	1.75	0.12
Residual income	0.05	6.55	0.23^*	0.18	25.56	0.42^{**}
Residual income return on investment	0.29	49.16	0.54^{**}	0.17	24.68	0.42^{**}
Asset turnover	0.00	0.45	0.06	0.19	27.08	0.43^{**}
Liabilities to total assets	0.00	0.11	-0.03	0.09	11.88	-0.30^{**}
Operating cash flow to equity	0.21	30.71	0.45^{**}	0.21	31.12	0.46^{**}
Altman's Z-score	0.00	0.04	0.02	0.59	172.73	0.77^{**}
Price-to-book ratio	0.01	0.99	0.09	0.35	63.97	0.59^{**}
Cost of equity capital	0.40	77.76	-0.63^{**}	0.09	11.12	-0.29^{**}

Notes:
[a] $n = 300$.
[b] $n = 120$.
$** \, p<0.01; * \, p<0.05; \, ^+ p<0.10.$

average balances. However, the formulation of the ratios using average balances provided marginally more information, so for the purposes of this research, the average balance formulation of the four measures is used.

As the first step in developing a model of organizational financial performance, a set of 32 annual and 27 three-year variables were identified that discriminated between high- and low-performing companies, with respect to the referent market-adjusted return to shareholders, at $p < 0.01$. Of these variables, those that provided the most information about the referent with respect to the sample of all companies, not just the high and low performers, should provide the most power for research where shareholder value creation is the phenomenon of interest.

The relative information content of the measures that discriminated between high- and low-performing companies was tested. This study found that the change in Altman's Z-score was the single variable that provided the most relative information about market-adjusted return to shareholders. The market-based measures' change in price-to-book value and the change in the cost of equity capital provided the next most relative information. For each category of financial performance measures, the relative information content of each measure found to discriminate between the high- and low-performing companies was determined and presented.

Next, the incremental and relative information content of static measures as compared to change scores was tested. The results indicated that there were statistically significant differences between the static and the change scores for the same measure in almost every case. This implies that static and change scores represent distinct dimensions of financial performance and generally should not be included in the same construct. The change in point-in-time measures, such as price-to-book value, generally provided greater relative information than the corresponding static measure. However, for measures that incorporate periods of time, such as return on equity, there was no specific pattern as to whether the static or the change score measures provided greater relative information. Accordingly, in testing a multidimensional model of organizational financial performance, separate constructs for both the static and the change scores should be included and tested.

9. Developing and testing an overall model of organizational financial performance

This chapter presents the exploratory work performed to develop and test different potentially useful models of organizational financial performance for annual and three-year timeframes. These models are inferred from empirical data, and include primary constructs representing separate dimensions of organizational financial performance as well as the measures of those constructs. The first section of this chapter discusses the selection and grouping of various individual measures into financial performance constructs, as discussed in Chapter 5. Separate models are proposed for annual and three-year timeframes. The results of convergent and discriminant validity testing of the proposed constructs and their measures are presented in this section for both annual and three-year data. Based upon the findings of this validity testing, revised measurement models of organizational financial performance are proposed. The second section of the chapter discusses the results of testing the revised models of organizational financial performance using return to shareholders as the referent. Based upon the results of this test of the proposed models, revisions to the models are proposed and tested using a second high/low sample, and then retested again using all records in the database. The third section of the chapter discusses the development and testing of a composite measure representing organizational financial performance.

PROPOSING AND TESTING INDIVIDUAL CONSTRUCTS OF ORGANIZATIONAL FINANCIAL PERFORMANCE

The first step in empirically inferring a model of organizational financial performance was to group the variables that differentiated between the high- and low-performing companies into separate constructs and then to test the validity of the constructs. Each construct represents a statistically distinct dimension of organizational financial performance. Those constructs that were found to be valid, and their corresponding observable measures, constitute an initial model of organizational financial performance.

The measures that were found to discriminate between the high- and low-performing companies in Chapter 8 were grouped into 13 constructs according to the categories of performance developed and discussed in Chapters 4 and 5. Separate constructs were presented for static and change scores where the statistical analysis performed in Chapter 8 indicated that the change scores provided statistically significant incremental information over the corresponding static measures. The variables representing the growth rate of operating expenses and the change in the growth rate of employees were eliminated from their respective constructs for annual data, because of the low relative information the measures provided about return to shareholders.

Separate measurement models were proposed for annual and three-year timeframes. Table 9.1 presents the measures used for each construct for each timeframe. Based upon the grouping of measures into constructs, the following hypotheses were proposed with respect to convergent validity of the constructs:

H5a: The static measures return on assets, return on equity, return on investment, return on sales, EBITDA return on investment and operating margin load into a single profitability factor for both annual and three-year periods.

H5b: The change in the measures return on assets, return on equity, return on investment, return on sales, EBITDA return on investment and operating margin load into a single profitability change factor for both annual and three-year periods.

H5c: The static measures representing the growth rate of sales, growth rate of total assets and growth rate of employees load into a single growth factor for annual and three-year periods.

H5d: The change in the measures representing the growth rate of sales, growth rate of operating expenses and growth rate of total assets load into a single growth change factor for both annual and three-year periods.

H5e: The static measure operating cash flow to equity loads into a single cash flow construct for annual and three-year periods.

H5f: The change in the measure operating cash flow to equity loads into a single cash flow change construct for three-year periods.

Table 9.1 Measures by construct

Variable	Static measures			Change scores		
	Abbreviation	Annual	Three-year	Abbreviation	Annual	Three-year
Profitability						
Return on assets	ROA	✓	✓	CROA	✓	✓
Return on equity	ROE	✓	✓	CROE	✓	✓
Return on sales	ROS	✓	✓	CROS	✓	✓
Return on investment	ROI	✓	✓	CROI	✓	✓
EBITDA return on investment	EROI	✓	✓	CEROI	✓	✓
Operating margin	OpM	✓	✓	COpM	✓	✓
Growth						
Growth rate of sales	GR Sales	✓	✓	CGR Sales	✓	✓
Growth rate of operating expenses	GR OpX			CGR OpX	✓	✓
Growth rate of total assets	GR Ast	✓	✓	CGR Ast	✓	✓
Growth rate of employees	GR Emp	✓	✓	CGR Emp		
Cash flow						
Growth rate of operating cash flow	GR OCF			CGR OCF		
Operating cash flow to equity	OCF/E	✓	✓	COCF/E		✓
Liquidity						
Liabilities to total assets	Liab/Ast			Cliab/Ast		✓
Survival						
Altman's Z-score	Alt Z	✓		CAlt Z	✓	✓
Efficiency						
Asset turnover	ATO			CATO	✓	✓
Economic value						
Residual income	RI	✓		CRI	✓	✓
Residual income return on investment	RI ROI	✓	✓	CRI ROI	✓	✓
Cost of equity capital						
Cost of equity capital	COC	✓	✓	CCOC	✓	✓
Market						
Price-to-book ratio	P/B	✓		CP/B	✓	✓

Note: The abbreviations in this table will be used to represent the variables in the following discussion.

H5g: The change in the measure total liabilities to total assets loads into a single leverage construct for three-year periods.

H5h: The static measure Altman's Z-score loads into a single survival construct for annual periods.

H5i: The change in the measure Altman's Z-score loads into a single survival change construct for both annual and three-year periods.

H5j: The change in the measure asset turnover loads into a single efficiency change construct for both annual and three-year periods.

H5k.1: The static measures residual income and residual income return on investment load into a single economic value construct for annual periods.

H5k.2: The static measure residual income return on investment loads into a single economic value construct for three-year periods.

H5l: The change in the measures residual income and residual income return on investment load into a single economic value change construct for both annual and three-year periods.

H5m: The static measure cost of equity capital and the change in the measure cost of equity capital load into a single cost of capital construct for both annual and three-year periods.

H5n: The static measure price-to-book ratio loads into a single market construct for annual periods.

H5o: The change in the price-to-book ratio loads into a single market change construct for three-year periods.

With respect to discriminant validity, it was hypothesized that:

H6: The constructs of financial performance are discriminant from each other for annual and three-year periods.

Results of Convergent Validity Tests of the Proposed Measures of Various Financial Performance Constructs Using Annual Data

Figure 9.1 depicts the initial set of constructs that was tested for both convergent and discriminant validity for annual data. The results of the

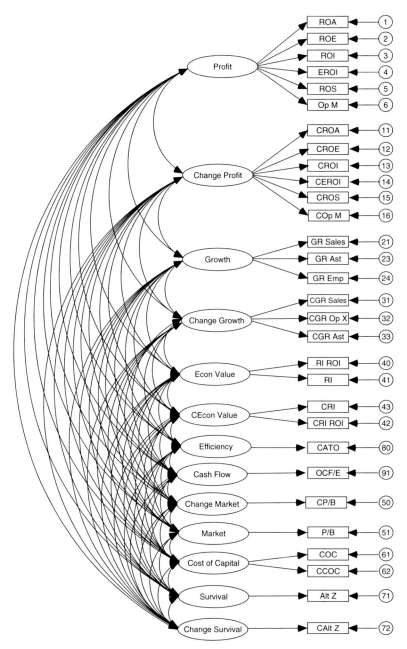

Figure 9.1 Proposed constructs and measures for a model of financial performance for annual data

convergent validity tests are presented in this subsection while the discriminant validity tests are presented in the next subsection.

Confirmatory factor analysis (CFA) was used to test the convergent validity of the measures chosen to represent each construct (Bollen, 1989; Bagozzi et al., 1991). The CFA framework uses a maximum-likelihood approach in its statistical analysis of construct validity and a decomposition of the measurement variance into its constituent components. Such an analysis estimates the variance in the observed measure explained by the construct (Arbuckle and Wothke, 1999).

AMOS 5.0 software was used to test whether the annual data fit the proposed model. Constructs with only one observed measure were constrained to exactly equal the value of the measure, as suggested by Bollen (1989). The variance of each construct was constrained to unity so that the parameters for each observed variable could be freely estimated. The assumptions of structural equation modeling require that the estimated variance of each measure must be positive and the covariance matrices must be positive definite. The three fit indices used to evaluate the prior models in this research were used to evaluate if the data fit the model (RMSEA, CFI and TLI). Please refer to page 140 for acceptable values for these indices. Arbuckle and Wothke suggest that a value of 0.90 or greater for both the CFI and the TLI indicates a reasonable fit of the data with a model, and an RMSEA value of about 0.08 or lower, but certainly no greater than 0.10 indicates an acceptable error rate for a model. Accordingly, a model that met all three criteria was considered to have an acceptable fit.

The annual data did not fit the model as proposed in Figure 9.1, since the covariance matrix for the constructs that comprise the model was not positive definite. This indicates that there was a specification error in the model or that the sample size was too small (Jöreskog and Sörbom, 1996). As the sample in this case had 300 observations, it is reasonable to conclude that the model had a specification error.

An examination of the correlations between variables across constructs revealed that RI ROI was more highly correlated with the profitability construct than with RI in the economic value construct. The model specification error was eliminated by moving the RI ROI measure to the profitability construct. The revised model had $\chi^2 = 2,213.4$ with $df = 334$ and $n = 300$. The CFI for the model was 0.83, the TLI was 0.78 and the RMSEA was 0.14. All three measures indicate that the data do not acceptably fit the model. Accordingly, the measures included in the model were reexamined to determine which should be kept and which should be excluded from a revised model. The following discussion addresses why individual variables may and may not have loaded onto constructs as anticipated.

Hypotheses supported

Hypotheses H5c, H5i, H5m, H5n and H5o were all supported by the CFA model. However, single-measure constructs, by definition, always load with an *R*-squared equal to 1.0. The only multiple-measure construct that loaded as originally hypothesized was cost of equity capital. This is not totally surprising since a large number of variables were selected for testing and the nature of this research is exploratory.

Hypothesis H5e was supported by definition, since it was a construct represented by a single variable. However, including this construct in the overall convergent validity model caused the model to have specification errors. This was a result of the correlation with this single construct with ROE as a result of the common denominator. Retesting the model with OCF/E included in the profit construct did eliminate the specification errors in the model. However, the fit of the model was unacceptable. Accordingly, the measure and the associated construct were eliminated from the model.

Hypothesis H5j was supported by definition since it had only a single indicator. However, the construct was highly correlated with both the growth and the survival change construct. With respect to the former, the growth rate of assets is the denominator for CATO and is also a measure in the growth construct. Further, asset turnover is a component of Altman's *Z*-score, so the change in asset turnover would naturally be correlated with the change in Altman's *Z*-score. Consequently, CATO was correlated with three constructs, and resulted in a model specification error. Accordingly, CATO was eliminated from the model.

Hypotheses not supported

Hypothesis H5a was not supported for annual data. Only ROA, ROE, EROI and ROS loaded on the profit construct with convergent validity with respect to the overall model. Both RI ROI and ROI were eliminated because the modification indices indicated that they were highly correlated with the cost of capital construct. This is reasonable for RI ROI since the charge for equity included in the calculation of RI ROI is based upon the cost of equity capital. However, the association with ROI and cost of equity capital is not obvious, but since ROI is highly correlated with RI ROI, the covariation did cause a problem in the model. ROS was eliminated from the construct because it was highly correlated with the change in profitability construct.

Hypothesis H5b was not supported for annual data. Only the change in ROA, ROE, ROI and ROS loaded on the profit change construct with convergent validity with respect to the overall model. The correlation of CEROI and COpM with the other measures in the construct was not sufficient to conclude that these measures were part of the same construct. This was supported by the low R-squared of each variable with constructs of 0.08 and 0.16, respectively.

Hypothesis H5d was not supported for annual data. The change in the growth rate of assets did not load well on the growth change construct because of its low correlation with the other growth change measures. This was evidenced by the low R-squared with the construct of 0.12. Further, as reported in Table 8.7, the results of the test of the incremental information provided by the change in the growth rate of assets over the static measure indicated that the incremental information was not statistically significant.

Hypothesis H5h was not supported. The correlation of Altman's Z-score with the market construct (0.54) represented by the price-to-book-value ratio suggested that the survival construct was not discriminant. This is understandable because of the market component used in calculating Altman's Z-score. Given the need to eliminate either ALT Z or P/B, ALT Z was removed because P/B provides significant information about unrealized market opportunities that is otherwise hidden within a composite measure. Accordingly, ALT Z was not retained in the annual model.

Hypothesis H5k.1 was not supported. RI ROI correlated highly with the profit construct. This is reasonable as the measure has a common denominator with ROI and EROI. Consequently, it was eliminated from the annual model.

Hypothesis H5l was not supported for annual data. The change in residual income was correlated with more than one performance construct including cost of equity capital and change in profitability. This was a violation of convergent validity, so the measure was eliminated.

Because ROS and OpM did not load well on the profit or profit change constructs, it was possible that they represented a separate and distinct construct. This possibility was tested by creating a separate construct using these variables and retesting the model. The data did not fit the revised model, with all of the fit indices falling to unacceptable levels. This was further evidence that one static and one change score measure should be excluded from the profit and profit change constructs.

Of the original 30 variables included in the first model, 20 were retained. Variables should be retained in a measurement model if they provide significant incremental information about the referent, or if they provide for better representation of the construct being tested. While Bollen (1989) suggests that more measures of a construct are better than fewer, this is only true when there is convergent validity for the set of indicators. The fit of a model is lessened by adding variables to a construct that reduce convergent validity without improving its explanation of the referent. The revised model was developed as indicated in Figure 9.2.

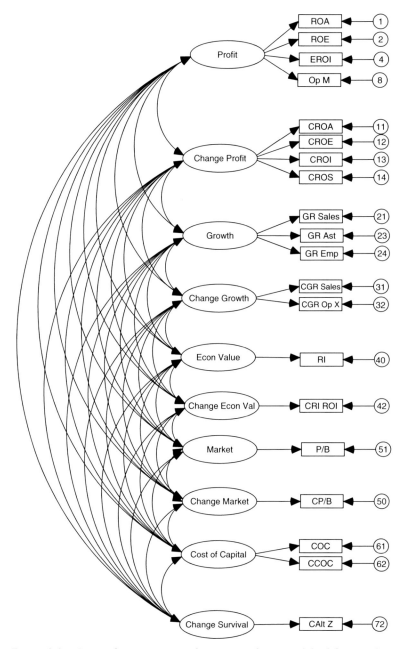

Figure 9.2   Revised constructs and measures for a model of financial performance for annual data

Results of the Discriminant Validity Tests of the Constructs Using Annual Data

Hypothesis H6 was not supported. As discussed with respect to the convergent validity testing of the original measurement model, three financial performance constructs (cash flow, efficiency and survival) were eliminated because the potential measures of these constructs correlated with other constructs. Accordingly, the remaining ten constructs in the revised model, as depicted in Figure 9.2, were tested for discriminant validity.

Using a confirmatory factor analysis framework, discriminant validity is achieved when the correlations between the separate constructs are statistically significantly lower than unity (1.0) (Bollen, 1989). Any correlations that appeared 'high' were tested by setting the correlation between the two constructs equal to unity, and then testing the statistical significance of the change in χ^2 between the two models.

For the revised model, only two constructs, growth and growth change, were correlated in excess of 0.60. Accordingly, the correlation between the two constructs was constrained to unity and the model was retested. The result was $\chi^2 = 414.0$ with $df = 131$. The change in χ^2 was 8.6 with $df = 1$ and $p < 0.01$. Accordingly, for the revised model, hypothesis H6 was supported, since the constructs were found to be discriminant. All other combinations of constructs had correlations below 0.52, which indicates that all constructs met the requirements for discriminant validity.

Summary of Findings for Annual Data

As a result of these changes in the specification of the model, the data fit the revised 10-construct model presented in Figure 9.2. The model had $\chi^2 = 405.4$ with $df = 130$ and $n = 300$. The CFI for the revised model was 0.95, the TLI was 0.93 and the RMSEA was 0.08. All three measures indicate that the data fit the model. Accordingly, the model met the requirements of convergent validity (Bollen, 1989; Jöreskog and Sörbom, 1996; Arbuckle and Wothke, 1999).

Ten of the original 13 constructs and 20 of the original 30 measures were retained in the annual financial performance measurement model. It was also demonstrated that these constructs were discriminant and that the measures of the constructs met the test for convergent validity. Accordingly, these constructs, and their corresponding measures, will be used as the basis for testing a model of organizational financial performance that utilizes annual market-adjusted return to shareholders as the dependent measure.

Results of Convergent Validity Tests of the Proposed Measures of Various Financial Performance Constructs Using Three-year Data

Figure 9.3 presents a diagram of the initial set of financial performance constructs and their corresponding measures, for three-year data. The convergent validity of the measures for each construct was tested using confirmatory factor analysis, as was done with the annual data model. AMOS 5.0 software was used to test whether the three-year high/low sample fit the proposed model using maximum-likelihood estimation. Again, constructs with only one measure were constrained to exactly equal the value of the measure representing it. The variance of each construct was constrained to unity so the parameters for each observed variable could be freely estimated.

The three-year data did not fit the proposed model. The model had $\chi^2 =$ 1,013.2 with $df = 307$ and $n = 120$. The fit indices were CFI $= 0.81$, TLI $= 0.74$ and RMSEA $= 0.14$. There were specification errors in the model, as indicated by estimated negative residuals for four measures including ROI, CROI, GR Sales and COC. Consequently, adjustments to the base model were necessary, as was the case with the annual data model. Accordingly, the measures included in the three-year model were reexamined in order to determine which should be retained in a revised model. The following discussion addresses why individual variables may not have loaded onto constructs as anticipated.

Hypotheses supported
Hypotheses H5c, H5d, H5g, H5i, H5l, H5m and H5o were supported by the CFA model. However, single-measure constructs, by definition, always load with an *R*-squared equal to 1.0. The multiple-measure constructs that loaded as originally hypothesized were growth, growth change, economic value change and cost of equity capital. The following discussion addresses why individual variables may not have loaded onto constructs as anticipated.

Hypothesis H5e was supported by definition, since it was a construct represented by a single variable. However, including this construct caused the model to have specification errors. This was a result of the correlation of OCF/E with ROE, as a result of the common denominator and with EROI because of the similarity between EBITDA and OCF. As with the annual data, including OCF/E with the profitability construct worsened the fit of the model. Accordingly, the measure and the construct were eliminated from the model.

Hypothesis H5f was supported by definition, since it was a construct represented by a single variable. However, as with OCF/E, COCF/E was

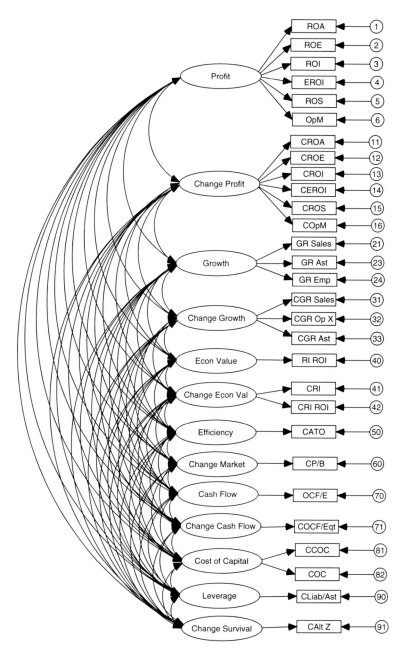

Figure 9.3 Proposed constructs and measures for a model of financial performance for three-year data

correlated with the profit change construct through CROE and CEROI. Accordingly, the measure and the construct were eliminated from the model.

Hypothesis H5j was supported by definition, since it was a construct represented by a single variable. However, CATO was highly correlated with the growth construct since the denominator is the change in assets and the numerator is the change in sales. Accordingly, the construct and the associated measure were eliminated from the model.

Hypothesis H5k.2 was supported by definition, since it was a construct represented by a single variable. However, RI was highly correlated with the profit construct (0.95). Adding RI to the profit construct rather than having it as a separate construct significantly worsened the model fit. Accordingly, the economic value construct, and the corresponding measure RI, were removed from the model.

Hypotheses not supported

Hypothesis H5a was not supported for three-year data. The maximum-likelihood estimate for the residuals for ROI was negative, indicating a possible specification error. Consequently, ROI was eliminated from the model. The residuals of ROS and ROA were also estimated as being highly correlated. Since one of the assumptions underlying structural equation modeling is that residuals are uncorrelated, ROS was eliminated from the model.

Hypothesis H5b was not supported for three-year data. CROI was eliminated for the same reason that ROI was eliminated, estimated negative residuals. With CROI eliminated from the model, CROA was estimated to have negative residuals, so it was eliminated as well. CROS was eliminated because of its correlation with GR Sales. This relationship is intuitively reasonable since the denominator or CROS is the change in sales.

Of the original 29 variables included in the first model, 20 were retained. Variables should be retained in a measurement model if they provide significant incremental information about the referent or if they provide for better representation of the construct being tested. As stated earlier, while more measures of a construct are better than fewer, this is only true when there is convergent validity for the set of indicators. The fit of a model is lessened by adding variables to a construct that reduce convergent validity without improving its explanation of the referent. The revised model was developed as depicted in Figure 9.4.

Results of the Discriminant Validity Tests of the Financial Performance Constructs Using Three-year Data

Hypothesis H6 was not supported for three-year data. As discussed with respect to the convergent validity testing of the original measurement

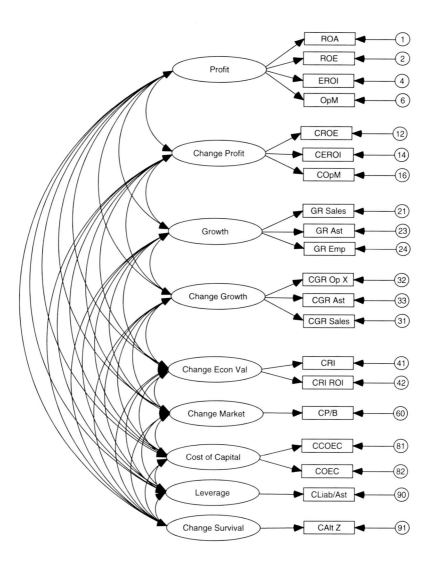

Figure 9.4   Revised constructs and measures for a model of financial performance for three-year data

model, three constructs were eliminated because the measures of the constructs correlated with other constructs. Accordingly, the constructs in the revised model presented in Figure 9.4 were tested for discriminant validity.

As with the testing of the measurement model for annual data, any correlations that appeared 'high' were tested by setting the correlation between the two constructs equal to unity, and then testing the statistical significance of the change in χ^2 between the two models. Two pairs of constructs appeared to possibly be highly correlated. They were the change in profitability and the change in survival and the cost of equity capital and the change in survival.

First, the correlation between the change in profitability and the change in survival was constrained to unity, and the model was retested. The result was $\chi^2 = 251.1$ with $df = 138$. The change in χ^2 was 39 with $df = 1$ and $p < 0.001$. Accordingly, the constructs were deemed to be discriminant.

Next, the correlation between the cost of equity capital and the change in survival was constrained to unity and the model was retested. The result was $\chi^2 = 230.0$ with $df = 138$. The change in χ^2 was 17.9 with $df = 1$ and $p < 0.001$. Accordingly, for the revised model, the constructs were deemed to be discriminant.

Summary of Findings for Three-year Data

As a result of the changes in the model specification, the data fit the revised, nine-construct model depicted in Figure 9.4. The model had $\chi^2 = 212.1$ with $df = 137$ and $n = 120$. The fit indices were CFI $= 0.93$, TLI $= 0.91$ and RMSEA $= 0.07$. All three measures indicate that the data fit the model. Further, modification indices do not indicate that any significant improvement in fit would be achieved by including a measure with an additional construct. Accordingly, the measures meet the requirements for convergent validity (Bollen, 1989; Jöreskog and Sörbom, 1996; Arbuckle and Wothke, 1999).

Nine of the original 13 constructs and 20 of the original 29 measures were retained in the measurement model. It was demonstrated that these nine constructs were discriminant and that the revised set of measures of the constructs met the test for convergent validity. Accordingly, these constructs, and their corresponding measures, will be used as the basis for testing a model of organizational financial performance that utilizes three-year market-adjusted return to shareholders as the dependent measure.

TESTING MODELS OF ORGANIZATIONAL FINANCIAL PERFORMANCE FOR ANNUAL AND THREE-YEAR DATA

Having constructs that are discriminant and corresponding measures that meet the test for convergent validity is a necessary, but not a sufficient, condition for developing a measurement model that represents organizational financial performance. Demonstrating that these constructs and measures explain a significant amount of the variance in the higher-order construct, organizational financial performance, is still necessary. Accordingly, the next step in this research was to test annual and three-year models of organizational financial performance, using return to shareholders as the referent.

The following subsections present the results of the statistical tests of both revised models. Based upon these findings, a second set of revised models are developed and tested using a second high/low sample, and tested again using all records in the database. The results of these confirmatory tests are presented and discussed for both the annual and the three-year models.

Results of the Tests of the Annual Organizational Financial Performance Measurement Model

Figure 9.5 presents a diagram of the proposed measurement model for financial performance for annual timeframes. As discussed in Chapter 7, return to shareholders was the referent used to represent organizational financial performance. A single structural equation was tested for each model in the form:

$$\eta_1 = \gamma_{11}\xi_1 + \gamma_{12}\xi_2 + \ldots + \gamma_{1i}\xi_i + \zeta_1,$$

where:

η_1 = organizational financial performance,
γ_{1i} = the coefficient representing the direct influence of one variable upon another,
ξ_i = a latent variable representing a first-order performance construct, and
ζ_1 = represents equation error (random disturbances) in the structural relationship between the referent η and the first-order performance constructs ξ.

To make the model easier to read, the paths representing the covariances between the latent constructs (the phi matrix) were excluded. However, in

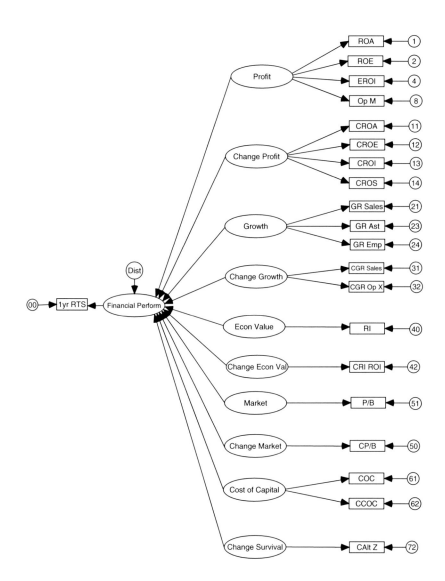

Figure 9.5   Proposed model of financial performance for annual data

testing the model, these parameters were allowed to be freely estimated and the results are reported.

All of the ten constructs included in the model were expected to positively affect organizational financial performance, with the exception of cost of equity capital and leverage. Profitability and growth are generally associated with positive financial performance and are the most frequently used measures to represent positive financial performance in the survey of empirical research in Chapter 2 (Drucker, 1954; Venkatraman and Ramanujam, 1987; Penman, 2001). Economic value measures are, by definition, positively associated with financial performance since these measures represent the return on invested capital over and above the cost of all invested capital (Stewart, 1991; Copeland et al., 2000; Barney, 2002). Cash flow measures are also positively associated with financial performance as discussed in Chapter 4 and as evidenced by the dividend discount model used for valuing companies (Brealey et al., 2001). Further, efficiency measures are included in most financial analysis textbooks as having a positive association with financial performance (see Brealey et al., 2001; and Penman, 2001 as examples). Survival is obviously positively associated with financial performance and, accordingly, Altman developed his Z-score with increasingly positive values representing better financial condition (Altman, 1968). Finally, market-based measures are positively associated with financial performance as demonstrated by Chen and Dodd (2001) and Cheng and Cheung (1993).

Cost of equity capital was expected to be negatively associated with financial performance for several reasons. First, increased cost of capital raises the hurdle rate to achieve positive economic value creation (Stewart, 1991; Copeland et al., 2000). Second, higher costs of equity capital are associated with greater financial risks (Brealey et al., 2001). Consequently, as the cost of equity capital rises, it becomes more difficult to achieve positive financial performance.

Leverage was also expected to be negatively associated with financial performance. For example, if it is assumed that a company is losing money, and if it is assumed that the company has not executed any additional equity financings, then leverage must increase. However, borrowed capital is generally less expensive than equity capital (ibid.), so if a company adjusts its capital structure to have a higher percentage of debt, without significantly lowering its credit standing, it can achieve positive economic value creation. This can also occur in stable, profitable companies with positive free cash flow that is used for share repurchases or dividends. However, the latter case is far less frequent than the former, making the expected association between leverage and financial performance negative.

Based upon the preceding discussion, it was hypothesized that:

H7a: Organizational financial performance is a multidimensional construct with subdimensions including profitability, the change in profitability, growth, the change in growth, economic value creation, the change in economic value creation, survival, the cost of equity capital, market value relative to book value, and the change in market value relative to book value for annual periods.

H7b: There is a positive relationship between organizational financial performance and profitability, the change in profitability, growth, the change in growth, economic value, the change in economic value, survival, the market value relative to the book value, and the change in the market value relative to the book value for annual periods. There is a negative relationship between financial performance and the cost of equity capital for annual periods.

The results of the test of the financial performance model for annual periods are presented in Figure 9.6. Path coefficients are presented in each model on the appropriate path. The squared multiple correlations are indicated to the upper right of each observed measure. This model will be referred to as FPA 1. The path coefficients are standardized, maximum-likelihood estimates. The model had $\chi^2 = 425.3$ with $df = 140$ and $n = 300$. The fit indices were CFI = 0.95, TLI = 0.93 and RMSEA = 0.08. All three measures indicate that the data fit the model. Accordingly, hypothesis H7a was supported. Table 9.2 summarizes the correlations between the first-order performance constructs.

Table 9.3 presents the squared multiple correlations for each of the 'predicted' variables (those at the termination of an arrow) in the annual model. Overall, this annual model accounts for 71 percent of the variance in the financial performance construct. The estimate for each individual measure represents the estimated variance in the measure explained by the associated construct. The greater the explained variance for a measure, the greater the evidence that it is rightly part of the construct, and the better the model fit.

For the proposed annual financial performance model FPA 1, the path coefficients indicate that hypothesis H7b was not supported for the relationships between financial performance and profitability, the change in growth, and economic value. Each of the respective path coefficients was negative, suggesting that there was an inverse relationship between the constructs. However, this conclusion should not be acceptable because all of the correlations between the individual performance measures and the

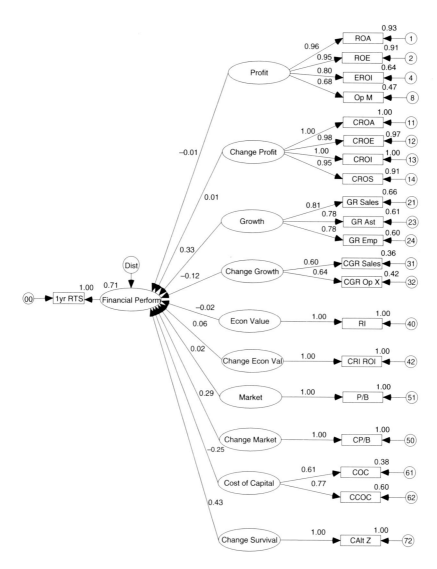

Figure 9.6   FPA 1: proposed model of financial performance for annual data

Measuring organizational performance

Table 9.2 Correlations between financial performance constructs

			Estimate
Profit	↔	Change profit	0.31
Profit	↔	Growth	0.42
Profit	↔	Change growth	0.35
Profit	↔	Econ value	0.39
Profit	↔	Change econ val	0.32
Profit	↔	Market	0.38
Profit	↔	Change market	0.15
Profit	↔	Cost of capital	−0.18
Profit	↔	Change survival	0.34
Change profit	↔	Growth	0.17
Change profit	↔	Change growth	0.39
Change profit	↔	Econ value	0.12
Change profit	↔	Change econ val	0.20
Change profit	↔	Market	0.06
Change profit	↔	Change market	0.26
Change profit	↔	Cost of capital	−0.16
Change profit	↔	Change survival	0.33
Growth	↔	Change growth	0.79
Growth	↔	Econ value	0.15
Growth	↔	Change econ val	0.19
Growth	↔	Market	0.32
Growth	↔	Change market	0.00
Growth	↔	Cost of capital	−0.08
Growth	↔	Change survival	0.13
Change growth	↔	Econ value	0.20
Change growth	↔	Change econ val	0.25
Change growth	↔	Market	0.16
Change growth	↔	Change market	0.23
Change growth	↔	Cost of capital	−0.31
Change growth	↔	Change survival	0.41
Econ value	↔	Change econ val	0.23
Econ value	↔	Market	0.16
Econ value	↔	Change market	0.15
Econ value	↔	Cost of capital	−0.22
Econ value	↔	Change survival	0.22
Change econ val	↔	Market	0.09
Change econ val	↔	Change market	0.24
Change econ val	↔	Cost of capital	−0.25
Change econ val	↔	Change survival	0.20
Market	↔	Change market	0.27
Market	↔	Cost of capital	−0.19

Table 9.2   (continued)

			Estimate
Market	↔	Change survival	0.29
Change market	↔	Cost of capital	−0.48
Change market	↔	Change survival	0.52
Cost of capital	↔	Change survival	−0.47

Table 9.3   *Squared multiple correlations for the annual data model*

	Construct	Estimate
Financial perform		0.71
1yr RTS	Financial perform	1.00
ROA	Profit	0.93
ROE	Profit	0.91
EROI	Profit	0.64
OpM	Profit	0.47
CROA	Change profit	1.00
CROE	Change profit	0.97
CROI	Change profit	1.00
CROS	Change profit	0.91
GR Sales	Growth	0.66
GR Ast	Growth	0.61
GR Emp	Growth	0.60
CGR Sales	Change growth	0.36
CGR Op X	Change growth	0.42
RI	Econ value	1.00
CRI ROI	Change econ val	1.00
P/B	Market	1.00
CP/B	Change market	1.00
COC	Cost of capital	0.38
CCOC	Cost of capital	0.60
CAlt Z	Change survival	1.00

market-adjusted return to shareholders, as reported in Table 8.8, were positive and significant. Further, the correlations reported in Table 9.2 support the hypothesized relationships, since all of the negatively correlated pairs of constructs include cost of equity capital. A more plausible explanation for the results is that there was significant shared variance between other constructs in the model and these constructs.

Chakravarthy (1986) found that Altman's Z-score provided the same amount of discrimination between 'excellent' and 'non-excellent' firms as the model he developed in his research. However, he criticized the use of such a measure as being 'more of an empirical artifact than a performance vector anchored in theory' (p. 447). Accordingly, he argued that a function that has a theoretical basis is superior because it provides greater information about the underlying dimensions of performance.

Following Chakravarthy's reasoning, to obtain greater information from a model of financial performance, individual measures of the dimensions of performance should be preferable to a composite measure to be able to understand the unique explanatory power of the different financial performance dimensions included, but unobservable, in the composite measure. Accordingly, model FPA 1 was revised to eliminate those measures that had the greatest collinearity with the other performance measures.

The change in Altman's *Z*-score includes a profitability component, a market value multiple, a liquidity component and an asset turnover component. Consistent with the approach suggested by Chakravarthy, this composite measure was eliminated rather than its individual components. Consequently, the financial performance model was retested without the change in survival construct. The data fit the revised model with $\chi^2 = 390.3$ with $df = 130$ and $n = 300$. The fit indices were CFI = 0.96, TLI = 0.94 and RMSEA = 0.08. This represented a slightly improved fit over the previous model. However, the *R*-squared for the financial performance construct measured using this model was reduced from 0.71 to 0.62. Even though the explanatory power of the model was reduced, the revised model provides greater insight into the individual dimensions of financial performance, as compared to the dimensions being obscured in the composite measure CALT Z.

All of the standardized path coefficients were positive in the revised model with the exception of the economic value construct, and that path coefficient was not statistically significant. Accordingly, the economic value construct was eliminated, and the resulting model retested. The data fit this revised model with $\chi^2 = 375.5$ with $df = 120$ and $n = 300$. The fit indices were CFI = 0.96, TLI = 0.94 and RMSEA = 0.08. The change in χ^2 between the two models was 14.8 with $df = 10$. The change in the model was not significant at $p < 0.10$, thus the two models cannot be considered statistically significantly different. Further, the *R*-squared for financial performance remained unchanged at 0.62. Consequently, the revised annual financial performance model excluded both the survival change and the economic value constructs as presented in Figure 9.7, as FPA 1a, including the standardized maximum-likelihood path coefficient and the *R*-squared values for the observed variables.

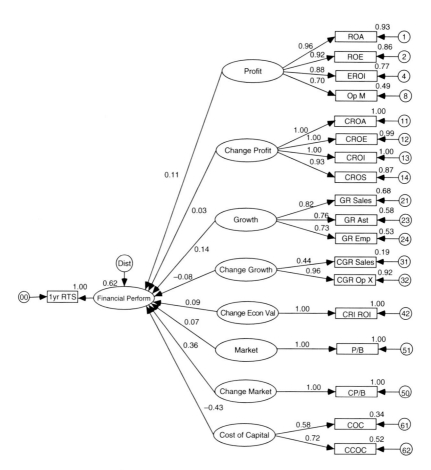

Figure 9.7   Revised model FPA 1a of financial performance for annual data

This revised financial performance model FPA 1a was tested with a second random sample of 300 annual firm years of data from the high/low database. This sample excluded all firm years that were used in the exploratory phase of building the model. The data fit the revised model with $\chi^2 = 418.6$ with $df = 120$ and $n = 300$. The fit indices were CFI $= 0.95$, TLI $= 0.93$ and RMSEA $= 0.09$. The R-squared for the model was 0.62. Figure 9.8, as FPA 1b, presents the standardized path coefficients for the retest of the model. The standardized path coefficient for the change in growth became negative in the retested model, suggesting that there is potentially an issue with covariation with some of the other constructs.

The final test of the revised financial performance model (FPA 1b) was with the entire database of annual firm years of data. The data fit the revised model with $\chi^2 = 2,405.9$ with $df = 120$ and $n = 2894$. The fit indices were CFI $= 0.96$, TLI $= 0.94$ and RMSEA $= 0.08$. The R-squared for the model was 0.47. The signs of standardized path coefficients were consistent with the results from the second high/low sample.

Once again the sign of the coefficient for change in growth was negative. This indicates either that over an annual period, a change in the rate of growth is negatively received by the market, or that the variance in the construct, relative to the criterion, is shared with another construct in the model. A review of the correlations between individual constructs indicated that the most likely source of such covariance is the growth construct, with an estimated correlation of 0.79. The two constructs were tested for discriminant validity using all annual firm years of data. The results indicated that the two constructs were discriminant at $p < 0.001$, with a change in $\chi^2 = 102.6$ with $df = 1$ and $n = 2,894$. Accordingly, while the two constructs may have significant shared variance with respect to the criterion, they are discriminant constructs within the model of financial performance.

A retest of the model using all annual data and eliminating the change in growth construct resulted in $\chi^2 = 1,889.7$ with $df = 95$ and $n = 2,894$. The fit indices were CFI $= 0.97$, TLI $= 0.95$ and RMSEA $= 0.08$. The R-squared for the model was 0.47. In short, this model of annual financial performance had a slightly better fit without the growth change construct and equal explanatory power for the variance in the criterion. Further, of the coefficients for the constructs retained in the model, the coefficient of the growth construct reflected the majority of the change in the model. This suggests that while the change in growth construct is discriminant from the growth construct, in the context of the full model of financial performance, there is no unique variance in the criterion explained by this construct. After eliminating the change in growth construct, the market construct was no longer significant and its sign was negative. Consequently, this construct was also removed from the final model of annual financial performance.

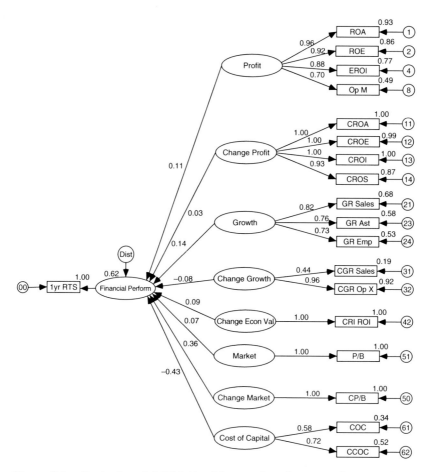

Figure 9.8   Revised model FPA 1b of financial performance for annual data using an independent sample

Figure 9.9 presents the standardized maximum-likelihood path coefficients and *R*-squared values for the final revised model of annual financial performance using all annual firm years and eliminating the change in growth and the market constructs. Table 9.4 presents the final correlations between the individual performance constructs. The final fit indices for this model were $\chi^2 = 1,647.7$ with $df = 86$ and $n = 2,894$. The fit indices were CFI $= 0.97$, TLI $= 0.96$, RMSEA $= 0.08$ and *R*-squared of 0.47.

In summary, the final model of annual financial performance included six constructs and 15 performance measures. The constructs were demonstrated to be discriminant and the measures of the constructs were demonstrated to meet the test of convergent validity. The model explained 62 percent of the variance for the high/low sample, and 47 percent of the variance of all annual firm years for the criterion market-adjusted return to shareholders. All of the path coefficients were significant at $p < 0.001$, with the exception of the change in profitability and the change in economic value, which were both significant at $p < 0.05$. A model that included the change in Altman's *Z*-score accounted for greater explanation of variance in the criterion. However, it did not provide easily interpreted information about which subdimensions contributed to the financial performance. As suggested by Chakravarthy, a model that has a theoretical basis is preferable to one that is purely empirical. The development of an empirically based, composite measure of financial performance is discussed later in this chapter.

Results of the Tests of the Three-year Period Organizational Financial Performance Measurement Model

Figure 9.10 presents a diagram of the initial measurement model for financial performance (FP3.1) for three-year timeframes. As with the annual model of financial performance, market-adjusted return to shareholders was the referent used to represent financial performance. Following the same reasoning presented for the annual model, it was hypothesized that:

H8a: Organizational financial performance is a multidimensional construct with subdimensions including profitability, the change in profitability, growth, the change in growth, the change in economic value creation, the change in market value relative to book value, the cost of equity capital, the change in leverage and the change in survival for three-year periods.

H8b: There is a positive relationship between three-year organizational financial performance and profitability, the change in profitability, growth, the change in growth, the change in economic value, the change

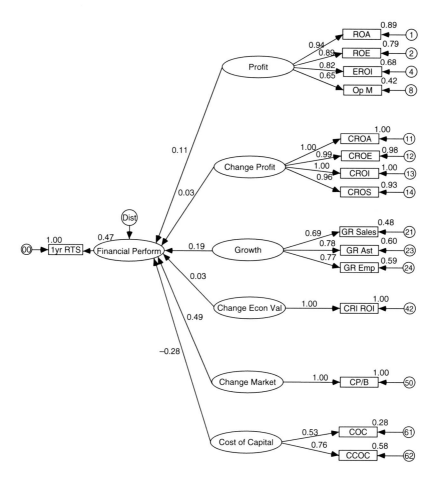

Figure 9.9   Revised model of financial performance using all annual firm years

Table 9.4   Correlations between the final financial performance constructs

			Estimate
Profit	↔	Change profit	0.26
Profit	↔	Growth	0.30
Profit	↔	Change econ val	0.29
Profit	↔	Change market	−0.01
Profit	↔	Cost of capital	−0.11
Change profit	↔	Growth	0.10
Change profit	↔	Change econ val	0.22
Change profit	↔	Change market	0.11
Change profit	↔	Cost of capital	−0.09
Growth	↔	Change econ val	0.12
Growth	↔	Change market	−0.07
Growth	↔	Cost of capital	0.04
Change econ val	↔	Change market	0.09
Change econ val	↔	Cost of capital	−0.17
Change market	↔	Cost of capital	−0.28

in survival and the change in the market value relative to the book value for three-year periods. There is a negative relationship between financial performance and the cost of equity capital and the change in leverage for three-year periods.

The results of the test of the financial performance model for three-year periods (FP3.1) are presented in Figure 9.10. The path coefficients are standardized maximum-likelihood estimates and the R-squared values are indicated to the upper right of each observed measure. Table 9.5 presents the correlations between the financial performance constructs. The model had $\chi^2 = 225.4$ with $df = 148$ and $n = 120$. The fit indices were CFI = 0.94, TLI = 0.91, RMSEA = 0.07 and an R-squared of 0.73. All three fit indices indicate that the data fit the model. Accordingly, hypothesis H8a was supported.

For the proposed FP3.1 model, the path coefficients indicate that hypothesis H8b was not supported for the relationships between financial performance and leverage and the change in profitability. As with the annual model, the signs of the coefficients were the inverse of the correlations between the measures of the constructs, indicating that there was significant shared variance between other constructs in the FP3.1 model and these two constructs. Altman's Z-score was eliminated from the FP3.1 model for the same reasons it was eliminated from the annual model. Further, the coefficient for the change in economic value was not statistically significant, so the construct was eliminated. However, the correlation

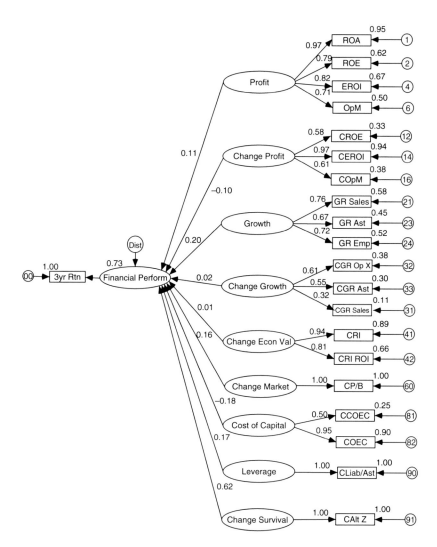

Figure 9.10   Proposed model of financial performance FP3.1 for three-year periods

Table 9.5   Correlations between financial performance constructs

			Estimate
Profit	↔	Change profit	0.33
Profit	↔	Growth	0.28
Profit	↔	Change growth	0.37
Profit	↔	Change econ val	0.26
Profit	↔	Change market	0.23
Profit	↔	Cost of capital	−0.51
Profit	↔	Change leverage	−0.38
Profit	↔	Change survival	0.49
Change profit	↔	Growth	0.48
Change profit	↔	Change growth	0.46
Change profit	↔	Change econ val	0.49
Change profit	↔	Change market	0.57
Change profit	↔	Cost of capital	−0.53
Change profit	↔	Change leverage	−0.24
Change profit	↔	Change survival	0.71
Growth	↔	Change growth	0.44
Growth	↔	Change econ val	0.32
Growth	↔	Change market	0.11
Growth	↔	Cost of capital	−0.04
Growth	↔	Change leverage	0.06
Growth	↔	Change survival	0.22
Change growth	↔	Change econ val	0.40
Change growth	↔	Change market	0.43
Change growth	↔	Cost of capital	−0.54
Change growth	↔	Change leverage	−0.03
Change growth	↔	Change survival	0.43
Change econ val	↔	Change market	0.43
Change econ val	↔	Cost of capital	−0.40
Change econ val	↔	Change leverage	−0.10
Change econ val	↔	Change survival	0.44
Change market	↔	Cost of capital	−0.57
Change market	↔	Change leverage	−0.13
Change market	↔	Change survival	0.56
Cost of capital	↔	Change leverage	0.32
Cost of capital	↔	Change survival	−0.67
Change leverage	↔	Change survival	−0.62

of the change in residual income return on investment was considerably more significant than was the change in operating margin, so the change in operating margin was eliminated and the change in residual income was added as a measure for the change in profit construct.

The revised financial performance model is presented in Figure 9.11, as FP3.2, which shows the standardized path coefficients and the R-squared values for the observed variables. The model had $\chi^2 = 154.3$ with $df = 110$ and $n = 120$. The fit indices were CFI $= 0.95$, TLI $= 0.93$, RMSEA $= 0.06$ and R-squared of 0.67. All three fit indices indicate that the data fit the model. Further, all of the path coefficients are consistent with the correlations of the observed variables with the criterion.

The revised FP3.2 model was retested with a new random sample of 120 three-year firm periods of data from the high/low database. This sample excluded all three-year periods that were used in the exploratory phase of building the model. The data fit the revised model only with respect to two of the three fit indices with $\chi^2 = 201.1$, $df = 110$ and $n = 120$. The fit indices were CFI $= 0.92$, TLI $= 0.88$ and RMSEA $= 0.08$. Although TLI was below the rule-of-thumb level of 0.90, it was very close. The R-squared for the retested model increased to 0.72. Figure 9.12 presents the standardized path coefficients and the R-squared values for the retested FP3.2 model.

Because of the difference in the results between the two high/low samples, the model was retested with all of the high/low three-year periods. The model had $\chi^2 = 236.6$ with $df = 110$ and $n = 267$. The fit indices were CFI $= 0.94$, TLI $= 0.91$, RMSEA $= 0.07$ and R-squared of 0.70. Accordingly, for the entire high/low sample, the data fit the model.

Next, the revised FP3.3 model was tested using the complete three-year period database. The model had $\chi^2 = 638.1$ with $df = 110$ and $n = 925$. The fit indices were CFI $= 0.91$, TLI $= 0.87$, RMSEA $= 0.07$ and R-squared of 0.60. Once again TLI was just below the desired level to accept that the data fit the model. Further, the coefficient for the change in growth construct was negative and not significant at the $p < 0.05$ level. Also, the modification indices suggested that the variance of GR Sales was correlated with the change in profitability construct. Accordingly, both the change in growth construct and the GR Sales measure were eliminated from the model.

The revised FP3.4 model had $\chi^2 = 247.2$ with $df = 59$ and $n = 925$. The fit indices were CFI $= 0.96$, TLI $= 0.94$, RMSEA $= 0.06$ and R-squared of 0.61. The data fit the revised model, with a slight increase in explanatory power for the criterion. All of the path coefficients were significant at the $p < 0.001$ level. Figure 9.13 presents the revised FP3.4 model of financial performance for three-year periods, using all three-year periods in the database including the standardized path coefficients and the R-squared values for each observed variable. Table 9.6 presents the correlations between the individual constructs in the final model.

In summary, the revised model of financial performance for three-year periods included six constructs and 13 performance measures. The constructs were demonstrated to be discriminant and the measures of these

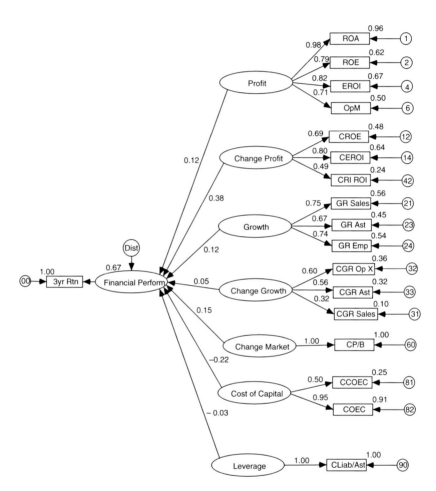

Figure 9.11   Revised model FP3.2 of financial performance for three-year periods

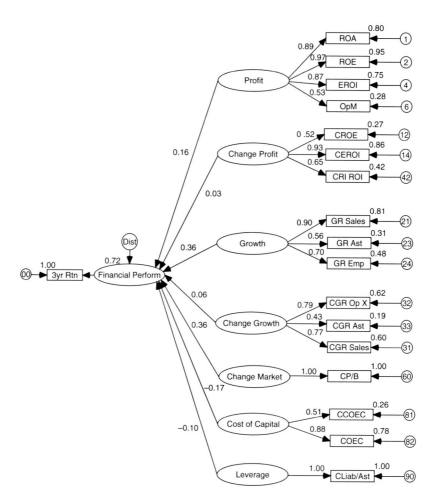

Figure 9.12   Revised model FP3.3 of financial performance for three-year periods using an independent sample

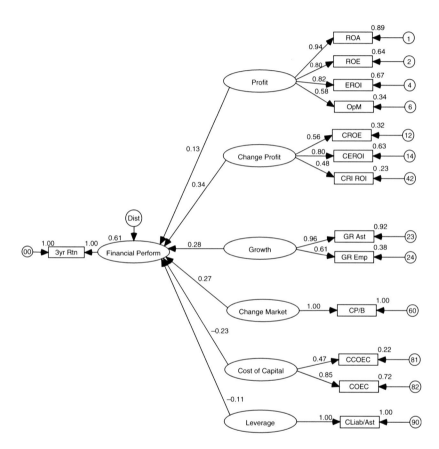

Figure 9.13   Revised model FP3.4 of financial performance using all three-year period data

Table 9.6   Correlations between the final three-year financial performance constructs

			Estimate
Profit	↔	Change profit	0.29
Profit	↔	Growth	0.21
Profit	↔	Change market	0.08
Profit	↔	Cost of capital	−0.17
Profit	↔	Leverage	−0.24
Change profit	↔	Growth	−0.01
Change profit	↔	Change market	0.55
Change profit	↔	Cost of capital	−0.53
Change profit	↔	Leverage	−0.09
Growth	↔	Change market	−0.21
Growth	↔	Cost of capital	0.22
Growth	↔	Leverage	0.05
Change market	↔	Cost of capital	−0.62
Change market	↔	Leverage	0.03
Cost of capital	↔	Leverage	−0.05

constructs were demonstrated to meet the test of convergent validity. The FP3.4 model explained 67 percent of the variance for the entire high/low sample, and 61 percent of the variance of all three-year firm periods, for the criterion market-adjusted return to shareholders. All of the path coefficients were significant at the $p < 0.001$ level. Finally, the signs of all the regression coefficients were consistent with the correlations between the individual measures of the constructs and the criterion.

THE DEVELOPMENT AND TESTING OF A COMPOSITE MEASURE OF ORGANIZATIONAL FINANCIAL PERFORMANCE

The next step in this research was to try to develop a composite measure of organizational financial performance that maximized the explanatory power of the variance in the referent. Such a composite measure would be invaluable for representing organizational financial performance when market-based information is not available, as is the case for companies that are not publicly traded such as new ventures, family businesses and closely held companies. Consequently, correlation with the referent was considered to be the most important factor in developing a composite measure of financial performance. In other words, the aim of developing a composite measure of organizational financial performance was to explain as much variance in the referent market-adjusted return to shareholders, with as parsimonious a set of variables as possible. In short, the underlying motivation was the accuracy of prediction, not the completeness of explanation.

To this point, the focus in developing a measurement model of organizational financial performance was: (i) to examine the subdimensions of the financial performance construct and (ii) to determine a set of measures that best represent the financial performance construct and its various subdimensions. Accordingly, composite measures, such as Altman's Z-score, that obscured the underlying dimensions of financial performance were omitted at the expense of some of the model's explanatory power *vis-à-vis* variance in the referent. However, since the primary focus of this part of the research was to maximize the explanatory power of variance in the referent, all variables initially included were considered. The one exception involved the elimination of the market measures price-to-book value, the change in price-to-book value, cost of equity capital and the change in the cost of equity capital. These were eliminated because one of the primary benefits of the composite measure would be its use when market information about organizational performance is unavailable. In addition, the cost of equity capital was excluded because, even though it is possible to calculate a cost of equity capital by using a proxy for a firm's specific beta (by using a sample of similar companies from the same industry that are publicly traded (Copeland et al., 2000)), the cost of equity capital variable used in this research was calculated using the actual beta for each company in the database, so the measure was excluded.

Economic value measures also use the cost of equity capital as the basis for the charge for equity capital. However, these measures were retained in this analysis because the impact of the market component is significantly diluted by the other aspects of these measures, and because the information provided by the inclusion of a charge for the cost of equity capital has been found to be considered significant in the accounting and finance literatures (see Stewart, 1991; Chen and Dodd, 1997 as examples).

Another variable that was retained in the analysis that contains market information was Altman's Z-score. The primary reason for retaining this measure was that there is an alternative formulation of Altman's Z-score that does not include a market component. Moreover, this alternative formulation has been demonstrated to provide similar reliability in the prediction of bankruptcies (Altman, 1993).

Two initial composite models for organizational financial performance were developed using multiple regression analysis for both annual and three-year timeframes. The following subsections discuss the results of the statistical tests used for each model.

Development of a Composite Model of Organizational Financial Performance for Annual Periods

An initial regression model was developed and tested that incorporated the variables that provided the greatest information about each of the significant constructs, as indicated by the standardized regression coefficient, based upon the model of financial performance for annual periods developed in the last subsection. The initial set of variables selected were return on assets, change in the return on investment, growth rate of assets and change in residual income return on investment. The change in Altman's Z-score was added to this variable set, since it had previously been shown to be significant. Only one variable from each construct was selected to avoid collinearity problems. The entire annual database was used, since the regression equation was being developed for use on the entire population of companies ($n = 2,894$).

Overall results

The results of this regression indicated that return on assets and the change in return on investment were not significant at $p < 0.10$. The R-squared for the equation was 0.42. Accordingly, the regression was rerun with the two insignificant variables excluded. All of the revised model coefficients were significant at $p < 0.001$ and the revised model R-squared was 0.42, which was significant at $p < 0.001$. The standardized coefficients for the resulting model were:

$$SWC1 = 0.220 \text{ GR AST} + 0.075 \text{ CRI ROI} + 0.617 \text{ CALT Z}.$$

Stepwise linear regression was used with all remaining variables in the dataset that were not part of the same construct as the variables already included in the model, in order to determine what level of improvement was possible beyond the three-variable model. Only one variable from each construct was included to avoid collinearity problems. These results indicated that the addition of the change in liabilities to assets significantly improved the model. With the addition of this variable (the change in liabilities-to-assets ratio), the change in residual income return on investment was no longer significant at the $p < 0.10$ level, so it was eliminated. All of the coefficients of the revised model were significant at the $p < 0.001$ level and the model had an R-squared of 0.46. The standardized coefficients for the resulting model were:

$$SWC1 = 0.208 \text{ GR AST} + 0.244 \text{ CLIAB/AST} + 0.739 \text{ CALT Z}.$$

The explanatory power of the values calculated using this model (the 'annual composite measure') was significantly higher than that of any individual measure. Individually, as indicated in Table 8.11, the change in Altman's Z-score had the highest individual R-squared value of 0.36. A predicted value was calculated for each record in the annual database and was used to classify each firm year of data as high, low or medium performance using the same criteria used to establish the high/low sample. Any predicted score of 1.0 or greater was classified as 'high' performance. Predicted scores equal to or less than -1.0 were classified as 'low' performance. All others were classified as 'medium'. Table 9.7 presents the results of this classification into performance categories.

The classification results indicate that the regression equation predicted high- and low-performance group membership with about 50 percent accuracy. All high- and low-performance annual periods that were misclassified were included in the medium-performance category with the exception of one high- and one low-performance annual period. The equation predicted 93 percent of the medium-performance annual periods accurately, with an almost equal percentage misclassified as either high or low performance. Overall, 83.7 percent of the annual periods were classified correctly. This represented a 55.7 percent improvement over classification by chance.

In summary, the regression model used to calculate the annual composite measure accounted for 46 percent of the variance in the criterion, market-adjusted return to shareholders, and classified 83.7 percent of the annual periods correctly as high, medium or low performance. Almost exclusively, the classification errors using the composite measure were including annual periods as average, rather than appropriately as high or low. These results suggest that using the annual composite measure, when market returns are not available, provides significantly more information

Table 9.7   Classification results using an annual composite measure

	Group	Predicted group membership			Total
		Low	Medium	High	
Count	Low	175	155	1	331
	Medium	75	2,092	87	2,254
	High	1	154	154	309
	Total	251	2,401	242	2,894
Percent	Low	52.9	46.8	0.3	100.0
	Medium	3.3	92.8	3.9	100.0
	High	0.3	49.8	49.8	100.0

about market-adjusted return to shareholders than any individual measure of financial performance.

Development of a Composite Model of Organizational Financial Performance for Three-year Periods

An initial regression model of organizational financial performance was tested that incorporated the variables that provided the greatest information about each of the financial performance constructs, indicated by the statistically significant standardized regression coefficients, based upon the final model (FP3.4) of financial performance developed for three-year periods. The initial set of variables selected for this regression model was return on assets, change in the EBITDA return on investment, growth rate of assets and change in liabilities to assets. The change in Altman's Z-score was added to this variable set, since it had previously been shown to be significant. Only one variable from each construct was selected to avoid collinearity problems. The entire three-year database was used, since the regression equation was being developed for use on the entire population of companies ($n = 925$).

The results of the regression indicated that all of the coefficients were significant at $p < 0.001$. The R-squared for the equation was 0.62. However, the tolerance and variable inflation factors for the model indicated a possible collinearity problem between the change in EBITDA return on investment and the change in Altman's Z-score. Accordingly, the regression was rerun without EBITDA return on investment. All of the revised model coefficients were significant at $p < 0.001$ and the revised model R-squared was 0.62 which was significant at $p < 0.001$. The standardized coefficients for the resulting model were:

$$SWC3 = 0.275 \text{ GR AST} + 0.317 \text{ CLIAB/AST} + 0.846 \text{ CALT Z} + 0.115 \text{ ROA}.$$

Stepwise linear regression was used with all remaining variables in the dataset that were not part of the same construct as the variables already included in the model, to determine what level of improvement was possible beyond the three-variable model. The change in residual income return on investment was significant in the revised model. All of the coefficients of the revised model were significant at the $p < 0.001$ level and the model had an R-squared of 0.63. The standardized coefficients for this model were:

$$SWC3 = 0.278 \text{ GR AST} + 0.296 \text{ CLIAB/AST} + 0.810 \text{ CALT Z} + 0.106 \text{ ROA} + 0.102 \text{ CRI ROI}$$

The effect of adding the extra variable was an increase of 0.01 in the R-squared of the model. This suggests that the variable was statistically significant only because of the large sample size. As the calculation of residual income requires the estimation of the cost of equity capital, the effort to gather the necessary information for non-publicly traded companies might exceed the benefit from this slight increase in explanatory power. Accordingly, the inclusion of the change in residual income return on investment is a matter of judgment by a researcher or practitioner.

The explanatory power of the values calculated using both models (the 'three-year composite measure') were significantly higher than that of any individual measure. Individually, as indicated in Table 8.12, the change in Altman's Z-score had the highest individual R-squared value of 0.45. A predicted value was calculated for each record in the three-year database using the more parsimonious four-variable model. The predicted value was then used to classify each three-year period of data as high, low or medium performance, using the same criteria used to establish the high/low sample. Any predicted score of 1.0 or greater was classified as 'high' performance. Predicted scores equal to or less than –1.0 were classified as 'low' performance. All others were classified as 'medium'. Table 9.8 presents the results of this classification into performance categories.

The classification results indicate that the regression equation predicted high- and low-performance group membership with approximately 50 percent accuracy. All of the high- and low-performance three-year periods that were misclassified were included in the medium-performance category with the exception of one high-performance three-year period. The equation predicted 92.4 percent of the medium-performance three-year periods accurately, with an almost equal percentage misclassified as either high or low performance. Overall, 80.0 percent of the three-year periods were

Table 9.8 Classification results using three-year composite measure

	Group	Predicted group membership			Total
		Low	Medium	High	
Count	Low	71	72	0	143
	Medium	28	608	22	658
	High	1	62	61	124
	Total	100	742	83	925
Percent	Low	49.7	50.3	0.0	100.0
	Medium	4.3	92.4	3.3	100.0
	High	0.8	50.0	49.2	100.0

classified correctly. This represented a 54.2 percent improvement over classification by chance.

In summary, the regression model used to calculate the three-year composite measure accounted for 62 percent of the variance in the criterion, market-adjusted return to shareholders, and classified 80 percent of the three-year periods correctly as high, medium or low performance. Again, almost all of the classification errors made using the three-year composite measure were including three-year periods as average, rather than their correct classification as high or low. These results suggest that using the three-year composite measure, when market returns are not available, provides significantly more information about market-adjusted return to shareholders than any individual measure of financial performance.

CHAPTER SUMMARY AND CONCLUSIONS

Chapter 9 presented the exploratory work performed to develop and test models of organizational financial performance for annual and three-year periods inferred from empirical data. A financial performance measurement model for annual periods was developed that included 10 separate constructs representing distinct dimensions of financial performance. The model included 20 separate measures for the constructs. A nine-construct financial performance measurement model including 20 measures was also developed for three-year periods.

Both financial performance measurement models were tested using market-adjusted return to shareholders as the referent representing organizational financial performance. A six-construct model including 15 measures was developed for annual timeframes. Four of the separate dimensions of annual financial performance developed in the initial model were not found to provide sufficient incremental information to warrant including them in the final model. Similarly, a six-construct model including 13 measures was developed for three-year timeframes. Again, four of the separate dimensions of three-year financial performance developed in the initial model were not found to provide sufficient incremental information to warrant including them in the final model. The aim in developing these models was not just to maximize the explanatory power of the models, but also to provide the greatest amount of information about individual dimensions of financial performance as possible.

Finally, financial performance composite measures were developed for annual and three-year timeframes using as few variables as possible to achieve the maximum explanation of variance in the referent. While the models used to calculate the composite measures were different for the two timeframes, the primary explanatory power of these models was provided by three variables, the change in Altman's Z-score, the growth rate of total assets and the change in the ratio of liabilities to assets. Both financial performance composite measures represented a significant improvement over any single measure of financial performance.

The survey of performance measures used in recent research in Chapter 2 indicated that the most commonly used objective performance measures for annual studies were return on assets and the growth rate of sales. However, no study in the survey used these two measures to form a composite financial performance measure. They were used just as separate criteria for testing the same set of independent variables. As indicated in Table 8.11, individually return on assets explained 4 percent and the growth rate of sales explained 2 percent of the variance in the criterion annual market-adjusted return to shareholders. In combination, these two variables explained only 5 percent of the variance in market-adjusted return to shareholders using all of the annual periods in the database for this study. By comparison, the annual composite measure developed in this chapter explained 46 percent of the variance in market-adjusted return to shareholders for the same sample. Similarly, these two variables (return on assets and sales growth) individually explained 12 and 7 percent of the three-year market-adjusted return to shareholders, respectively, and 17 percent in combination. By comparison, the composite measure developed in this study explained 62 percent of the three-year market-adjusted return to shareholders for the same sample.

10. Summary, conclusions and implications for theory and practice

This chapter summarizes the findings and conclusions of this research. It also includes a discussion of the limitations of the research, and some ways that it can be extended in the future. In addition, it discusses the implications of these findings for future research in the fields of entrepreneurship and strategic management and for management practice. The chapter concludes with a summary of the major contributions of this research.

SUMMARY OF KEY FINDINGS AND CONCLUSIONS

This section presents a summary of the individual findings regarding the exploratory work in this research pertaining to: (i) the relative information content of profitability measures calculated using ending balances versus average balances; (ii) the financial measures that discriminated between high- and low-performing companies with respect to shareholder value creation; (iii) the relative information content of individual measures of financial performance with respect to shareholder value creation; (iv) the relative and incremental information content of static performance measures versus the change in the value of that measure; (v) the major statistically significant dimensions of financial performance, and appropriate measures of those dimensions; (vi) a model of financial performance using market-adjusted return to shareholders as a referent; and (vii) the development of two composite measures of financial performance that incorporate multiple financial performance dimensions.

The Relative Information Content of Profitability Measures Calculated Using Ending versus Average Balances

The relative information content of return on assets, return on equity, return on investment and EBITDA return on investment was examined in this research using ending versus average balances in the denominator of the ratios. The results indicated that the correlation between the paired variables was between 0.95 and 0.99, and that all the correlations were significant at $p<0.001$. The adjusted R-squared values for the individual regressions of each variable against the common referent market-adjusted return to shareholders indicated almost no difference between the two formulations for each of these four measures, although in almost every case, the F-statistic was higher for the formulation using average balances. Approximately 10 percent of the annual sample had a difference of 20 percent or greater between the formulations, and approximately 12 percent of the three-year sample had a difference of 20 percent or greater.

There was a difference between the two formulations for each of the four variables. However, the difference was not sufficiently significant to conclude that one approach was consistently superior to another. Nonetheless, if a researcher can gather the data needed to calculate these measures using average balances, the higher F-statistic suggests that this approach should yield marginally more statistical power. Further, the use of average balances better matches the timeframe of the numerator with the timeframe of the denominator, which is intuitively more appealing. In short, both methods of calculating these measures should be acceptable, and the judgment of the observer should prevail.

The Financial Measures that Discriminated between High- and Low-performing Companies

One paradox of management research described by Cameron (1986) was that most empirical studies tend to use measures and methods that explain average performance, while the primary focus should be on understanding what makes firms either very successful or very unsuccessful. It is, therefore, essential to select performance metrics that can discriminate sufficiently among companies that perform at different levels of performance.

This research found that, for annual periods, 35 of the 40 financial performance measures tested discriminated between high- and low-performing companies at $p<0.10$, using market-adjusted return to shareholders as the basis for classification. For three-year periods, 32 of the 40 financial performance measures tested discriminated between high- and low-performing companies at $p<0.10$. Table 10.1 summarizes the variables that did, and the variables that did not discriminate between high- and low-performing companies for both annual and three-year periods.

More specifically, this study identified 32 annual and 27 three-year financial performance measures that discriminated between high- and low-performing companies at $p<0.01$ with respect to market-adjusted return to shareholders. Of these measures, those that provided the most information about the return

Table 10.1 Measures that discriminate between high- and low-performing companies by construct

Variables	Static measures		Change scores	
	Annual	Three-year	Annual	Three-year
Profitability				
Return on assets	**	**	**	**
Return on equity	**	**	**	**
Return on sales	**	**	**	**
Return on investment	**	**	**	**
EBITDA return on investment	**	**	**	**
Operating margin	**	**	**	**
Growth				
Growth rate of sales	**	**	**	*
Growth rate of operating expenses	**	*	**	**
Growth rate of total assets	**	**	**	**
Growth rate of employees	**	*	**	NS
Cash flow				
Growth rate of operating cash flow	*	*	*	NS
Operating cash flow to equity	**	**	NS	**
Free cash flow to equity	NS	NS	NS	NS
Liquidity				
Liabilities to total assets	NS	NS	NS	**
Survival				
Altman's Z-score	**	NS	**	**
Efficiency				
Asset turnover	+	NS	**	**
Economic value				
Residual income	**	+	**	**
Residual income return on investment	**	**	**	**
Cost of equity capital				
Cost of equity capital	**	**	**	**
Market				
Price-to-book ratio	**	NS	**	**

Notes:
** $p<0.01$.
* $p<0.05$.
+ $p<0.10$.
NS $p>0.10$.

to shareholders' referent with respect to the sample of all companies, not just high- and low-performing ones, should provide the most statistical power for research where shareholder value creation is the phenomenon of interest.

The Relative Information Content of Financial Performance Measures

Those variables that have the highest correlation with a construct are considered to be the 'best' measures of the construct (Cheng and Cheung, 1993). Accordingly, those variables that had the highest correlation with the referent market-adjusted return to shareholders in this study were considered to provide the most relative information about the organizational financial performance construct.

The best overall measures
Overall, this study found that a survival measure and two market measures were the best overall measures of shareholder value creation.

More specifically, the *change in Altman's Z-score* was the single variable that provided the most relative information about market-adjusted return to shareholders for both annual and three-year timeframes. This suggests that if a researcher can use only one dependent measure, the change in Altman's Z-score would provide the greatest power with respect to shareholder value creation.

The market-based measures *change in price-to-book value* and *change in the cost of equity capital* provided the next best information about the market-adjusted return to shareholders for both annual and three-year timeframes. However, when market information is not available, these measures are not observable, although the change in the cost of equity capital can be approximated using proxies for the individual company betas. In cases where market information is available, the use of these measures to represent shareholder value creation would generally be inappropriate because market-adjusted return to shareholders can be calculated.

The best profitability measures
This research examined 12 'accounting' measures of profitability – specifically: (i) return on assets; (ii) return on equity; (iii) return on sales; (iv) return on investment; (v) EBITDA return on investment; (vi) operating margin; and the six annual changes in each of these variables – as well as four 'economic value' profitability measures: (i) residual income; (ii) residual income return on investment; and the two annual changes in these variables.

Among these profitability measures, *residual income return on investment* provided the most relative information about market-adjusted return to shareholders for both annual and three-year timeframes. However, this economic value measure provided only slightly more relative information than other profitability measures, including return on assets, return on investment and return on equity. This suggests that researchers should weigh the effort necessary to calculate the charge for the cost of equity capital against the loss of explanatory power between residual income return on investment and alternative profitability measures.

Return on assets, the most commonly utilized profitability measure in the survey of recent empirical studies in this research, provided the greatest explanatory power of the other profitability measures tested in this study.

The change in the economic value measures residual income and residual income return on investment provided the greatest relative information about market-adjusted return to shareholders of the annual change in profitability measures. The annual measures – change in return on investment, change in return on assets, change in return on equity and change in return on sales – provided less relative information than the change in the economic value measures, but approximately the same relative information as one another. Accordingly, the change in economic value should be the preferred metric for the annual change in profitability. However, if in the judgment of the researcher, the cost of calculating an economic value measure exceeds the benefit of the increased relative information, then the results of this study suggest that any of the other four profitability change measures should provide equivalent relative information.

The change in EBITDA return on investment provided significantly more relative information about three-year market-adjusted return to shareholders than any other three-year profitability change measure. The change in return on investment, return on assets and the return on equity all provided greater relative information than either of the two economic value profitability measures. The change in all of the three-year profitability measures, with the exception of residual income return on investment, provided greater relative information about market-adjusted return to shareholders than their corresponding static measure. This suggests that over the longer term, the change in the state of organization has a greater association with the change in shareholder value. However, this same conclusion cannot be made for annual timeframes.

The best growth measures
This research examined eight measures of growth, specifically: (i) growth rate of sales; (ii) growth rate of operating expenses; (iii) growth rate of total assets; (iv) growth rate of employees; and the four changes in each of these variables.

The growth rate of total assets provided the most relative information among annual growth measures, although only slightly more than the growth rate of sales or the growth rate of employees. However, for three-year timeframes, the growth rate of sales measure provided significantly more information than the next most significant measures, the growth rate of total assets and the growth rate of employees.

The change in the growth rate of operating expenses was the most significant of the annual growth change measures, while the change in the growth rate of total assets provided the most relative information about three-year market-adjusted return to shareholders of the three-year growth change measures. In general, the growth measures provided greater relative information about the referent than the change in growth measures. This suggests that growth itself is a better indicator of shareholder value creation than the change in the rate of growth.

The best cash flow and leverage measures
This research examined six measures of cash flow and two measures of liquidity, specifically: (i) growth rate of operating cash flow; (ii) operating cash flow to equity; (iii) free cash flow to equity; (iv) liabilities to total assets; and the four annual changes in each of these variables.

In general, annual cash flow and leverage measures provided limited relative information about market-adjusted return to shareholders. However, over the three-year timeframe cash flow, change in cash flow and the change in leverage provided significantly more information about the referent. Of the three-year measures, operating cash flow to equity provided the most relative information. However, researchers should consider using EBITDA return on investment in place of operating cash flow to equity since EBITDA is often used as a proxy for operating cash flow, and the measure provides greater relative information.

The best efficiency measure
This research examined two efficiency measures, specifically asset turnover and the annual changes in this variable. The change in asset turnover was significant for both annual and three-year periods. For both periods the change in the measure provided significantly more relative information than the static measure. This implies that a change in operating efficiency provides greater relative information about shareholder value creation. Again, the change in state of the organization provided greater explanation of the market-adjusted return to shareholders than its static efficiency condition.

The Relative and Incremental Information Content of Static Measures versus Change Scores

The survey of empirical literature conducted in this study, and the surveys reported in previous studies, found that only static measures of financial performance were used in prior research. However, this study argued that if organizational performance involves a change in the state of the organization, either good or bad, then it follows that the change in financial performance measures should provide statistically significant incremental information about market-adjusted return to shareholders, but as noted above, this research's literature review did not find any previous study that empirically examined this hypothesis.

Key findings

This research found that 14 out of 18 annual change scores provided statistically significant incremental information beyond that provided by the corresponding static financial performance measure at $p < 0.05$. The four variables for which change scores did not add incremental information were: (i) the growth rate of operating cash flow; (ii) the growth rate of total assets; (iii) the growth rate of employees; and (iv) operating cash flow to equity. Three of these four variables are growth measures. This indicates that the growth rates provided more information about the change in the condition of the organization than the change in the growth rates.

The three-year change scores for each corresponding static measure also provided statistically significant incremental information for 15 out of 19 financial performance measures at $p < 0.05$. The change scores that did not add significant incremental information were: (i) the growth rate of sales; (ii) the growth rate of employees; (iii) the growth rate of operating cash flow; and (iv) the cost of equity capital. Once again, three of these four variables are growth measures. In the three-year high/low sample, no change score was correlated with the corresponding underlying variable at greater than 0.50. Again, it is reasonable to surmise that the change scores not only provide incremental information, but are part of a separate organizational performance construct.

Annual and Three-year Period Measurement Models of Financial Performance

Annual and three-year multidimensional models of financial performance were inferred empirically. The annual model consisted of ten constructs represented by 20 measures, as indicated in Table 10.2. The ten constructs were demonstrated to be discriminant and the measures of each construct met the test for convergent validity. The three-year model consisted of nine constructs represented by 20 measures, also as indicated in Table 10.2. The nine constructs were demonstrated to be discriminant and the measures met the test for convergent validity.

Table 10.2   Annual and three-year measurement models of financial performance

	Annual models		Three-year models	
	Without referent	With referent	Without referent	With referent
Profitability				
Return on assets	✓	✓	✓	✓
Return on equity	✓	✓	✓	✓
Return on investment				
EBITDA return on investment	✓	✓	✓	✓
Operating margin	✓	✓	✓	✓
Profitability change				
Δ return on assets	✓	✓		
Δ return on equity	✓	✓	✓	✓
Δ return on investment	✓	✓		
Δ return on sales	✓	✓		
Δ EBITDA return on investment			✓	✓
Δ residual income return on investment			✓	✓
Growth				
Growth rate of sales	✓	✓	✓	
Growth rate of total assets	✓	✓	✓	✓
Growth rate of employees	✓	✓	✓	✓
Growth change				
Δ growth rate of sales	✓		✓	
Δ growth rate of operating expense	✓		✓	
Δ growth rate of total assets			✓	
Economic value				
Residual income	✓			
Economic value change				
Δ residual income			✓	
Δ residual income return on investment	✓	✓	✓	
Market				
Price-to-book value	✓			

Table 10.2 (continued)

	Annual models		Three-year models	
	Without referent	With referent	Without referent	With referent
Market change				
Δ price-to-book value	✓	✓	✓	✓
Cash flow change				
Δ operating cash flow to equity				
Cost of equity capital				
Cost of equity capital	✓	✓	✓	✓
Δ cost of equity capital	✓	✓	✓	✓
Leverage				
Δ liabilities to total assets			✓	✓
Survival change				
Δ Altman's Z-score	✓		✓	

The annual financial performance measurement model was tested using the referent annual market-adjusted return to shareholders. Six of the ten constructs were found to be statistically significant and discriminant relative to the referent. These constructs were measured by 15 financial variables that met the tests for convergent validity. This model explained 62 percent of the variance in market-adjusted return to shareholders for a sample of high- and low-performing companies. The same model explained 47 percent of the variance in market-adjusted return to shareholders for a large sample of firms that represented all levels of performance.

The three-year financial performance measurement model was tested using the referent three-year market-adjusted return to shareholders. Six of the nine constructs were found to be statistically significant and discriminant relative to the referent. These constructs were measured by 13 financial variables that were demonstrated to meet the tests for convergent validity. This model explained 67 percent of the variance in market-adjusted return to shareholders for a sample of high- and low-performing companies. The same model explained 61 percent of the variance in market-adjusted return to shareholders for a large sample of firms that represented all levels of performance. Table 10.2 summarizes the financial performance constructs and the measures for the annual and three-year financial performance models both with and without the referent market-adjusted return to shareholders.

While previous researchers have proposed organizational financial performance is a multidimensional construct, and some researchers have demonstrated the discriminant properties of profitability and growth, this is the first research to methodically examine all of the primary categories of organizational financial performance. The annual and three-year models that were developed are the first to empirically test the discriminant properties of each category of financial performance.

Annual and Three-year Composite Measures of Financial Performance

One annual and one three-year financial performance composite measures were developed that maximized the explanation of the variance in market-adjusted return to shareholders, as well as the discrimination between high-, medium- and low-performing companies. These financial performance composite measures were developed based upon the annual and three-year financial performance measurement models developed in this research. However, while the measurement models were developed to provide as much information as possible about the underlying dimensions of financial performance, the aim of the composite measures was to explain as much variance in the shareholder value creation criterion, with as parsimonious a set of variables as possible. In other words, the purpose of the financial performance composite measures was prediction, not explanation.

The annual financial performance composite measure, called SWC1 (annual shareholder wealth creation) explained 46 percent of the variance in market-adjusted return to shareholders, more than 10 times more than the most commonly used single-variable measure, and the standardized coefficients for this measure were all significant at $p < 0.001$. The SWC1 composite measure was:

$$SWC1 = 0.739 \text{ CALT Z} + 0.244 \text{ CLIAB/AST} + 0.208 \text{ GR AST}.$$

The SWC1 composite measure includes a change in survival, a change in leverage and a growth construct. All of these measures actually track changes in the condition of the company. This is consistent with the conceptualization of performance in this research.

By comparison, the survey of recent empirical studies found that most studies utilized only one variable to represent organizational performance, and return on assets was the most frequently used measure of organizational performance. However, return on assets explained only 4 percent of the variation in market-adjusted return to shareholders and classified substantially all companies in the sample as average, results consistent with the findings of previous studies.

Overall, the SWC1 annual financial performance composite measure classified 83.7 percent of the annual periods correctly as high, average or low financial performance. This represented a 55.7 percent improvement over chance. Moreover, almost all of the classification errors involved classifying a high- or a low-performance company as medium, rather than appropriately as high or low. These results suggest that using the SWC1 financial performance composite measure as an indicator of annual performance provides significantly more information about market-adjusted return to shareholders when market returns are not available, than any individual measure.

The three-year financial performance composite measure, called SWC3 (three-year shareholder wealth creation), explained 62 percent of the variance in market-adjusted return to shareholders and the standardized coefficients for this measure were all significant at $p < 0.001$. The three-year financial performance composite measure was:

$$\text{SWC } 3 = 0.846 \text{ CALT Z} + 0.317 \text{ CLIAB/AST}$$
$$+ 0.275 \text{ GR AST} + 0.115 \text{ ROA}.$$

This composite measure includes a change in survival construct, a change in leverage construct, a growth construct and a profitability construct. The SWC3 composite measure classified 80.0 percent of all three-year periods correctly as high, medium or low financial performance. This represented a 54.2 percent improvement over classification by chance. Again, almost all of the classification errors involved incorrectly classifying three-year performance as medium, rather than appropriately as high or low performance.

In both the annual SWC1 and the three-year SWC 3 financial performance composite measures, the change in Altman's Z-score provided the greatest explanatory power for the referent market-adjusted return to shareholders. The change in leverage, represented by the change in the ratio of liabilities to assets provided slightly more relative information than the growth rate of assets, and for the three-year composite measure, a profitability measure was also significant.

In summary, the SWC1 and SWC3 financial performance composite measures developed in this research provided between five and 20 times the explanatory power of the variance in market-adjusted return to shareholders, as compared to the most frequently used dependent measures in prior entrepreneurship and strategic management studies, return on assets, return on equity and the growth rate of sales. Further, the constructs represented in the SWC1 and SWC3 financial performance composite measures indicate that performance is multidimensional. Finally, the primary components of the SWC1 and SWC3 composite measures were change scores, representing a change in the condition of the organization.

LIMITATIONS OF THIS RESEARCH

There are three primary sources of limitations to this research: (i) the research design; (ii) the sample; and (iii) the operationalization of variables.

Research Design Limitations

The research design of this study limits the generalization of the findings in several ways. These limitations include: (a) a focus on only one primary organizational performance dimension, namely financial performance; (b) the choice of referent; (c) the use of a single measure for the referent used to develop and test the models of financial performance; (d) the use of only two timeframes; and (e) the omission of risk as a dimension of financial performance.

Only one primary organizational performance dimension
Organizational performance is a multidimensional construct. This research focused on only one of the primary dimensions, namely financial perform-ance. Operational and stakeholder dimensions were not examined. As a consequence, the relative importance of financial performance to the two other performance dimensions was not examined. A model of organiz-ational performance that includes all major performance dimensions might require a different set of financial dimensions or different measures of the identified dimensions due to overlapping information across the higher-order constructs.

Choice of referent
The referent selected was return to shareholders. While this is perhaps the most commonly used for-profit referent, it does not represent the goals and objectives of all organizational stakeholders. Further, it limits the application of the results primarily to for-profit companies. The meas-urement of financial performance in non-profit organizations is not addressed. In addition, this research may not even apply to all for-profit business. For example, it is quite common that family businesses have goals and objectives that are not solely financial in nature. These other objectives are not considered in this research. Finally, the use of return to shareholders as a referent assumes, at least implicitly, that the referent

itself is not biased in any systematic way, that is, that the 'traditional' finance assumption of 'efficient' markets is valid over the periods covered by the study. While a substantial body of research does shows that the assumption is reasonably accurate over the long term, it is also clear that some market inefficiencies do exist, witness the relatively recent dot.com 'boom' and 'bust'.

Use of a single measure of the chosen referent
Using a single, objective measure to represent financial performance limits the interpretation of the results. Utilizing multiple measures of a construct is preferable, in particular measures that are calculated using different methods (Campbell and Fiske, 1959; Dess and Robinson, 1984). For instance, using both objective and subjective measures is preferable to using just objective ones. As a consequence, method bias could not be statistically addressed in this research.

Use of only two timeframes
An additional limitation of the research design was the selection of only two timeframes, one and three years. While these two timeframes are those most frequently used in entrepreneurship and strategic management research, 21 percent of the empirical studies summarized in Chapter 2 used other timeframes, most notably single point-in-time measures and five-year measures. Also, the annual and three-year models of financial performance developed in this research were not the same, implying that different dimensions of financial performance are more or less important at different times. Accordingly, the generalization of the results to other timeframes requires additional testing.

Omission of risk
A final limitation of the research design of the study was the omission of risk in the financial performance model. Even though financial risk is indirectly included through the calculation of the cost of equity capital, strategic risk was not calculated or included in any way. Many, including Bromiley (1990), have suggested that risk should be a component of the analysis of organizational performance. However, the addition of risk would have added significantly to the complexity of this study. Since this was an exploratory study, it was ultimately decided to exclude risk, with the understanding that it is one of the factors that must be considered in follow-on research. In addition, it should be up to the discretion of the researcher whether it is appropriate to capture the effects of risk as an independent measure or as a component of the dependent measure.

Sample Limitations

The sample utilized in this study limits the generalization of the findings in several ways: (a) only US companies were included in the sample; (b) only publicly traded companies were included; (c) financial services firms such as banks and insurance companies were disproportionately eliminated from the sample because they did not report sufficient information to calculate the measures tested in this research; (d) only one three-year period was used to develop and test the three-year financial performance model; (e) the annual data were from the same timeframe as the three-year data; (f) one primary source was used to gather most of the financial data; (g) outliers were omitted rather than recoded and included; and (h) the three-year sample did not include any companies that went out of business during the three-year period.

Only US publicly traded companies were used

The sample included only US companies that were publicly traded on US stock exchanges. More specifically, the sample included only companies in the Standard and Poor's 500, Mid Cap 400 and Small Cap 600. While this represents a cross-section of public companies by size, even the smallest of the Small Cap 600 companies is substantially larger than most for-profit enterprises. For example, the median annual sales of the companies in the sample were $1.2 billion and the median total assets were $1.6 billion. As a consequence, this is a small subset of the companies in the world and limits the generalizability of the findings of this research to publicly traded, US companies. This limitation is not as serious for strategic management researchers as it is for entrepreneurship researchers. However, the problems of gathering equivalent data from a set of initial public offerings eliminated the inclusion of such firms from this study. This limitation is counterbalanced by the fact that the SWC1 and SWC 3 financial performance measures developed in this study offer the prospect of ultimately measuring the performance of privately held firms, although additional research will need to be done before these measures can be used in this fashion.

Financial services firms were disproportionately excluded

Company data were included only if all of the measures to be used in this study could be calculated. As a consequence, companies that did not report classified balance sheets (separately disclosing short- and long-term assets and liabilities) did not have sufficient information to calculate all the measures used. In particular, almost half of the incomplete data was for banking, financial service and insurance companies, which do not generally report classified balance sheet values. Consequently, the findings may not be generalizable to these industries.

Only one three-year period was included

Only one three-year period was used to develop and test the three-year model of performance. Using limited three-year data was a consequence of the limitations of the Compustat® database. In particular, betas were not readily available in the Compustat® database to calculate the cost of equity capital for years prior to 1999. Also, the change in the accounting for goodwill was not reflected for earlier years, making comparability difficult without significant adjustments to individual company data.

The same timeframe for the one- and three-year periods was used

Even though the annual data had the advantage of covering three separate annual periods, it was still from the same three-year period as the three-year data. Additional testing would need to be done over a longer timeframe to determine whether the findings of this research are generalizable across longer periods of time. Further, the three-year period over which the data spanned was a particularly volatile time in the US markets. Significantly different results may have been found for another period in history.

A single primary source for the data was used

The primary data source for this research was Standard and Poor's Compustat® database. While Standard and Poor's has an excellent reputation, any bias or systemic errors that they may make in data collection would clearly impact the findings of this study. In particular, one of the findings was that Standard and Poor's does not correct their calculations of return on equity for companies that have both losses and negative equity. No other systematic computational errors in the database were noticed, but reliance on a single source for data does introduce potential measurement errors.

Outliers were excluded

Primarily because of the use of change scores, a significant number of firm-years of data and three-year periods were omitted because they included values that were outliers. These observations could have been retained if the measure deemed to be an outlier was recoded to a set value such as 10 standard deviations. This would have preserved the information from those firm years of data for the other measures that were not outliers. The decision to omit the data was made because of the assumed effect on the distribution of the variables for which the outliers were recoded. However, had these firm-years of data been retained, the statistical results may have varied from those reported.

Firms that failed were excluded from the three-year database
Finally, the three-year sample did not include any companies that went out
of business during the three years or that started business during the three
years involved in this research. To maintain comparability across the
sample, only firms that were in business and reported complete information
for the three years were included. However, this introduces some potential
bias, since firms that went out of business during the three years were
omitted from the analysis. Very few of these firms that were not included
for the full three years failed. In most cases, they were purchased by or
merged with another company. Consequently, some of the firms that were
excluded were successful and some were unsuccessful, mitigating some of
the direction of the effect of the bias.

Limitations Arising from the Operationalization of Variables

The operationalization of variables used in this study limits the generalization of the findings in several ways. These limitations include: (a) the
calculation of return to shareholders assuming that all dividends are reinvested in the stock of the issuing company; (b) the use of reported
accounting information as the basis for most of the financial performance
measures; and (c) the floor and ceiling effects on change scores used in this
research.

Method of calculating the return to shareholders' referent
The referent return to shareholders was operationalized using the assumption that all dividends were reinvested in the stock of the company. This
assumption does not necessarily reflect the actual investment choices that
would be made by shareholders. However, companies that do not pay dividends, reinvest all cash generated back into the business, yielding compound returns on invested capital. The assumption that dividends are
reinvested in the company tends to smooth the variation in returns across
companies over longer periods of time.

**Using reported accounting numbers to calculate financial performance
measures**
Most of the measures used in this research were based upon accounting
numbers. As previously discussed, and in particular over shorter timeframes, accounting numbers are subject to manipulation through management estimates and the choice of accounting methods. Further, while the
most frequently cited financial measures were used, other less frequently
used measures were not calculated or used.

Floor and ceiling effects on the change scores

Change scores by their nature are subject to floor and ceiling effects. Consequently, the change score measures were subject to significant variability and extreme values were frequent. The result is values that appear to be outliers. However, if extreme values are common, they should not be eliminated from the sample (Pedhazur, 1997). The effect on the statistical tests of keeping these extreme values in the sample for analysis was greater variance in some of the observed measures in the measurement models, resulting in lower-fit statistics.

IMPLICATIONS FOR FUTURE RESEARCH

This research generated several findings of importance to future research in the fields of entrepreneurship and strategic management. They include: (i) confirmation that organizational financial performance has nine separate dimensions, each of which may be impacted by different independent variables; (ii) the finding that these different financial performance dimensions differ with respect to their relative and incremental information, which affects the dependent measures that researchers should select to represent organizational performance; (iii) the fact that change scores provide both more information and supplementary information about overall organizational financial performance than static measures; (iv) the fact that, in general, the three-year measurement models of overall organizational financial performance were statistically stronger than the one-year measurement models with respect to their ability to explain or predict the stockholder wealth creation referent; and (v) the fact that the composite measurement models of overall financial performance developed in this research are four to 20 times more effective 'predictors' of shareholder wealth creation than any of the single variable measures used in over 99 percent of the research studies conducted in the fields of entrepreneurship and strategic management to date.

Implications of the Multiple Dimensions of Organizational Financial Performance

This research empirically demonstrated that organizational financial performance is a multidimensional construct. Consequently, if the unit of analysis for a study is the entire organization, and if the phenomenon of interest is overall organizational performance, it is incumbent upon the researcher to consider the effects of the independent variable(s) being studied on multiple performance dimensions simultaneously.

However, if only one dimension of organizational performance is examined in a study, it is then inappropriate to claim to be studying the effects of the independent variables on 'organizational performance'. In such situations, it would be more appropriate to specify the specific dimensions of organizational performance being studied, which would provide both better context and understanding to the readers of the research.

The theory being tested should help guide the researcher in selecting the dimensions of organizational performance to examine. Specifically, those dimensions of organizational performance that are hypothesized to create value for the constituents of interest should be used as the dependent variables. In general, dependent measures representing the phenomenon of interest should be selected with great care, and a full explanation for the selection criteria should be provided for users of the research.

Implications for Selecting the Dependent Measures Used to Represent Organizational Financial Performance

The importance of change scores

In most cases, the changes in the values of the financial performance measures were found to provide statistically significant incremental information about market-adjusted return to shareholders. In particular, the change in profitability measures for three-year timeframes provided greater information than the corresponding static measures. Specifically, the change in EBITDA return on investment generally provided more than twice the relative information about market-adjusted return to shareholders than any static three-year profitability measure. Accordingly, researchers should consider using change scores either in place of static measures or in addition to them. This finding supports the proposition that organizational performance involves a change in condition.

The importance of survival measures

For both annual and three-year timeframes, the single measure that provided the greatest explanation of the variance in market-adjusted return to shareholders was the change in Altman's Z-score. Altman (1993) proposed that the change in this measure was more meaningful than the static value, which is consistent with this study's findings. The explanatory power of Altman's Z-score was many times greater than the most commonly used financial measure, return on assets. Residual income return on investment provided the most power of the annual and three-year profitability measures and the growth rate of sales individually provided the most relative information about market-adjusted return to shareholders of the growth measures for both annual and three-year timeframes.

The importance of the composite financial performance measures
The composite annual and three-year financial performance measures, SWC1 and SWC3, that were developed in this research provided far greater relative information about the market-adjusted return to shareholders than any individual performance measure, including Altman's Z-score. The composite annual financial performance measure, SWC1, included components representing three separate financial performance dimensions, namely change in the likelihood of survival, change in leverage and organizational growth. The composite three-year financial measure, SWC3, included components that represented four different financial performance components – the three components of the composite annual financial performance measure and profitability. If a researcher is interested in management actions that impact returns to shareholders, and if market information is unavailable, the use of these composite annual and three-year financial performance measures, SWC1 and SWC3, should provide considerably greater statistical power to the researcher than any of the traditional one-dimensional measures of financial performance traditionally used in such research in the past.

Implications for Selecting the Timeframe to be Studied

The timeframe selected for any research should be appropriate to the anticipated lag between the hypothesized cause and effect. However, the findings of this research suggest that the shorter the timeframe involved, the more volatile the measures of overall organizational financial performance. Thus, the annual measures, in general, provided relatively less information about annual returns to shareholders than the three-year measures provided about three-year returns to shareholders. This implies that in studies that use annual timeframes, non-financial or perceptual measures (such as management's perception of performance) should be considered as possible avenues for augmenting the information about overall organizational performance.

The statistical significance of the relative information provided by the change in price-to-book value suggests that the creation of options provides a considerable amount of value to shareholders. Further, the greater relative information that financial measures provide over three-year periods suggests that execution on existing opportunities may be valued more in the market over the longer term than over the shorter term. However, additional work still needs to be done to better understand these dynamics.

Implications of the Exploratory Nature of This Research

This study was exploratory in its design. Moreover, even though there was a theoretical basis for the various choices made, in general it was driven by the data. This condition is typical of exploratory research, but one or more replications of this research with an a priori specification of a measurement model of financial performance will be necessary to confirm these findings. In addition, the statistical power of the SWC1 and SWC3 composite measures of overall financial performance developed in this research should be compared with other financial performance measures using known relationships with other sets of independent measures, similar to Robinson's (1998) research on alternative measures of new venture performance.

IMPLICATIONS FOR MANAGEMENT PRACTICE

This research provides several important findings for management practice, especially for entrepreneurs and general managers. These include the findings that: (i) changes in financial performance metrics may be more important than the value of the metric itself; (ii) the composite annual and three-year financial performance measures, SWC1 and SWC3, can be used as proxies for market-based measures when no market information or inefficient market information is available; (iii) the importance of monitoring changes in Altman's Z-score; (iv) the importance of using financial performance metrics that are appropriate to the timeframe being examined; and (v) the importance of using a combination of financial and non-financial metrics that are tailored to the specific circumstances of the manager's organization to predict and explain the change in shareholder returns.

The Importance of Changes in Financial Performance Metrics

One of the most important findings of this research for practitioners is the fact that changes in performance metrics should be considered of equal, if not greater importance, than the value of the metric itself. Management already places some emphasis on changes in performance metrics as demonstrated by the content of management discussion and analysis (MD&A) sections in annual reports and SEC filings. Typically, changes in performance period-over-period is the focus of MD&A. However, while changes may be explained post hoc, management planning should focus on actions that accomplish organizational change.

The Importance of Composite Financial Performance Metrics

While market-based measures may provide management with the best indication of the value they are creating for shareholders, markets react only to information that is available outside the company. During the interim periods between public disclosure of performance information, management needs metrics to estimate the probable market response to new financial information when it is disclosed. The composite measures of shareholder wealth creation, SWC1 and SWC3, developed in this research should provide managers with useful information about anticipated market performance during interim periods, prior to the release of financial information.

In addition, these composite measures could prove to be even more important to non-public companies that have no accurate gauge of shareholder wealth creation, since they provided significantly more relative information about shareholder returns than any other single measure. In particular, the SWC1 and SWC3 composite measures provided many times more information about shareholder returns than the most frequently used performance metrics return on assets, return on equity and the growth rate of sales.

In addition, the components of these two metrics indicate that the ability of the organization to obtain and retain resources is a key driver of shareholder wealth creation. Thus, the financial risk of the organization, as indicated by changes in Altman's Z-score, changes in financial leverage, and the growth rate of total assets were more important to short-term shareholder wealth creation than were more traditional profitability metrics. However, over three-year periods, profitability also became an important metric associated with increasing shareholder returns, but even here the most important metric was return on assets, not the return on investment or return on equity measures that are emphasized in the financial press and in most finance courses.

The bottom line is that the performance metrics that have been shown in this research to discriminate between high- and low-performing companies should receive the primary attention of management and users of financial statements. Those companies that attain and sustain competitive advantage in the market do not strive to be average. Therefore, the metrics they use to gauge performance should focus on outcomes that set them apart from the competition.

The Importance of Altman's Z-score

Very few non-public companies monitor the change in their Altman Z-score. However, the findings of this research indicate that this is the single most powerful measure for monitoring shareholder returns for both annual and three-year timeframes. Since this is a survival measure that is also important to creditors, management should pay particular attention to this financial performance metric. Interestingly, this is one of the very first metrics examined by turnaround managers when they are called on to 'turn around' troubled organizations. In fact, an understanding of this metric is not only called for in the Turnaround Management Association's Management Body of Knowledge, but questions about it are usually included in that organization's Certified Turnaround Professional (CTP) examination. The findings of this research suggest that knowledge of this metric should be even more widespread.

The Importance of Timeframes

Another key finding of this research is that management should consider using different performance metrics over different timeframes. More specifically, the data suggest that non-financial considerations may be more important in the shorter term, and that financial metrics are usually more informative in the longer term. These findings also suggest that perform-ance over the short term and the cumulative performance of the organiz-ation over the longer term should both be monitored on a regular basis, using different metrics for the differing timeframes.

The Importance of Understanding What We Don't Know

SWC1 and SWC3, the two composite financial performance measures developed in this research are far (400 to 2000 percent) better predictors of shareholder wealth creation than any other financial performance metrics in common use in management today. Nevertheless, a not insignificant portion of the variance in return to shareholders was left unexplained even by these financial measures for both annual and three-year timeframes. Hopefully, future extensions of this research will improve these measures, and reduce this unexplained variance. However, until this happens man-agement should monitor other operational and stakeholder metrics tail-ored to the strategic and operational objectives of their organizations in addition to the various financial performance measures suggested by this research.

THE CONTRIBUTIONS OF THIS RESEARCH

This research makes several unique contributions to the understanding of financial performance measurement for both research and manage-ment practice. Specifically, it (i) identified the most frequently used financial performance measures that discriminated between high- and low-performing companies with respect to shareholder returns; (ii) tested the relative information content of individual financial performance measures with respect to shareholder returns; (iii) identified several distinct dimensions of financial performance and measures of them; (iv) demonstrated that changes in performance metrics provide unique and significant information about shareholder returns; (v) developed and tested two multi-dimensional models of overall organizational financial performance; and (vi) developed two composite measures of overall organizational financial performance that effectively predict shareholder wealth creation and can be used when market data are not available.

Financial Performance Measures Used in Prior Research

The summary of performance measures presented in this research found that the changes in financial performance metrics are not generally used in empirical research. This is consistent with the results of prior research that examined the performance measures used in entrepreneurship and strategic management research. Further, no previous research specifically tested and quantified the information content of the changes in financial performance measures. This research is the first and only study in the fields of entrepreneurship and strategic management to demonstrate that the change in financial performance metrics provides significant and unique information about shareholder returns.

Cameron discussed in 1986 what he called 'a paradox in management research'. Management researchers are interested in what causes firms to be successful or unsuccessful. However, most management research studies use methods that tend to focus on the mean of the population, rather than on those companies that are exemplars of good and bad performance. This research specifically addressed this issue by identifying financial performance measures that discriminated between firms that are good and bad exemplars with respect to shareholder returns.

Testing the Information Content of Financial Performance Measures

While several prior studies have examined the relative information content of a few financial performance measures, this is the first study that systematically compared the most frequently used financial measures against a common referent. The findings of this research indicate that there are several individual measures that provide more relative information content about shareholder returns than those commonly used in entrepreneurship and strategic management research. These findings allow researchers to make an informed decision about individual performance measures that they may select as dependent measures for their research.

The Multidimensionality of Organizational Financial Performance

For over 50 years, management scholars have suggested that organizational performance is a multidimensional construct. However, this is the first study that has undertaken to empirically identify both distinct dimensions of organizational financial performance and the measures that represent those dimensions. The identification of different dimensions and measures of financial performance for annual and three-year timeframes is also a unique contribution.

This research used a common referent, market-adjusted return to shareholders, to test the different dimensions of financial performance identified and the measures of those constructs. The findings indicated that not all of the identified financial performance constructs provided statistically significant incremental information about shareholder returns. The final models developed for annual and three-year timeframes each included six distinct dimensions of financial performance that, in conjunction, provided the most relative information about shareholder returns.

Two Improved Composite Measures of Shareholder Wealth Creation

Finally, this research empirically developed two composite financial performance measures, SWC1 (an annual measure) and SWC3 (a three-year measure), that provided much greater (400 to 2,000 percent better) explanatory power for the variance in market-adjusted return to shareholders than any previously tested measures. The use of these composite financial performance measures in future research in the fields of entrepreneurship and strategic management may provide researchers with much greater understanding of the causal relationships between management actions and changes in shareholder value.

Bibliography

Agle, B.R. and R.K. Mitchell (1999), 'Who matters to CEOs? An investigation of stakeholder attributes and salience, corporate performance, and CEO values', *Academy of Management Journal*, **42** (5), 507–25.

Alchian, A. and H. Demsetz (1972), 'Production, information costs, and economic organization', *American Economic Review*, **62**, 777–95.

Allison, P.D. (1990), 'Change scores as dependent variables in regression analysis', in C.C. Clogg (ed.), *Sociological Methodology*, Oxford: Basil Blackwell, 93–114.

Altman, E. (1968), 'Financial ratios, discriminant analysis, and the prediction of corporate bankruptcy', *Journal of Finance*, **23** (4), 589–609.

Altman, E. (1993), *Corporate Financial Distress and Bankruptcy* (2nd edn), New York: John Wiley & Sons.

Andrews, K.R. (1987), *The Concept of Corporate Strategy*, Homewood, IL: Richard D. Irwin.

Ansoff, H.I. (1965), *Corporate Strategy: An Analytic Approach to Business Policy for Growth and Expansion*, New York: McGraw-Hill.

Arbuckle, J.L. and W. Wothke (1999), *Amos 4.0 User's Guide*, Chicago: SmallWaters Corporation.

Babbie, E. (1998), *The Practice of Social Research* (8th edn), New York: Wadsworth.

Bagozzi, R.P., Y. Yi and L.W. Phillips (1991), 'Assessing construct validity in organizational research', *Administrative Science Quarterly*, **36**, 421–58.

Bain, J.S. (1959), *Industrial Organization*, New York: John Wiley & Sons.

Ball, R. and P. Brown (1968), 'An empirical evaluation of accounting income numbers', *Journal of Accounting Research*, Autumn, 159–78.

Bamber, L.S. and T.E. Christiansen (2000), 'Do we really "know" what we think we know? A case study of seminal research and its subsequent overgeneralization', *Accounting Organizations and Society*, **25** (2), 103–30.

Barnard, C. (1938), *The Functions of the Executive*, New York: John Wiley & Sons.

Barney, J.B. (2002), *Gaining and Sustaining Competitive Advantage* (2nd edn), Upper Saddle River, NJ: Pearson Education.

Basu, S. (1983), 'The relationship between earnings' yield, market value and return for NYSE common stocks: further evidence', *Journal of Financial Economics*, **12** (1), 129–56.

Baucus, D., J Golec and J. Cooper (1993), 'Estimating risk–return relationships: an analysis of measures', *Strategic Management Journal*, **14**, 387–96.

Baum, J.A., T. Calabrese and B.S. Silverman (2000), 'Don't go it alone: alliance network composition and startups' performance in Canadian biotechnology', *Strategic Management Journal*, **21** (3), 267–94.

Beaver, W. (1968), 'The information content of annual earnings announcements', *Journal of Accounting Research*, Supplement, 67–92.

Bentler, P.M. (1989), *Structural Equations Program Manual*, Los Angeles: BMDP Statistical Software.

Bentler, P.M. (1990), 'Comparative fit indexes in structural models', *Psychological Bulletin*, **107**, 238–46.

Bentler, P.M. and D.G. Bonett (1980), 'Significance tests and goodness of fit in the analysis of covariance structures', *Psychological Bulletin*, **88**, 588–606.

Berman, S.L. and A.C. Wicks (1999), 'Does stakeholder orientation matter? The relationship between stakeholder management models and firm financial performance', *Academy of Management Journal*, **42** (5), 488–506.

Bettis, R.A. (1983), 'Modern financial theory, corporate strategy and public policy: three conundrums', *Academy of Management Review*, **8**, 406–15.

Biddle, G.C., R.M. Bowen and J.S. Wallace (1998), 'Evidence on the relative and incremental information content of EVA®, residual income, earnings and operating cash flow', *Journal of Accounting and Economics*, **24** (3), 301–36.

Birchard, B. (1999), 'Metrics for the masses', *CFO*, **15**, 64–72.

Birley, S. and P. Westhead (1990), 'Growth and performance contrasts between "Types" of small firms', *Strategic Management Journal*, **11** (7), 535–57.

Blackman, I.L. (1992), *Valuing the Privately-Held Business: The Art and Science of Establishing a Company's Worth*, Chicago: Probus.

Blyth, M.L., E.A. Friskey and A. Rappaport (1986), 'Implementing the shareholder value approach', *Journal of Business Venturing*, **6** (3), 48–58.

Bollen, K.A. (1989), *Structural Equations with Latent Variables*, New York: John Wiley & Sons.

Boulding, W. (1990), 'Unobservable effects and business performance: do fixed effects matter?', *Marketing Science*, **9** (1), 88–91.

Bourgeois, L.J., III. (1979), 'Toward a method of middle-range theorizing', *Academy of Management Review*, **4**, 443–7.

Boyd, B., G. Dess and A. Rasheed (1993), 'Divergence between archival and perceptual measures of the environment: causes and consequences', *Academy of Management Review*, **18** (2), 204–26.

Bracker, J.S. and J.N. Pearson (1986), 'Planning and financial performance of small, mature firms', *Strategic Management Journal*, **7** (6), 503–22.

Brealey, R.A., S.C. Myers and A.J. Marcus (2001), *Fundamentals of Corporate Finance* (3rd edn), New York: McGraw-Hill.

Bromiley, P. (1986), 'Shareholder value and strategic management: some caveats', in W.D. Guth (ed.), *Handbook of Business Strategy: 1986/1987 Yearbook*: 6:1–6:6, New York: Warren, Gorham & Lamont.

Bromiley, P. (1990), 'On the use of finance theory in strategic management', *Advances in Strategic Management*, **6**, New York: JAI Press, 71–98.

Brown, M.W. and R. Cudeck (1993), 'Alternative ways of assessing model fit', in K.A. Bollen and J.S. Long (eds), *Testing Structural Equation Models*, Newbury Park, CA: Sage, 136–62.

Brush, T.H., P. Bromiley and M. Hendrickx (1999), 'The relative influence of industry and corporation on business segment performance: an alternative estimate', *Strategic Management Journal*, **20**, 519–47.

Brush, C., P. Bromiley and M. Hendrickx (2000), 'The free cash flow hypothesis for sales growth and firm performance', *Strategic Management Journal*, **21** (4), 455–72.

Brush, C. and R. Chaganti (1999), 'Business without glamor? An analysis of resources on performance by size and age in small service and retail firms', *Journal of Business Venturing*, **14** (3), 233–57.

Brush, C.G. and P.A. VanderWerf (1992), 'A comparison of methods and sources for obtaining estimates of new venture performance', *Journal of Business Venturing*, **7** (March), 157–70.

Buzzell, R. (1990), 'Commentary on "Unobservable effects and business performance"', *Marketing Science*, **9** (1), 86–7.

Buzzell, R.D. and B.T. Gale (1987), *The PIMS Principles: Linking Strategy to Performance*, New York: Free Press.

Callard, C.G. and D.C. Kleinman (1985), 'Inflation-adjusted accounting: does it matter?', *Financial Analysts Journal*, May–June, 51–9.

Cameron, K. (1978), 'Measuring organizational effectiveness in institutions of higher education', *Administrative Science Quarterly*, **23**, 604–32.

Cameron, K. (1980), 'Critical questions in assessing organizational effectiveness', *Organizational Dynamics*, **9** (2), 66–80.

Cameron, K. (1986), 'Effectiveness as paradox: consensus and conflict in conceptions of organizational effectiveness', *Management Science*, **32** (5), 539–53.

Cameron, K.S. and D.A. Whetten (1981), 'Perceptions of organization effectiveness across organization life cycles', *Administrative Science Quarterly*, **26**, 525–44.

Cameron, K.S. and D.A. Whetten (1983), 'Organizational effectiveness: one model or several?', in K.S. Cameron and D.A. Whetton (eds),

Organizational Effectiveness: A Comparison of Multiple Methods, New York: Academic Press, 1–24.

Cameron, K.S., D.A. Whetton and M.Kim (1987), 'Organizational dysfunctions of decline', *Academy of Management Journal*, **30** (1), 126–38.

Campbell, D.T. and D.W. Fiske (1959), 'Convergent and discriminant validation by the multitrait–multimethod matrix', *Psychological Bulletin*, **56**, 81–105.

Capon, N., J.U. Farley and S. Hoenig (1990), 'Determinants of financial performance: a meta-analysis', *Management Science*, **36** (10), 1143–59.

Castrogiovanni, G. (1991), 'Environmental munificence: a theoretical assessment', *Academy of Management Review*, **16** (3), 542–65.

Caves, R.E. (1972), *American Industry: Struture, Conduct, and Performance* (3rd edn) Englewood Cliffs, NJ: Prentice-Hall.

Chakravarthy, B.S. (1986), 'Measuring strategic performance', *Strategic Management Journal*, **7**, 437–58.

Chandler, G.N. and S.H. Hanks (1993), 'Measuring the performance of emerging businesses: a validation study', *Journal of Business Venturing*, **8** (5), 391–408.

Chandler, G.N. and S.H. Hanks (1994a), 'Founder competence, the environment, and venture performance', *Entrepreneurship Theory and Practice*, **18** (3), 77–89.

Chandler, G.N. and S.H. Hanks (1994b), 'Market attractiveness, resource-based capabilities, venture strategies, and venture performance', *Journal of Business Venturing*, **9** (4), 331–49.

Chandler, G.N. and E. Jansen (1992), 'The founder's self-assessed competence and venture performance', *Journal of Business Venturing*, **7** (3), 223–36.

Chen, S. and J.L. Dodd (1997), 'Economic value added (EVA®): an empirical examination of a new corporate performance measure', *Journal of Managerial Issues*, **9** (3), 319–33.

Chen, S. and J.L. Dodd (2001), 'Operating income, residual income, and EVA® which metric is more value relevant?', *Journal of Managerial Issues*, **13** (1), 65–86.

Cheng, C.S.A. and J.K. Cheung (1993), 'On the usefulness of operating income, net income, and comprehensive income in explaining security returns', *Accounting and Business Research*, **23** (91), 195–203.

Chung, K.H. and S.W. Pruitt (1994), 'A simple approximation of Tobin's *Q*', *Financial Management*, **23** (3), 70–74.

Clinton, B.D. and S. Chen (1998), 'Do new performance measures measure up?', *Management Accounting*, **38** (October), 40–43.

Cohen, A. and M. Quarrey (1986), 'Performance of employee-owned small companies: a preliminary study', *Journal of Small Business Management*, **24** (2), 58–63.

Cohen, J. and P. Cohen (1983), *Applied Multiple Regression/Correlation Analysis for the Social Sciences*, Hillsdale, NJ: Erlbaum.

Connolly, T., E.J. Conlon and S.J. Deutsch (1980), 'Organizational effectiveness: a multiple constituency approach', *Academy of Management Review*, **5** (April), 211–17.

Cook, T.D. and D.T. Campbell (1976), 'The design and conduct of quasi-experiments and true experiments in field settings', in M.D. Dunnette (ed.), *Handbook of Industrial and Organizational Psychology*, Chicago: Rand-McNally, 223–36.

Cook, T.D. and D.T. Campbell (1979), *Quasi-Experimentation: Design and Analysis Issues in Field Settings*, Boston, MA: Houghton Mifflin.

Cook, T.D., D.T. Campbell and L. Perrachio (1990), 'Quasi experimentation', in M.D. Dunnette and L.M. Hough (eds), *Handbook of Industrial and Organizational Psychology*, Palo Alto, CA: Consulting Psychologists Press, 491–576.

Cooper, A.C. (1993), 'Challenges in predicting new firm performance', *Journal of Business Venturing*, **8** (3), 241–53.

Copeland, T., T. Koller and J. Murrin (1996), *Valuation: Measuring and Managing the Value of Companies* (2nd edn), New York: John Wiley & Sons.

Copeland, T., T. Koller and J. Murrin (2000), *Valuation: Measuring and Managing the Value of Companies* (3rd edn), New York: John Wiley & Sons.

Cox, J.C., S.A. Ross and M. Rubinstein (1979), 'Option pricing: a simplified approach', *Journal of Financial Economics*, **7**, 229–63.

Cronbach, L.J. and L. Furby (1970), 'How should we measure "change" – or should we?', *Psychological Bulletin*, **74**, 68–80.

Cyert, R.M. and J.G. March (1963), *A Behavioral Theory of the Firm*, Englewood Cliffs, NJ: Prentice-Hall.

Daily, C.M. and D.R. Dalton (1992), 'The relationship between governance structure and corporate performance in entrepreneurial firms', *Journal of Business Venturing*, **7** (5), 375–86.

Daily, C.M. and D.R. Dalton (1993), 'Board of directors leadership and structure: control and performance implications', *Entrepreneurship Theory and Practice*, **17** (3), 65–81.

Dambolina, I. and J. Shulman (1988), 'A primary rule of bankruptcy: watch the cash', *Financial Analysts Journal*, September–October, 66–70.

Davies, M. (2000), 'Value-based management in practice: a critical review', in G. Arnold and M. Davies (eds), *Value-based Management: Context and Application*, New York: John Wiley & Sons, 37–58.

de Waal, A. (2001), *Power of Performance Management: How Leading Companies Create Sustained Value*, New York: John Wiley & Sons.

Desmond, G.M. and J.A. Marcello (1988), *Handbook of Small Business Valuation Formulas* (2nd edn), Marina del Rey, CA: Valuation Press.

Dess, G.G., R.D. Ireland and M.A. Hitt (1990), 'Industry effects and strategic management research', *Journal of Management*, **16** (1), 7–27.

Dess, G. and R.B. Robinson, Jr. (1984), 'Measuring organizational performance in the absence of objective measures: the case of the privately-held firm and conglomerate business unit', *Strategic Management Journal*, **5** (3), 265–73.

Drucker, P. (1954), *The Practice of Management*, New York: Harper & Row.

Dwyer, H.J. and R. Lynn (1989), 'Small capitalization companies: what does financial analysis tell us about them?', *Financial Review*, **24** (3), 397–415.

Edelstein, J. (1992), *Adjustment and Decline in Hostile Environments*, New York: Garland.

Eisenhardt, K.M. and M.J. Zbaracki (1992), 'Strategic decision making', *Strategic Management Journal*, **13**, 17–37.

Etzioni, A.W. (1960), 'Two approaches to organizational analysis: a critique and suggestion', *Administrative Science Quarterly*, **5**, 257–78.

Etzioni, A.W. (1964), *Modern Organizations*. Englewood Cliffs, NJ: Prentice-Hall.

Finegan, P.T. (1989), 'Financial incentives resolve the shareholder-value puzzle', *Corporate Cashflow*, October, 27–32.

Fink, R. (2000), 'Minding the gap: when earnings and cash flow diverge, danger may lurk', *CFO*, **16**, 46–54.

Ford, J. and D. Schellenberg (1982), 'Conceptual issues of linkage in the assessment of organizational performance', *Academy of Management Review*, **7** (1), 49–58.

Freeman, R.E. (1984), *Strategic Management: A Stakeholder Approach*, Boston, MA: Pitman.

Gartner, W.B. (1990), 'What are we talking about when we talk about entrepreneurship?', *Journal of Business Venturing*, **5**, 15–28.

Ghiselli, E.E., J.P. Campbell and S. Zedeck (1981), *Measurement Theory for the Behavioral Sciences*, San Francisco: Freeman.

Gifford, D. (1998), 'After the revolution: Miller and Modigliani at 40', *CFO*, **14** (7), 75–9.

Giles, W.F. and H.S. Feild (1978), 'Effects of amount, format, and location of demographic information on questionnaire return rate and response bias of sensitive and nonsensitive items', *Personnel Psychology*, **31** (3), 549–59.

Hall, R.H. (1972), *Organizations: Structure and Process*, Englewood Cliffs, NJ: Prentice-Hall.

Harrigan, K. (1983), 'Research methodologies for contingency approaches to business strategy', *Academy of Management Review*, **8** (3), 398–405.

Helfert, E.A. (1994), *Techniques of Financial Analysis* (8th edn), Boston, MA: Irwin.

Herron, L. and R.B. Robinson Jr. (1993), 'A structural model of the effects of entrepreneurial characteristics on venture performance', *Journal of Business Venturing*, **8** (3), 281–94.

Higgins, R.C. (1995), *Analysis for Financial Management* (4th edn), Boston, MA: Irwin.

Hitt, M.A., R.E. Hoskisson and H. Kim (1997), 'International diversification: effects on innovation and firm performance in product-diversified firms', *Academy of Management Journal*, **40**, 767–98.

Hofer, C.W. (1975), 'Toward a contingency theory of business strategy', *Academy of Management Journal*, **18** (4), 784–811.

Hofer, C.W. (1983), 'ROVA: a new measure for assessing organizational performance', in R. Lamb (ed.), *Advances in Strategic Management*, Vol. 2, New York: JAI Press, 43–55.

Hofer, C.W. and D. Schendel (1978), *Strategy Formulation: Analytic Concepts*, St. Paul, MN: West.

Hoskisson, R.E., M.A. Hitt, R.A. Johnson and D.D. Moesel (1993), 'Construct validity of an objective (entropy) categorical measure of diversification strategy', *Strategic Management Journal*, **14** (3), 215–35.

Ittner, C.D. and D.F. Larcker (1998), 'Innovations in performance measurement: trends and research implications', *Journal of Accounting Research*, **10**, 205–39.

Jacobsen, R. (1988), 'The persistence of abnormal returns', *Strategic Management Journal*, **9**, 415–30.

Jacobsen, R. (1990a), 'Unobservable effects and business performance', *Marketing Science*, **9** (1), 74–85.

Jacobsen, R. (1990b), 'Unobservable effects and business performance: reply to the comments of Boulding and Buzzell', *Marketing Science*, **9** (1), 92–5.

Jahera, J.S., Jr. and W.P. Lloyd (1992), 'Additional evidence on the validity of ROI as a measure of business performance', *Mid-Atlantic Journal of Business*, **28** (2), 105–12.

Jensen, M. and W. Meckling (1976), 'Theory of the firm: managerial behavior, agency costs, and ownership structure', *Journal of Financial Economics*, **3** (4), 305–60.

Jöreskog, K. and D. Sörbom (1996), *Lisrel 8 User's Reference Guide* (2nd edn), Chicago: SSI Scientific Software.

Kamin, J.Y. and J. Ronen (1978), 'The effects of corporate control on apparent profit performance', *Southern Economic Journal*, **45** (1), 181–91.

Kaplan, R. (1984), 'Yesterday's accounting undermines production', *Harvard Business Review*, July/August, 95–101.

Kaplan, R.S. and D.P. Norton (1992), 'The balanced scorecard – measures that drive performance', *Harvard Business Review*, January–February, 71–9.

Katz, D. and R.L. Kahn (1978), *The Social Psychology of Organizations*, New York: John Wiley & Sons.

Keeley, M. (1978), 'A social-justice approach to organizational evaluation', *Administrative Science Quarterly*, **23**, 272–92.

Keppel, G. and S. Zedeck (1989), *Data Analysis for Research Designs: Analysis of Variance and Multiple Regression/Correlation Approaches*, New York: W.H. Freeman.

Kerlinger, F.N. (1986), *Foundations of Behavioral Research* (3rd edn), Fort Worth, TX: Harcourt Brace Jovanovich.

Kim, W.S., J.W. Lee and J.C. Francis (1988), 'Investment performance of common stocks in relation to insider ownership', *Financial Review*, **23** (1), 53–64.

Kirchhoff, B.A. and B. Phillips (1988), 'The effect of firm formation and growth on job creation in the United States', *Journal of Business Venturing*, **3** (4), 261–72.

Kotey, B. and G.G. Meredith (1997), 'Relationships among owner/manager personal values, business strategies, and enterprise performance', *Journal of Small Business Management*, **35** (2), 37–64.

Kuhn, T.S. (1970), *The Structure of Scientific Revolutions* (2nd edn), Chicago: University of Chicago Press.

Kunkel, S.W. (1991), 'The impact of strategy and industry structure on new venture performance', unpublished doctoral dissertation, University of Georgia, Athens, GA.

Kunkel, S. and C.W. Hofer (1991), 'Why study the determinants of new venture performance: a literature review and rationale', paper presented at the Academy of Management 51st Annual Meeting Miami, FL, August.

Lawley, D.N. and A.E. Maxwell (1971), *Factor Analysis as a Statistical Method*, London: Butterworth.

Lehn, K. and A.K. Makhija (1997), 'EVA, accounting profits, and CEO turnover: an empirical examination', *Journal of Applied Corporate Finance*, **10** (Summer), 90–97.

Lev, B. (1989), 'On the usefulness of earnings and earnings research: lessons and directions from two decades of empirical research', *Journal of Accounting Research*, **27** (Supplement), 153–201.

Lev, B. and J.A. Ohlson (1982), 'Market-based empirical research in accounting: a review, interpretation, and extension', *Journal of Accounting Research*, **20**, 249–322.

Lindberg, E.G. and S.A. Ross (1981), 'Tobin's Q ratio and industrial organization', *Journal of Business*, **54**, 1–32.

Lingle, J.H. and W.A. Schiemann (1996), 'From balanced scorecard to strategic gauges: is measurement worth it?', *Management Review*, March, 56–61.

Lubatkin M. and S. Chatterjee (1991), 'The strategy–shareholder value relationship: testing temporal stability across market cycles', *Strategic Management Journal*, **12** (4), 251–71.

Madden, B.J. (1999), *CFROI Valuation: A Total System Approach to Valuing the Firm*, Woburn, MA: Butterworth-Heinemann.

McDougall, P.P., R.B. Robinson and A.S. DeNiso (1992), 'Modeling new venture performance: an analysis of new venture strategy, industry structure, and venture origin', *Journal of Business Venturing*, **7**, 267–89.

McGrath, J.E., J. Martin and R.A. Kulka (1981), 'Some quasi-rules for making judgment calls in research', *American Behavioral Scientist*, **25** (2), 211–14.

Miller, C.C. and L.B. Cardinal (1994), 'Strategic planning and firm performance: a synthesis of more than two decades of research', *Academy of Management Journal*, **37** (6), 1649–65.

Miller, D. (1987), 'Strategy making and structure: analysis and implications for performance', *Academy of Management Journal*, **30** (1), 7–32.

Miller, D. and J. Lee (2001), 'The people make the process: commitment to employees, decision making, and performance', *Journal of Management*, **27** (2), 163–90.

Miller, M.H. and F. Modigliani (1961), 'Dividend policy, growth and the valuation of shares', *Journal of Business*, **33** (October), 411–33.

Milunovich, S. and A. Tsuei (1996), 'EVA in the computer industry', *Journal of Applied Corporate Finance*, **9** (Spring), 104–15.

Murphy, G.B., J.W. Trailer and R.C. Hill (1993), 'Measuring performance in entrepreneurship research: a review of the empirical literature', paper presented at the Eighth Annual United States Association for Small Business and Entrepreneurship National Conference, Baltimore, Maryland, October.

Murphy, G.B., J.W. Trailer and R.C. Hill (1996), 'Measuring performance in entrepreneurship research', *Journal of Business Research*, **36**, 15–23.

Nunnally, J.C. (1978), *Psychometric Theory*, New York: McGraw-Hill.

O'Byrne, S.F. (1999), 'EVA and its critics', *Journal of Applied Corporate Finance*, **12** (2), 92–6.

O'Hanlon, J. (1991), 'The relationship in time between annual accounting returns and annual stock market returns in the UK', *Journal of Business Finance and Accounting*, **18** (3), 305–14.

Ottoo, R.E. (2000), *Valuation of Corporate Growth Opportunities: A Real Options Approach*, New York: Garland.

Pedhazur, E.J. (1997), *Multiple Regression in Behavioral Research: Explanation and Prediction* (3rd edn), Fort Worth, TX: Harcourt Brace.

Penman, S.H. (2001), *Financial Statement Analysis and Security Valuation*, New York: McGraw-Hill.

Peter, J.P. (1979), 'Reliability: a review of psychometric basics and recent marketing practices', *Journal of Marketing Research*, **18**, 133–45.

Peteraf, M.A. (1993), 'The cornerstones of competitive advantage: a resource-based view', *Strategic Management Journal*, **14**, 179–88.

Peters, T.J. and R.H. Waterman (1982), *In Search of Excellence: Lessons from America's Best Run Companies*, New York: Harper & Row.

Pfeffer, J. and G.R. Salancik (1978), *The External Control of Organizations: A Resource Dependence Perspective*, New York: Harper & Row.

Porter, M.E. (1980), *Competitive Strategy*, New York: Free Press.

Porter, M.E. (1985), *Competitive Advantage*, New York: Free Press.

Porter, M.E. (1987), 'From competitive advantage to corporate strategy', *Harvard Business Review*, **45** (3), 46–59.

Porter, M.E. (1996), 'What is strategy?', *Harvard Business Review*, **74**, 61–79.

Powell, J.D. and C.F. Bimmerle (1980), 'A model of entrepreneurship: moving toward precision and complexity', *Journal of Small Business Management*, **18** (1), 33–6.

Quinn, R.E. and K. Cameron (1983), 'Organizational life cycles and shifting criteria of effectiveness: some preliminary evidence', *Management Science*, **29** (1), 33–51.

Quinn, R.E. and J. Rohrbaugh (1983), 'A spatial model of effectiveness criteria: towards a competing values approach to organizational analysis', *Management Science*, **29** (3), 363–77.

Rappaport, A. (1986), *Creating Shareholder Value: The New Standard for Business Performance*, New York: Free Press.

Rawley, T. and M. Lipson (1985), *Linking Corporate Return Measures to Stock Prices*, St. Charles, IL: HOLT Planning Associates.

Reimann, B.C. (1989), *Managing for Value: A Guide to Value-Based Strategic Management*, Cambridge, MA: Basil Blackwell.

Robinson, K.C. (1995), 'Measures of entrepreneurial value creation: an investigation of the impact of strategy and industry structure on the economic performance of independent new ventures', unpublished doctoral dissertation, University of Georgia, Athens, GA.

Robinson, K.C. (1998), 'An examination of the influence of industry structure on eight alternative measures of new venture performance for high potential independent new ventures', *Journal of Business Venturing*, **14**, 165–87.

Ruefli, T.W., J.M. Collins and J.R. Lacugna (1999), 'Risk measures in strategic management research: auld lang syne?', *Strategic Management Journal*, **20**, 167–94.

Sackett, P.R. and J.R. Larson (1990), 'Research strategies and tactics in industrial and organizational psychology', in M.D. Dunnette and L.M. Hough (eds), *Handbook of Industrial and Organizational Psychology*, Palo Alto, CA: Consulting Psychologists Press, 419–89.

Scandura, T.A. and E.A. Williams (2000), 'Research methodology in management: current practices, trends, and implications for future research', *Academy of Management Journal*, **43** (6), 1248–64.

Schendel, D.E. and C.W. Hofer (1979), *Strategic Management: A New View of Business Policy and Planning*, Boston, MA: Little, Brown & Company.

Schriesheim, C.A., R.E. Kopelman and E. Solomon (1989), 'The effect of grouped versus randomized questionnaire format on scale reliability and validity: a three-study investigation', *Educational and Psychological Measurement*, **49** (3), 487–508.

Schwab, D.E. (1980), 'Construct validity in organizational behavior', in B.M. Staw and E.E. Cummings (eds), *Research in Organizational Behavior*, Vol. 2, Greenwich, CT: JAI Press, 2–43.

Schwenk, C.R. and C.B. Shrader (1993), 'Effects of formal strategic planning on financial performance in small firms: a meta-analysis', *Entrepreneurship Theory and Practice*, **17** (3), 53–64.

Scott, M.C. (1998), *Value Drivers: The Manager's Framework for Identifying the Drivers of Corporate Value Creation*, New York: John Wiley & Sons.

Seth, A. (1990), 'Value creation in acquisitions: a reexamination of performance issues', *Strategic Management Journal*, **11**, 99–115.

Shrader, R.C. and M. Simon (1997), 'Corporate versus independent new ventures: resource, strategy, and performance differences', *Journal of Business Venturing*, **12** (1), 47–66.

Shulz, W. and C.W. Hofer (2000), *Creating Value through Skill-Based Strategy and Entrepreneurial Leadership*, Amsterdam and New York: Pergamon.

Simon, H.A. (1976), *Administrative Behavior* (3rd edn), New York: Macmillan.

Slevin, D.P. and J.G. Covin (1995), 'Entrepreneurship as firm behavior: a research model', in J.A. Katz and R.H. Brokhaus (eds), *Advances in Entrepreneurship, Firm Emergence and Growth*, Greenwich, CT: JAI Press, 175–224.

Snow, C. and D. Hambirck (1980), 'Measuring organizational strategies: some theoretical and methodological problems', *Academy of Management Review*, **5** (4), 527–38.

Steers, R.M. (1975), 'Problems in the measurement of organizational effectiveness', *Administrative Science Quarterly*, **20** (December), 546–57.

Stevens, S.S. (1968), 'Measurement statistics and the schemapiric view', *Science*, **161**, 849–56.

Stewart III, G.B. (1991), *The Quest for Value: A Guide for Senior Managers*, New York: HarperCollins.

Stewart III, G.B. (2001), *Using EVA for Performance Measurement and Financial Management in the New Economy*, New York: Stern Stewart & Co.

Study, H.V.A.V. (1998), 'The pricing of successful venture capital-backed high-tech and life-sciences companies', *Journal of Business Venturing*, **13** (5), 333–51.

Thomas, A.S., R.J. Litschert and K. Ramaswamy (1991), 'The performance impact of strategy–manager coalignment: an empirical examination', *Strategic Management Journal*, **12** (7), 509–22.

Tsai, W.M., I.C. MacMillan and M.B. Low (1991), 'Effects of strategy and environment on corporate venture success in industrial markets', *Journal of Business Venturing*, **6** (1), 9–29.

Tully, S. (1993), 'The real key to creating wealth', *Fortune*, September 20, 38–50.

Van de Ven, A. (1989), 'Nothing is quite so practical as a good theory', *Academy of Management Review*, **14** (4), 486–9.

Venkatraman, N. (1989), 'The concept of fit in strategy research: toward a verbal and statistical correspondence', *Academy of Management Review*, **14** (3), 423–44.

Venkatraman, N. and J. Grant (1986), 'Construct measurement in organizational strategy research: a critique and proposal', *Academy of Management Review*, **11** (1), 71–87.

Venkatraman, N. and V. Ramanujam (1986), 'Measurement of business performance in strategy research: a comparison of approaches', *Academy of Management Review*, **11** (4), 801–14.

Venkatraman, N. and V. Ramanujam (1987), 'Measurement of business economic performance: an examination of method convergence', *Journal of Management*, **13** (1), 109–22.

Weick, K.E. (1989), 'Theory construction as disciplined imagination', *Academy of Management Review*, **14** (4), 516–31.

Weinberg, S. and K. Goldberg (1990), *Statistics for the Behavioral Sciences*, Cambridge and New York: Cambridge University Press.

Wesphal, J. (1999), 'Collaboration in the boardroom: behavioral and performance consequences of CEO–board social ties', *Academy of Management Journal*, **42** (1), 37–61.

West, T.L. and D.J. Jones (1999), *Handbook of Business Valuation* (2nd edn), New York: John Wiley & Sons.

White, R. and R. Hamermesh (1981), 'Toward a model of business unit performance: an integrated approach', *Academy of Management Review*, **6** (2), 213–23.

Woo, C.Y. and G. Willard (1983), 'Performance representation in strategic management research: discussions and recommendations', paper presented at the Academy of Management, Dallas, August.

Yuchtman, E. and S.E. Seashore (1967), 'A system resource approach to organizational effectiveness', *American Sociological Review*, **32** (December), 891–903.

Zahra, S.A. and W.C. Bogner (2000), 'Technology strategy and software new ventures' performance: exploring the moderating effect of the competitive environment', *Journal of Business Venturing*, **15** (2), 135–73.

Index

proposed model 2–9, 205, 211, 213, 215
value creation *see* value creation
see also accounting measures; return on investment
effectiveness
assessment of 113–17, 119–26
attributes of 110–11
construct validity 23, 24, 36–7, 62, 75, 111–12, 115, 121
content validity 114, 118
convergent validity 23, 24, 116, 118, 139, 189–94, 195, 196–8, 201, 221, 235–40
criterion-related 114–15, 118
discriminant validity 17, 23, 24, 116–17, 139–40, 146–59, 189–91, 195, 198–201, 235–40
evolution of concept 4, 47–51
face validity 113–14, 117, 118
perspectives 39–59, 71
predictive validity 114–15, 118
statistical conclusion validity 114–15
tradeoffs 57
and uniqueness, organizational 47
efficiency measures
asset turnover 188, 189
discriminant validity tests 195
and growth 56–7
information content 166–7, 174
as market-based measure 76, 77
as performance measurement 21, 22, 28–35, 48, 58, 62, 73–4, 188, 190, 197, 203, 231, 234
proposed model 188, 190, 197, 203
in strategic management perspective 43, 44
employee
attitude 43
costs 22, 30, 58, 71
performance 43, 74
retention 48
satisfaction 45
employee growth
convergent validity 116, 154–5
correlations 26–7, 150–51, 162–3, 166–7
in data sample 134
discriminatory validity 146–59

information content 179, 180, 183, 184
means and standard deviations 26, 147–8, 158, 160
as performance measurement 17, 22, 24, 28, 31, 58, 71, 83, 90, 231, 233–5
proposed model 181, 187, 188, 190, 194, 197, 199, 202, 205, 209, 211, 213, 215
regression analyses 161, 171, 175, 179, 180, 183, 184
revised model 209, 211, 213
size dimensions 35
t-test results 170
entrepreneurship 21–4
equity, return on
cash flow 91, 93, 130, 146–61, 162–70, 172, 176, 180, 184, 187–8, 190, 197, 234
convergent validity 139, 196, 198
correlations 26–7, 145, 150–51, 154–5, 162–4, 166–8, 207
denominator value 132, 143–4
dependent variables 29
discriminatory validity 146–58
DuPont analysis 86
economic value measures 80, 101
information content 40, 174, 179, 183
leverage of 88–9, 91, 92
means and standard deviations 26–7, 147–8, 158, 160
as performance measurement 1, 5, 15, 18–22, 24, 58, 83, 84, 105, 138, 143, 188, 231–3, 236, 239, 249
and profitability 57, 61, 129, 175
proposed model 187, 190, 192, 194, 197, 199, 202, 203, 204, 205
and R&D 64
regression analyses 145, 171, 175, 179, 183
revised model 209, 211, 212–15, 218–20, 222
strengths and weaknesses 85–7
t-test results 170
EVA (economic value added) 64, 97, 100–102

research design and methods
128–31, 141
revised model 222, 224
and risk 68, 69
and sales change 20
see also return on equity
size 22, 34, 35, 58, 61, 83, 89, 116
stakeholders 5–6, 28, 45, 53–4, 57, 88,
122
goals 53, 55, 78–9
influence 44
performance 33, 42, 75
relationships with 44, 47
static measures versus change scores
127–8, 133, 177–84, 187–93, 234–5
Steers, R.M. 5, 7, 47, 48, 52–3, 54, 56
survival
Altman's Z score *see* Altman's Z
score
discriminatory validity 195
as performance measurement 15, 34,
35, 56, 66, 121–2, 231, 237, 246,
249–50
strategic management perspective
43–4
strengths and weaknesses 94–5
see also debt; liquidity
systems model 50, 54–5

t-test 137, 146, 170
Tobin's Q ratio 14, 34, 62, 76, 99
Tucker–Lewis coefficient 140
turnover ratios 74

validity measures *see* effectiveness
value creation 3–4, 5, 6, 53, 57
competing 50, 52
and earnings *see* accounting
literature perspective
economic rent 46–7
and return on assets *see* return on
assets
shareholder *see* shareholder
see also economic value measures
Venkatraman, N. and V. Ramanujam
'Measure of business economic
performance' (1987) 8, 9, 16–17,
36, 44–5, 53, 56, 70, 71, 90, 105,
114, 116, 123, 139, 203
'Measure of business performance in
strategy' (1986) xii, 6, 54, 56, 57,
74, 120, 173
venture capital 45

weighted average cost of capital
(WACC) 99, 100